Researching the Psychothei

Researching the Psychotherapy Process

A Practical Guide to Transcript-based Methods

Georgia Lepper
Nick Riding

First published 2006 by
PALGRAVE MACMILLAN
Houndmills, Basingstoke, Hampshire RG21 6XS and
175 Fifth Avenue, New York, N.Y. 10010
Companies and representatives throughout the world

PALGRAVE MACMILLAN is the global academic imprint of the Palgrave
Macmillan division of St. Martin's Press, LLC and of Palgrave Macmillan Ltd.
Macmillan is a registered trademark in the United States, United Kingdom
and other countries. Palgrave is a registered trademark in the European
Union and other countries.

ISBN-13: 978–1–4039–2206–9
ISBN-10: 1–4039–2206–3

This book is printed on paper suitable for recycling and
made from fully managed and sustained forest sources.

A catalogue record for this book is available from the British Library.

A catalog record for this book is available from the Library of Congress.

Printed in Great Britain by
Creative Print & Design (Wales), Ebbw Vale

This book is dedicated to our colleague Dr Alan Cartwright, whose imagination and determination led to the founding of psychotherapy training at the University of Kent. Alan's innovative and creative approach to training and research was an important early stimulus to the work on which this book is based.

Contents

List of Tables and Figures

Tables

Figures

Preface

Each time we teach our course, *Psychotherapy Process Research*, we are faced with the same dilemma. We find a wide variety of published research studies that are relevant to the topics we wish to teach; but they do not tell their readers *how* the research was done. We find a number of excellent books, but they tend to focus on one particular method or approach to research; or, if more general, to review the wider domain of psychotherapy research without helping the novice clinician/researcher to understand *how* to go about undertaking a clinically relevant research project. Much of the available literature is written in the specialized language of formal research, and is experienced by many clinicians as remote and irrelevant to their clinical concerns. Perhaps the most important purpose of psychotherapy process research, as we understand it, is to provide evidence for the critical evaluation, and development, of clinical practice. Our students are encouraged to use their own sessions for their research projects, and to examine critically both theory and their own practice on the basis of the evidence of their research project. In recent years, they have explored questions like:

- Has there been an improvement in the patient's capacity to reflect upon a core conflict?
- Is there a relationship between non-verbal vocalizations and anxiety-provoking topics?
- What is the effect of my interventions on the therapeutic process?

This book is intended primarily as a teaching and learning resource for both practising and student clinicians. They may be training or working in counselling or psychotherapy training institutes or university departments, or in the clinical or counselling psychology training programmes of a university. Within the field of psychotherapy process research, there are a wide variety of methods, varying in scope and complexity. The methods we have chosen to describe in detail are generally applicable to researching the psychotherapy process through detailed analysis of session transcripts, regardless of the modality of psychotherapy being practised. In the case of the coding approaches introduced in Part II, the underpinning concepts are derived from theories of psychotherapy; while the discourse approaches introduced in Part III are applications of more general theories of human interaction developed in the wider field of the social sciences. While we mention some of the research tools designed for the study of specific psychotherapy modalities, we have not discussed them in detail. Nor have we covered the rapidly developing research in attachment theory and its potential application to psychotherapy research. This is primarily because the methods involved are complex, and therefore beyond the scope of the student clinician/researcher engaged in small scale projects. We feel certain, however, that as this field of research develops, the relationship between attachment style and the psychotherapy process itself will become a major area of interest and inquiry.

The design of the book aims to provide step-by-step support for the student/clinician to undertake clinically relevant research on transcripts of his or her own psychotherapy or counselling sessions. Following an introduction to the research process, it provides a general historical background to the development of psychotherapy process research and its findings. Issues around ethical practice in research and the procedures for gaining ethical approval are addressed. The specific methods are introduced in separate chapters, which include examples of analysis in the text, accompanied by exercises that will help the reader to explore *how* the method is applied to a psychotherapy session text. The methods introduced are those most in use in formal research, and which therefore appear widely in the psychotherapy process literature. In each chapter, the student is directed to exemplar studies. The student will find support for modest projects based on transcripts taken from his/her own clinical practice, or more complex doctoral level research designs using transcribed data gathered specifically for the project. Also included is an overview of the kinds of research each method has been used for, with references to published research that illustrates the application of the method and its findings.

How to use this book

Researching the Psychotherapy Process can be used in two ways. For the novice clinician/researcher, new to psychotherapy process research methods, the book is structured in the form of a narrative, which takes the reader through the logic of the research process, and then introduces a variety of methods within this general framework. Those new to the subject would gain most from a sequential reading of the text. For those who are already doing research, the book is divided into clear chapter and sub-headings, in order to provide an introductory reference to the various aspects of the research process that might be of particular interest, and to methods which readers might want to add to their existing range of expertise. Each chapter is followed by specific references to further reading, which will direct the reader towards fuller accounts of specific research issues and methods, and towards examples of the most significant research studies that illustrate the methods introduced.

Part I provides a general introduction to psychotherapy research and the kinds of consideration which must be given to the initial phases of undertaking a project. In Chapter 1, we give a general background to psychotherapy research, and in Chapter 2 the core issues involved in starting any research project are introduced and discussed. Issues such as 'validity and reliability', and ethical issues, are introduced in separate sections, which can be used as reference resources for the student, as the project gets underway. Parts II and III then introduce two of the major methods in use in contemporary psychotherapy process research: the coding methods, and the discourse methods. Each part begins with a general introduction to the methods to be considered, in their historical context. Part II (Chapters 3–5) introduces the three major coding approaches: the transference-related methods, assimilation analysis, and the interpersonal methods. Part III (Chapters 6–9) introduces a variety of different methods that can be used to study the therapeutic discourse directly. Part IV reviews the process of managing and analyzing data and presenting it in the form of a research report. Chapter 10 provides an outline introduction to the different kinds of computerized tools and methods which can be used to help the process researcher manage and analyze data. Finally, in Chapter 11, a student's research report is reproduced in full, to illustrate what a student or practitioner project might look like: how it could be structured; how methods can be combined; and how the experience of data analysis can be used to explore and deepen clinical practice.

Acknowledgements

This book would not have been possible without the help and contributions of many people. In particular, we wish to thank trainees on the *Psychotherapy Process Research* module within the clinical psychotherapy training programme at the University of Kent – Christina Belcher, Janet Brown, Kimberley Carter, Sophia Chatzimitriou, Louise Coppin, Roseanne Culling, Dawn Devereux, Katrina Epps, Robert Ford, Howard Grassow, Laura Jacobs, Helly Langley, Sandra Lawrence, Carole Lynch, Louise May, Beverley Mears, Alla Reason, Philippa Shaddrach Long, John Spalding, Rosemary Tennant, Jon Willows. They have contributed ideas and material for the examples, which have not been identified for reasons of confidentiality. Philippa Shaddrach Long is particularly thanked for contributing her project as an example of small scale practitioner research.

We have also been helped through discussions with colleagues within the Society for Psychotherapy Research (SPR). SPR is an invaluable national, regional and international community which holds conferences with presentations from most active researchers in the field. The website address for the international organization is www.psychotherapyresearch. org. A number of colleagues have commented on chapters or given permission for us to use illustrations and examples from their models. In particular we would like to thank Lynn Angus, Lorna Benjamin, Tirril Harris, Lester Luborsky, James McDonald, Erhard Mergenthaler and Bill Stiles. We are grateful to Guilford Press for permission to reproduce Figure 5.1.

We would also like to thank colleagues at the University of Kent and within our families who have provided the help or tolerance to make this project possible. Catherine Gray – our editor – and the anonymous reviewers of the various drafts have contributed substantially to the form and structure of this book.

Finally, we would like to thank the psychotherapy clients who have given permission for taped material from their sessions to be used in supervision, teaching and research. Some extracts from this material is included in this book, although always in a disguised form which does not enable any identification.

GEORGIA LEPPER
NICK RIDING

PART I

Background to the field of psychotherapy research

Introduction: What is research?

In this practical introduction to psychotherapy process research methods, we will be exploring different ways of analyzing transcripts of therapeutic interaction in order to investigate how the therapeutic process works. The methods which will be discussed are, however, very varied in the way they tackle the kinds of questions we want to ask of the therapeutic process. This introduction presents a brief outline of the basic principles of the single, over-arching process called scientific inquiry, which underpins every research project, whatever method is chosen. It will introduce and define some of the main concepts of the research process, and how they govern the way in which a particular piece of research is undertaken. The important definitions will be set out in italics for easy reference.

The process of inquiry

Research is a process of inquiry. It is a 'dialogue between ideas and evidence' (Ragin, 1994), grounded in a common set of procedures, or **methods**: '*a (defined or systematic) way of doing a thing*' (Oxford English Dictionary). The ideas are based in a conceptual framework which informs the choices and interpretations of the investigator as he or she proceeds through the phases of the process. *This conceptual framework plus the procedures of analysis – the methods – constitute the* **methodology**. The dialogue between ideas and evidence is achieved through the methods chosen to organize the data into units for comparison. All scientific inquiry, whether natural or social science, numerical or text-based, or any combination of the two, relies on the principle of comparison (Glaser and Strauss, 1967). Thus, for example, patients presenting with symptoms of anxiety might be compared with patients presenting with depression; or sessions with high levels of interpretation compared with those with low levels.

The process of inquiry begins with a question of interest to the investigator. A specific hypothesis might be tested, and in this case, the way the research is carried out may be quite specific. Or a wider, more general question may be posed, where theory building is the objective of the analysis, and methods are chosen as the analysis proceeds. In either case, the investigator must begin the process of inquiry with a statement of intent, on the basis of which subsequent decisions will be made about the proposed strategy of analysis. Methods relevant and sufficient to the task at hand must be chosen, and a statement made which may be broad or narrow depending on the kind of inquiry to be undertaken. *Taken all together, this process of deciding what to investigate, and how to undertake the analysis of the data, is called the **research design**.*

The next phase of the process is the ***collection of data** which are sufficient to support the intended dialogue of ideas and evidence.* In some psychotherapy process studies, this will be a long and complex process, involving various sub-phases, which will be subject to ethical approval (see Chapter 2). In other cases, the source of the data may be more readily available, in the form of transcripts obtained from text databanks, for example. For the student or clinician researcher, for whom this book is intended, access to appropriate data may come from his or her own practice, or from resources within a university setting. Whatever the source of the data, it must be adequate to the question being asked.

Once the phase of data collection is complete, and even before, the investigator will be starting the process of data analysis. Transcripts may need to be prepared for entry into information processing software (see Part IV) or, if coded by hand using one of the coding methods in Part II, transcripts may be coded as the data collection proceeds. In the phase of data analysis, the dialogue of ideas and evidence begins in earnest, and its outcome is interpretation of the data. This may take the form of purely quantitative analysis, purely textual analysis, or any combination of the two. The important point here is that all ***data analysis** is an interpretive procedure which is undertaken in the context of the conceptual framework, or methodology, within which the study is undertaken.* The interpretation of data yields not 'truth', but demonstrable relations between phenomena (Bhaskar, 1989).

The final phase of the process is its documentation. It is at this point that the investigator writes up his or her findings, and presents them to the wider community for critical evaluation and discussion. ***Documentation** is the means of communication by which the wider dialogue of ideas and evidence which is scientific knowledge proceeds.* It normally takes a commonly accepted form, which is outlined in Part IV. In all kinds of research, documentation should include a description of each stage of the process, and the rationale made for the decisions presented in each phase.

The procedures outlined above, taken in turn, provide the framework for the grounding and objectivity of systematic analysis of evidence. Each stage provides the preparation for the next, and all together underpin the reliability and validity of the analysis (see Chapter 2 for a detailed discussion). Within psychotherapy process research, there is a vigorous debate concerning the nature of 'objectivity' in the domain of psychotherapy, where the focus of the clinical process is on human 'subjectivity'. This debate has a wider context in social sciences more generally, where the study of human action within the social domain has yielded new conceptions of what can be studied, and new methods of inquiry (see the Introduction to Part III for further discussion). In the following section, some of these issues are considered.

Naturalism vs. hermeneutics

Two quite different ideas about the nature of knowledge have dominated thinking about scientific method throughout the development of psychotherapy research. On the one hand is the tradition of naturalism, the basis of traditional scientific inquiry, which holds that there is a real, existing natural world, independent of our perceptions and thoughts, whose objective properties we can gain knowledge about through systematic observation and analysis. Early scientific endeavour was primarily observational and theory building. Darwins's theory of evolution is the paradigm example of this kind of research. Theory building, or *inductive* science, is one phase of the process of discovery. 'Analytic induction is the process of using evidence to formulate or reformulate a general idea. The process of constructing images (via the synthesis of evidence) is mostly inductive. Generally, whenever evidence is used as a basis for generating concepts, as in qualitative research, or empirical generalizations, as in quantitative research, induction has played a part' (Ragin, 1994, p. 188).

The complement of inductive science is theory testing science, by means of which hypotheses derived from theoretical principles are identified and tested. Much of this kind of scientific procedure is based on the study of generalities rather than specifics, populations rather than individual cases, and uses statistical analysis to compare groups. A problem for natural science is that the forms and processes of the material world are not necessarily visible. A good example is the earth's magnetic field, a property whose effects are observed but which is not in itself observable.

Most natural science, in addition to methods, requires tools or instruments for its success. Advances in technology (for example, the microscope) are often the drivers of new developments in scientific knowledge.

A second way of understanding and knowledge building is based on the notion that the real world is only known/knowable to us in the form of our subjective experience of it, and that all our knowledge is therefore an interpretation of what we experience. This understanding of knowledge has two important traditions: the phenomenological, which holds that it is the experience itself which is real; and the hermeneutic, which holds that knowledge is an interpretive process, rather than a representation of the real world. According to these traditions, concepts precede and shape our experience, and therefore our knowledge, of the natural world. As the social sciences developed, a division emerged between those investigators who hold that the human and social world is a part of the natural world, subject to its laws, and investigable by the principles of natural science; and those who hold that the human world is an entirely interpreted world, which can only be investigated through interpretive procedures. Broadly speaking, psychology has tended to follow the tradition of naturalism, while researchers in many of the other social science disciplines have moved towards an interpretive view of the human world and its processes.

The development of psychotherapy research has been affected by these schisms, with some researchers embedded in naturalist assumptions, while others promote opposing hermeneutic or phenomenological perspectives. We have taken a different position in organizing this introduction to process research, following a middle path between those apparently opposing camps. We take the view that in the natural sciences, no less than in the social sciences, observation is theory impregnated and that knowledge is socially organized; and that all systematic investigation deals with structures that set limits, not with determinacy (Bhaskar, 1989). Whether natural or social, structures and processes may be opaque to experiencing and knowing subjects, and it is only by adopting a coherent and structured approach to investigation that any kind of knowledge of phenomena, whether 'subjective' or 'objective', can be explored.

Therefore we have avoided using the terms 'quantitative' and 'qualitative' which are often seen as marking out the boundaries of this dispute, and have instead organized this volume in terms of commonalities around the objectives of the investigation of psychotherapy process: general theory testing (the coding strategies); and micro-theory building (the discourse strategies). The complete scientific process necessarily includes both these objectives at different points in its evolution.

The dialogue between ideas and evidence: comparative analysis

Research is a process by which the investigator chunks up the world – phenomenal or natural – in order to undertake some kind of comparative analysis. In order to compare, that which is being compared has to be established in an accountable way. That is, the researcher must be able to justify the choice of things to be compared with reference to a theory, and must proceed through **sampling:** *the selection of data to be analyzed through a coherent and transparent decision making process.* The transparency of the sampling procedure, the means by which it is conducted and communicated, provide the foundation for the **reliability and validity** *of the analysis: the consistency of the inferences which are made on the basis of the analysis.* A general discussion of reliability and validity in psychotherapy research follows in Chapter 2; and specific issues of reliability and validity are discussed throughout the chapters on method. The following sampling procedures are the major ones which are applied in research, and will be encountered in the discussion of psychotherapy process research methods:

- *Population sampling.* This ensures that where two or more populations are being compared, they are the same in other respects. This is a fundamental procedure in studies of the outcomes of particular kinds of therapies. In psychotherapy process research studies, a similar procedure is observed, where theories of change, for example, are being compared. If a population of patients is being studied in order to identify and compare change processes, it is important that the groups being compared are similar in all other important ways – i.e., that the kind or level of disturbance is similar; that their age, sex and general circumstances are similar.

- *Coding.* Using codes to sample data means that the investigator chooses to select some parts of the data by identifying similar elements and grouping them together, in order to compare them with other groups of elements. Codes are derived from theories, and, where they are successful, are developed into coding systems, or instruments, used to investigate texts and test theories. Many such coding systems have been developed by psychotherapy researchers, and some of the most important ones are introduced in Part II. The coding process itself must be conducted in a comprehensive and consistent way, so that all instances of the elements being sampled are included. Then, the identified elements can be compared (contrasted), either numerically, or textually, or both.

- *Theoretical sampling.* In the case of purely textual analysis, an additional constraint of the coding process must be observed. This process is termed *theoretical sampling* by Glaser and Strauss (1967) who developed an inductive, theory building method for textual analysis (see Chapter 6). Through the method of *constant comparative analysis* of observational or textual data, categories can be derived which correspond more closely to the experienced framework of subjects, rather than merely representing the conceptual framework of the initial theory. This basic principle of sampling underpins the validity of the analytic inductive process.

- *Sampling by type.* Another kind of theoretical sampling, used in observational strategies, is sampling by type. Darwin systematically collected bones, and sorted them into types in order to compare one against another, and to identify type groups, or species. He did this in the context of his provisional theory: that all the different species are related to each other in form and structure. This basic principle of sampling is also used by conversation analysts (see Chapter 7).

- *Random sampling.* A final method of sampling data, which may be vital for a project which involves large quantities of textual data, is random sampling. For example, in comparing a dataset of 26 session therapies, the researcher may sample the data by choosing the 3rd, 12th and 24th sessions to compare, assuming that this sample will adequately represent the early, middle and later stages of the therapy. Or alternatively, where a single case is being intensively analyzed, the researcher may employ the 'pond water' theory of sampling: that a random sample from the whole text will contain and reveal pervasive features of the entire text.

Conclusion

In the chapters which follow, we will explore a variety of different research methods which can be used to undertake psychotherapy process research. Their underpinning concepts and strategies differ in ways touched on in this introduction. They are all, however, linked by the common, shared basic process of inquiry and governed by the principles of reliability and validity. It is this adherence to this set of procedures which provides a secure grounding for the variety of approaches needed to research the complex process which is psychotherapy.

CHAPTER 1

Psychotherapy research: a brief overview

Introduction and origins

It sometimes surprises people who are new to the field of psychotherapy that there is a long and very productive history of empirical research into the outcome and process of the therapy relationship. Generally speaking, the efficacy of formal psychotherapy has become well established and the research agenda has moved on to more specific questions relating to particular therapeutic methods, client groups and the process of change. This section will give a broad overview of the history of psychotherapy research in order to provide a context for the methods introduced in the following chapters.

Modern schools of psychotherapy derive from psychoanalysis, which was based in the work of Sigmund Freud and his followers at the beginning of the 20th century. Freud developed the theory and practice of psychoanalysis from insights developed from his practice as a physician specializing in neurological disorders. His roots were in empirical science and he always emphasized the importance of seeing psychoanalysis as a science. However, in developing the new field he was not engaged in what would now be considered empirical science. The Freudian claim to scientific status came from the clinical observation in the consulting room of material which was seen as confirming psychoanalytic theory. Freud's laboratory was the analytic couch. Some may challenge the legitimacy of clinical observation as a basis for evaluating theory, but most will accept that this is legitimate so long as there are rigorous methods for ensuring that the observations are collected in a systematic and open minded way. This cannot be said of the observations and presentations of Freud and his followers in the standard format of the psychoanalytic case study, as documented by Spence (1993).

The main problems with this kind of data collection are that the observations are made by the therapist who has a particular perspective both on the course of the treatment and on a particular theoretical model. We only have to look at clinical commentaries, where proponents from particular analytic schools comment on data as presented by a clinician to see how one's theoretical perspective will colour the material and in some cases produce several very confident and contradictory accounts. This is not to undermine the value and creativity of the endeavour, or to say that the theory based upon this procedure is wrong, but merely to acknowledge that in order to have any confidence in theories based upon this form of observation there must be a more rigorous approach to its collection and evaluation.

The proponents of the founding theory of psychotherapy, those of the psychoanalytic schools, have not traditionally been supportive of empirical research into psychotherapy and have been slow to take up the mantle. Even now there is a lack of empirical support for psychoanalytic treatment which arises not from *negative* evidence (or superior support for alternatives) but rather *lack* of evidence of its efficacy. It was the new therapeutic modalities, set up as an alternative to the psychoanalytic hegemony of the early part of the 20th century, that were keen to establish the efficacy of their treatments through empirical research. Thus Carl Rogers, the founder of client-centred therapy, was actively engaged in research using audio recordings during the 1940s to find evidence of the core therapeutic factors that he felt produced changes. These were used as support for the importance of the facilitative elements: in particular, empathy. A more radical alternative to psychoanalysis came from learning-based approaches, which stressed the importance of patient behaviours and a more active role for the therapist. These were developed in the 1920s and 1930s and the proponents put great emphasis on empirical evaluation of the outcome of therapy. Both of these new therapy methods relied on a shorter intervention than did psychoanalysis and hence it was more feasible to conduct empirical research on their process and outcome. This was also the case with cognitive therapy, which developed in the 1960s and 1970s in response to the perceived limitations of approaches which only saw behaviour, as opposed to thought, as significant. These new approaches were also strongly committed to empirical research.

Research into psychotherapy outcome

The post Second World War years thus saw a great diversification of therapeutic approaches and a growth in the quantity and quality of research into therapy. A defining moment in the history of psychotherapy research came with Eysenck's review of 24 research studies, concluding that there was no evidence that psychotherapy treatment was more effective than no treatment (Eysenck, 1952). Eysenck's methodology has since been criticized (e.g. by Bergin and

Lambert, 1978) on the grounds that he was more stringent in his criteria for evaluating improvement in the treatment group than in the no-treatment group and also on the basis of the limitations of the studies included in his review. However, we can thank Eysenck for helping to establish the efficacy of psychotherapy because his review mobilized a great activity of research into the efficacy of treatment, most of which has been much more positive.

Barkham (1996) has characterized psychotherapy research generations, starting from the response to the Eysenck study, as follows:

- Generation I – 1950s to 1970s concerned with whether psychotherapy is effective and the process question of whether there are objective methods for evaluating process.
- Generation II – 1960s to 1980s concerned with which psychotherapy is more effective and the process question of what components are related to outcome.
- Generation III – 1970s to 1990s concerned with making treatments more cost effective and the process question of how change occurs.
- Generation IV – 1980s to present concerned with the issue of clinically significant change and the development of exploratory approaches to discover effective ingredients.

This is obviously somewhat simplified, with considerable overlap between research generations, but it does illustrate how the focus has changed over the post war period. It is also interesting to observe that the process research agenda has been there from the beginning, although often as a rather under-valued and under-funded alternative to outcome research. We will discuss the developments within process research separately. It should also be observed at this point that some of the research methodologies which have come to be important in psychotherapy process research – namely the discourse-based methods – were developed within other discipline areas. The antecedents of these approaches are reviewed in Part III.

The first generation research into efficacy was supported by the emergence of meta-analytic statistical methods to enable the collation of large numbers of research projects, which has further helped to establish efficacy. Smith and Glass (1977) used 475 trials of treatment versus no-treatment over 18 therapeutic modalities and found that the average treated person is better off than 80% of people who have not been treated. They found that the effects of therapy are better than no treatment or of placebo control, and that therapies generally seem to have equivalent effects when compared between different modalities. Since the ground-breaking Smith and Glass review there have been a large number of such studies and, although overall effect sizes vary, their findings have been replicated. Thus it is broadly agreed that psychotherapy treatments benefit the majority of (but not all) subjects. More detailed reviews can be found in publications such as Bergin and Garfield's authoritative studies of psychotherapy research, the *Handbook of Psychotherapy and Behaviour Change*, the most recent edition of which was issued in 2003 (Lambert, 2003).

Equivalence of treatments

The establishment of the efficacy of psychotherapy generally led to the 'equivalent outcome' finding, or what Luborsky has called the 'dodo bird verdict' (Luborsky and Singer, 1975). This is a reference to the caucus race in Alice in Wonderland where the dodo bird concludes that 'all have won and all shall have prizes'. This finding was the stimulus for the research developments that Barkham characterized as Generation II, namely investigations into particular therapeutic modalities with a view to demonstrating which treatment was most efficacious for which disorder. The standard methodology for this research was the randomized controlled trial (RCT), with a random allocation of patients into at least two treatment types and a control group. The largest of these was the National Institute of Mental Health Treatment of Depression Collaborative Research Program (Elkin, 1994), where 250 clients were randomly assigned to four treatment conditions, including cognitive behavioural, interpersonal, a pharmacological intervention and a placebo condition. This found no significant differences between the three active treatment groups, but superiority of the treatment groups over the placebo group. The Sheffield projects in the UK used this basic design to compare 8 and 16 session prescriptive (cognitive behavioural) and exploratory (psychodynamic interpersonal) treatment for patients with depression (Shapiro and Firth, 1987; Shapiro *et al.*, 1994). Findings showed a slight advantage of prescriptive over exploratory therapy, but only on one out of seven client self-report measures.

The attempt to establish the general superiority of one treatment modality over another has not been successful, causing Bergin and Garfield (1994) to conclude:

> One of the most difficult findings to conceptualise theoretically or to use practically is the continuing and frequent lack of difference in the outcomes of various techniques. With some exceptions, which we will consider, there is massive evidence that psychotherapeutic techniques do not have specific effects, yet there is tremendous resistance to accepting this finding as a legitimate one. (p. 822)

This is a judgement that is repeated in the 2003 edition of the *Handbook of Psychotherapy and Behaviour Change*, in which the authors launch a robust criticism of the movement to develop lists of 'empirically supported treatments' (ESTs) and treatment guidelines founded on psychotherapy research. It is argued that the research evidence does not support this approach, partly because of the overwhelming finding of equivalence of treatments (except in a very few matches of certain treatments with particular circumscribed conditions) and partly because of the methodological weaknesses in some of the research on which it is based. One telling finding in relation to this issue was that of Luborsky *et al.* (1999) who demonstrated that strong researcher allegiance produces large effect sizes in research studies: in other words there is systematic bias in research findings according to the therapeutic allegiance of the researchers. This therefore tends to favour those modalities which are more active in empirical research.

Cost effectiveness

The third generation of research as defined by Barkham has been particularly concerned with issues of cost effectiveness and service delivery, driven by the public sector service provision agendas in the United States and Europe. Given that the general efficacy of psychotherapy had been established, and that there was a demand for its provision within the public services, this raised the question of how much is enough. While a private treatment, like private sector psychoanalysis, is rationed by the willingness of the client to pay, when psychotherapy treatments became an important part of public sector provision there was naturally a need to provide evidence of what and how much was justified. It is generally the case in the UK that psychotherapy treatments available within the National Health Service (NHS) are limited – between six sessions and a year – and within the US there has been an even stronger trend towards briefer treatments. This is also true of the psychotherapies which have been systematically researched, which are almost all brief interventions. While this partly reflects the normal practice of the modalities which have been the subject of research, it also arises from the need for experimental control and for economy in research design.

Much of the discussion about length of treatment has focused upon 'dose-effect' research, which has been concerned to look at the incremental effect of therapy upon outcome. Howard *et al.* (1986) found that over 50% of clients showed measurable improvement after just eight sessions, and 74% after 26 sessions. In other words, most clients seem to gain quite quickly, with a minority needing a longer provision. Barkham (1996) stresses the importance for efficient service delivery for distinguishing between those clients who can be helped with a brief intervention and those who require a longer treatment. Within public sector provision this is possibly (in an ideal world) achieved through the provision of differing levels of speciality of psychological treatment, from primary care short-term counselling to more specialist and intensive psychotherapy treatments.

Howard *et al.* (1995) have built upon the dosage model to develop a three-phase model of psychotherapy which has been used as a basis for the widely used UK clinical audit instrument, the Clinical Outcomes in Routine Evaluation (CORE) (Barkham *et al.*, 2001). The phase model sees psychotherapy as progressing through phases in order:

- remoralization – usually a quick response reducing distress and enabling the mobilization of coping resources;
- remediation – concerned with refocusing coping skills to bring symptomatic relief;
- rehabilitation – a later stage focusing on unlearning maladaptive long-standing patterns.

The authors have demonstrated that the phases are sequentially dependent and that there may be different therapeutic processes that characterize each phase. Empirical support for the model comes from the large amount of data that has been accumulated from the CORE instrument based upon the phase model.

Clinically significant change

The research generation which Barkham defines as a possible fourth phase focuses on the area of clinically significant change. The standard procedure for determining whether psychotherapy 'works' is that there is a demonstrable difference in change between a non-treatment and a treatment group which is statistically significant: i.e. judged to have a less than 5% or 1% probability of having happened by chance. Jacobson and Truax (1991) challenge the use of the concept of statistical significance to determine whether change has taken place. They argue that statistical significance tests give no information on the variability of response within the sample and also that statistical effects have little to do with clinically significant changes. While the notion of effect size (the overall effect of the treatment) provides some fuller information, it is subject to the same limitations, in that the size of an effect is relatively independent of its clinical significance. Jacobson and Truax argue that a clinically significant change occurs when the client moves outside the range of a dysfunctional population into the range of a functional population. This approach has been used in conjunction with outcome measures to develop guidelines on standard scores for normal and pathological populations. For instance, developers of the CORE outcome measure (Barkham *et al.*, 2001; Evans *et al.*, 2002) have developed outcome benchmarks based upon data for clinical and normal populations which has enabled service providers to evaluate their provision in relation to national benchmarks for psychotherapy effectiveness.

The requirement of clinically significant change leads to a more rigorous test of efficacy, reducing the normal figure for improvement over a specified treatment period to a lower figure. Lambert and Ogles (2003) reviewed the recent research on clinically significant change in relation to the optimal duration of therapy. They conclude that 50% might expect to achieve clinically significant change with 21 sessions, but that over 50 sessions are needed for 75% of patients to achieve clinically significant change. This indicates a longer optimal treatment than the research of Howard *et al.* (1986) quoted above. On this basis Lambert and Ogles argue that the lengths of treatment offered within public services, particularly in the US, could be seen as sub-optimal. On a more encouraging note they confirm that there is good evidence that the effects of therapy are lasting.

Developments in process research

Process research methods are the topic of this book and hence the main focus from this point. However, it should first be acknowledged that the standard division between process and outcome research is not a satisfactory one. In its purest forms outcome research is only concerned with comparing where patients are at the end of therapy – using various instruments, mainly self report – with where they were before therapy started. In its purest form process research is concerned with what happens in the psychotherapy process itself without concern for the before/after outcome. In reality, practically all psychotherapy research conducted in recent years has combined elements from both. Consideration only of outcome had relevance in the days when establishing the efficacy of psychotherapy generally was the main aim. However, as soon as investigation moved to the comparison of treatments, process elements had to be taken into account. A fundamental question in comparing treatments is whether there is adherence to the technical requirements of the modality in the actual treatment. There has been a vast range of research which comes into the category of process-outcome. In their comprehensive recent review of this research Orlinsky *et al.* (2003) counted 2354 separate findings from hundreds of studies between 1950 and 1992, and a further 320 publications appearing between 1993 and 2001.

According to Orlinksy *et al.* (2003) there are two sources for the contemporary study of psychotherapy processes. The first was the use of sound recordings of sessions which began in the 1930s and 1940s. Previous to this the only available data from sessions was in the form of case studies written up by therapists for didactic purposes. The other approach to studying process came from those who developed rating scales and questionnaires to study the subjective experiences of clients and therapists. The main methods reviewed in this book clearly relate to the first tradition: the analysis of the raw data (sound or sound and video) or the session, by the therapist or by a third party. Much of the early research in this area was on the necessary and sufficient conditions for change, based upon Rogerian client-centred therapy (Rogers, 1957), which formed the foundation of research into the therapeutic relationship for decades to come.

The development of research into the therapeutic alliance, stimulated by Bordin's (1976) discussion of the 'working alliance' was probably the most significant process research innovation in the 1970s and 1980s. The work of Horvarth and Greenberg (1994) continues to the present day. Another significant development was the publication of Rice and Greenberg's *Patterns of Change* (1984) which described the task-analytic method for the intensive analysis of process, with markers for significant events. The development of robust concepts and methods to study the psychotherapy process, in combination with the equivalence of outcomes finding from outcome research, has led to an interest in the 'common factors' in the psychotherapy process, rather than technique specific factors.

Factors leading to change in psychotherapy

Despite many studies into the specific effects of psychotherapy modalities, the significant ingredients of the process of psychotherapy have been found to be common factors, namely those which may be expected to be present in some form or other in any therapy. This has led to a call for an abandonment of the movement for empirically supported treatments towards a greater exploration of the elements of therapy which seem to promote change. Lambert and co-workers (Asay and Lambert, 2000;

Lambert and Barley, 2002) reviewed the outcome research literature and found that the variables which affect progress can be divided into four main categories: extratherapeutic factors (those factors that come with the client, ego strength, spontaneous remission, outside events etc); expectancy (placebo, belief in treatment); techniques (factors specific to a particular modality); relationship factors (variables found in more therapies, such as empathy, understanding, alliance). The relative impact of these categories based upon this review has been judged to be: 40% extratherapeutic, 30% relationship, and 15% expectancy. Thus only 15% of therapeutic change is contributed by factors which are specific to a particular modality of therapy; the remaining 85% comprise common or extratherapeutic factors. The largest of the categories – the extratherapeutic factors brought by the client and his/her environment – is outside of the control of psychotherapy. These factors are very significant from the point of view of assessment of suitability for various interventions, and for adjusting treatments. Similarly, the area of pre-therapy expectancy is outside the control of treatment, although this is not to say that expectancy cannot be changed in treatment. The clear implication of this finding is that we should mainly focus upon relationship factors, rather than specific techniques, in order to maximize therapeutic gain.

Before discussing the relationship factors, it is useful to reiterate the issue of the lack of research support for specific techniques, which came up in the 'dodo bird verdict' in efficacy, as discussed above. Lambert and Barley (2002) point out that available research leads to the clear conclusion that psychotherapy in general has been shown to be effective, but that this does not lead us to what the healing components in the therapy relationship actually are. Despite attempts by particular schools of therapy to demonstrate the unique efficacy of their own techniques, meta-reviews have not demonstrated the superiority of any form of therapy in treating clients across broad categories of pathology. It can be argued that those studies that have shown differential effects do not seem representative of typical clinical practice: for instance, in using very restricted client groups with mild pathology. Obvservations by Luborsky et al. (1999) of the significant part played by researcher allegiance further undermines the confidence in any differences. While there are a few techniques that have shown clear superiority with particular diagnostic categories, such as exposure treatments for certain phobias, there is no clear evidence that the ingredients of particular modalities are more effective with the broad range of problems seen in normal clinical practice.

Lambert et al. (2003) point out that observations of practice across the modalities have revealed that, regardless of the type of therapy, it will include cognitive, emotional, behaviour and relationship elements.

Whatever the technique that is emphasized in the theories and manuals, there is a great degree of commonality between different modalities. The evidence seems to point to these common elements as the main ingredients of therapeutic change. The importance of common factors does not mean that formal therapy is ineffective, merely that we don't know precisely why it works. Learning theorists have attributed change to un-learning response patterns in the therapy relationship and acquiring new ones. Humanistic perspectives have emphasized the caring relationship, characterized by empathy and acceptance, as healing in itself. The psychodynamic view to some extent spans these two perspectives, in emphasizing maladaptive relational patterns acquired in childhood which are able to change in the therapeutic milieu. Where traditionally psychoanalytic theorists have emphasized the role of transference interpretation in developing insight and promoting change, the link between frequency of transference interpretation and outcome has not been supported by research evidence. The emphasis of most psycho-dynamic schools has now shifted to a more relational focus.

Relationship factors

The most robust finding from process-outcome research over the years has been the importance of the therapist and the therapeutic relationship. Lambert and Barley (2002) have divided these into therapist variables, facilitative conditions, and client–therapist relationship, while acknowl-edging that it is impossible to completely differentiate these issues. For instance, the facilitative conditions of psychotherapy are essential in forming the therapeutic alliance. Barkham (1996) points out that facilitative conditions have been viewed as the mechanism of change, whereas the alliance is maybe best seen as the mechanism through which the client is able to stay in therapy. The work of Safran and Muran (for instance, 1996) has looked in detail at the ebb and flow of the therapeutic alliance and importance of dealing with ruptures and bringing about reparation to enable therapies to work.

Research on facilitative conditions started with Rogers and others using taped sessions as mentioned above. Orlinsky *et al.*'s review of 1994 identified therapist credibility, skill, empathic understanding and affirmations of the client as consistently shown to have a positive impact. They also found that the ability to focus on the client's problems and to direct attention to the affective experience are strongly related to outcome. However, according to Lambert and Barley (2002), research into the facilitative conditions proposed by the person-centred model – empathy, warmth, positive regard, congruence – has provided little direct evidence of a cause–effect relationship. They suggest that the relationship between therapist attitudes and interpersonal skills and outcome is more ambiguous than originally thought. However, Elliott *et al.* (2003) quote a medium effect size linking empathy to outcome-based upon a meta-analysis. They conclude that empathy is better seen as a 'climate' variable created by the therapeutic dyad rather than a technique provided by the therapist. Client-perceived measures have achieved consistently more positive results than observer or therapist measures. This tends to reinforce the view that it is the relational aspects of the process that are important. It is not the objective level of skills of the therapist, but rather how the personality and skill of the therapist are experienced by the client, which supports the therapeutic relationship. This observation, of the importance of the client's perception of being liked, understood and helped, has been supported by many research studies. An example of this finding is provided in the study by Najavits and Strupp (1994) who used the structural analysis of social behaviour (SASB) methodology (discussed in detail in Chapter 5) to look at facilitative conditions as well as more subtle forms of negative behaviours exhibited by different therapists. They concluded:

> Thus, basic capacities of human relating – warmth, affirmation, and a minimum of attack and blame – may be at the center of effective psychotherapeutic intervention. Theoretically-based technical interventions were not nearly as often significant in this study (p. 121).

Orlinsky *et al.* (2003) conclude that effective therapy is more than a set of technical procedures, but also more than just a warm supportive relationship (p. 363).

Therapeutic alliance

The therapeutic alliance, or relationship, therefore has moved very much centre stage in process-outcome studies. Bordin (1976) conceived the alliance as comprising three components: tasks, bonds and goals. Modern views of the alliance are close to this formulation in incorporating the therapist's contribution, including the facilitative conditions, the therapist's ability to deal with ruptures, and to negotiate goals. Horvarth and Bedi (2002) provide the following definition of the concept:

The alliance refers to the quality and strength of the collaborative relationship between client and therapist in therapy. This concept is inclusive of: the positive affective bonds between client and therapist, such as mutual trust, liking, respect, and caring. Alliance also encompasses the more cognitive aspects of the therapy relationship; consensus about, and active commitment to, the goals of therapy and to the mean by which these goals can be reached. Alliance involves a sense of partnership in therapy between therapist and client, in which each participant is actively committed to their specific and appropriate responsibilities in therapy, and believes that the other is likewise enthusiastically engaged in the process. (p. 41)

While the alliance is specifically about the therapy relationship it is recognized that it will be affected by prior relational history or disposition. It is well known that patients with very chaotic or abusive relational histories are very difficult to engage in therapy.

Various instruments have been developed to measure the alliance, from a client, therapist or observer perspective. Most of this research has its origins in the psychodynamic and humanistic perspectives, although the alliance has received more emphasis from exponents of behavioural and cognitive therapies in recent years, leading to hopes that the concept can bring about real integration in the research field between the different approaches. Reviews have consistently found a positive relationship between alliance and outcome. The research is comprehensively reviewed in Horvarth and Bedi (2002) who found a substantial relationship between alliance and outcome. They found that the source of the data was significant, in that therapist, client and observer ratings are different: what we are dealing with in relation to the participants is the *perception* rather than something which can be precisely measured. Given that we also have ratings of outcome derived from therapist, client and observer, tracing the relationship between alliance and outcome is a complex process. Generally speaking, client rating of alliance has been a superior outcome predictor than therapist rating, although it seems that client and therapist ratings tend to move closer together as therapy progresses. A fairly robust finding of research into alliance is that early measures of alliance (often at the third session) are a slightly better predictor of outcome than mid-therapy measures, which is perhaps a reflection of the difficult issues that have to be worked through in the middle stages of therapy.

Horvarth and Bedi (2002) also look at the mediators of the therapeutic alliance: those factors which contribute to or impede the formation of an alliance. These include client factors with some (but not all) studies indicating that more severely disturbed clients have poorer alliances. They comment that one of the reasons that there is only weak evidence for this link is probably due to the fact that clients with poor alliance tend to drop out of therapy. There is also some evidence that patients with complex and entrenched pathologies, such as borderline and other personality disorders combined with the main diagnosis, are particularly challenging to engage. The quality of the client's attachment style is also significant, with poor attachment styles correlated with poor initial alliances, therapeutic ruptures and poor improvement in alliance over time (Eames and Roth, 2000). However, despite the difficulty experienced by patients with non-secure attachment styles in forming an alliance, there is some evidence that greater relative improvements can occur in patients with insecure forms of attachment (Fonagy *et al.*, 1996; Meyer and Pilkonis, 2002).

Research into the therapist contributions to the alliance give support to the role of interpersonal and communication skills, empathy and openness in helping to build the alliance. There is less unequivocal evidence for the contribution of experience and training to the ability to form an alliance. However, there has been increasing focus upon the therapist's own past, and the tendency to engage in covert negative process, by Henry, Strupp and co-workers (e.g. Henry *et al.*, 1990). They argue that even in carefully devised handbook-based therapies, the therapist's unresolved relationship patterns may engage negatively in therapy. Rubino *et al.* (2000) used attachment theory to find a link between therapist attachment style and the resolution of ruptures in the alliance. They found that more anxious therapists tended to respond less empathically with some patients. Meyer and Pilkonis (2002) conclude that research is beginning to demonstrate how therapist attachment styles influence treatment, with complementary matches between therapist and patient styles affecting the quality of the alliance. Investigations into the interactive elements of the therapy relationship has shown some support for the hypotheses of interpersonal theory (see Chapter 5 on interpersonal approaches), in that positive moment-to-moment interactions with greater complementarity are related to good alliance. The opposite is true for negative interactions, for instance covert criticism and hostility. Horvarth and Bedi (2002) conclude that 'it seems that what is most important is that the therapist–client transactions are not hostile, negative, or competing' (p. 59). Similarly they find preliminary evidence for the positive link between alliance and collaboration and cooperation.

In conclusion, the impact of relationship factors and the alliance is far in excess of the outcome variance that can be accounted for by techniques. Alliance, along with therapist variables, accounts for 'most of the systematic outcome variance in psychotherapy' (Horvarth and Bedi,

2002, p. 61). The alliance is a complex concept which can be seen as having various elements, measurable from the three different perspectives of therapist, client and observer, with a number of well established instruments. While the alliance itself is not the main aim of psychotherapy treatment, the well replicated robust finding of the link between alliance and outcome means that it has become a very important concept within psychotherapy process-outcome research, and certainly the most important generic therapy ingredient. Given the importance of the therapy relationship in therapeutic outcome, and the established influences on this of client and therapist factors and the interactional context itself, there are strong arguments for the focus on the therapeutic discourse which most of the process research methods discussed in this book involve.

Conclusion

The field of psychotherapy research is a rich one which draws upon a wide variety of disciplines and methodologies. The efficacy of psychotherapy has been broadly established to the satisfaction of all but the most sceptical of observers and the focus has shifted to the mechanisms of change: what actually happens in the psychotherapy relationship that enables clients to change in significant ways. Thus the field of process research has increased in importance and there is great potential for creative work in this area. In addition, findings from other disciplines are beginning to make an impact on process research. This is particularly the case in neuro-science, with researchers attempting to match cognitive and emotional phenomena with observable changes and events within the brain. Early evidence is beginning to emerge that experiences in psychotherapy – for instance, the mobilization of significant relationship or attachment experiences – may facilitate changes in schema or internal working models that can form the basis for significant and long lasting good outcome (see, for instance, Fonagy *et al.*, 2004). There is good evidence that psychotherapy works and emerging evidence that this might be enabled through the emotional experience of the therapy relationship, mediated by past attachment experiences and facilitated by the skill and attachment style of the therapist. The time is thus ripe for psychotherapists and researchers to develop creative and meaningful research focusing upon the psychotherapy relationship as manifested in the session recording or transcript.

   In the chapters which follow, a number of different research methods appropriate to psychotherapy process research will be introduced. Their underpinning concepts and strategies differ in the ways outlined in this introduction. They are all, however, linked by the common, shared basic process of inquiry: research design; data collection; data analysis, and documentation. It is this adherence to a set of procedures which provides a secure grounding for the variety of approaches needed to research the complex process which is psychotherapy.

SUGGESTIONS FOR FURTHER READING

Lambert, M.J. (ed.) (2003) *Bergin and Garfield's Handbook of Psychotherapy and Behaviour Change*, 5th edn. New York: Wiley.

Hubble, M.A., Duncan, B.L. and Miller, S.D. (eds) (1999) *The Heart and Soul of Change: What works in therapy.* Washington DC: American Psychological Association.

Roth, P. and Fonagy, P. (2005) *What Works for Whom: A critical review of psychotherapy research*, 2nd edn. London: Guilford Press.

CHAPTER 2

The research process

Introduction

It is not within the scope of this book to provide a detailed discussion of the various methodological issues and challenges within the psychotherapy research field. However, it is necessary to provide an overview before we go on to look at the specific area of process research. In the area of traditional quantitative efficacy research the perspective has been based on the principle of naturalism (as discussed in the introduction to Part I) and the dominant research paradigm has been that of the drug trial. This method is mainly concerned with testing the efficacy of a new treatment by comparing it with a control (no treatment or placebo), and often with another form of treatment. Research designs based around the single case have been slow to gain acceptance with the psychotherapy research field, but increasingly this form of research is being conducted and accepted as legitimate. The emphasis of this book is upon small scale research, often of a single case, based upon the psychotherapy session text. However, before focusing on this we will attempt to place this research practice within the wider context of psychotherapy research.

In this chapter we will follow the research process through the stages outlined at the end of Chapter 1. First, we start by looking at the research question, and specifically how we might approach three very different research questions. We will then discuss the issue of research design in relation to group and single case research and consider the question of validity and reliability specifically in relation to text-based research. This will enable us to return to the matter of our three research questions with a detailed discussion of the strategies for answering them. We will then go on to discuss data collection, research ethics, validity and reliability issues which need to be addressed in using an established (or inventing a new) method, and finally the process of drawing conclusions and documenting findings.

Asking a question

All research programmes and projects start with a question, or a set of questions. The feasibility of finding an answer to the question – or, using the more formal terminology, *falsifying a hypothesis* – depends upon many factors. A number of elements may make the research design inappropriate for the research question. The scope of the question may be too ambitious. For instance, the question 'how does psychotherapy work?' is too wide to yield any tangible results. Or, it could be that the methodology employed to address a question is not appropriate. For instance, patient completed self-report questionnaire data is not going to give any usable information on counter-transference. The problem could be the size and structure of the sample. A sample which is too small or which is not representative of the population under study will not give results that can be generalized with any confidence. Many of these issues come down to resources. While we may wish to produce the definitive randomized controlled trial on medium- or long-term psychotherapy, compared against medication and no treatment, the cost of undertaking such research is enormous and funding difficult to obtain.

This inevitably introduces the political into the equation. Research is normally only funded if there is a vested interest, usually by government or private industry, in the outcome. One consequence of this is that the issue of the lack of neutrality in research cannot be avoided. This is an issue that has been highlighted by Luborsky *et al.* (1999) in their finding that the modality allegiance of the researcher is a significant factor influencing outcome findings. While there are procedures that can be adopted to safeguard against this – for instance multi-modality research teams, guarantees that results can be published whatever the findings, non-interference by funding bodies in the research programme – nevertheless it is impossible to get around the problem that substantial funds will not be forthcoming for research which does not sit high on the agendas of funding agencies. In the field of psychotherapy research, one of the recurrent problems has been the tendency for medical research to be funded by pharmaceutical companies. It is unlikely that a pharmaceutical company will be enthusiastic about funding research into a potentially effective non-pharmacological alternative to anti-depressant medication.

Some of the important aims of this book are to help the psychotherapy researcher to refine the question, to adopt feasible strategies for data collection, and to utilize an appropriate research methodology so that the research goal is attainable. It is beyond our scope to advise on funding and it is a regrettable fact that funding for psychotherapy research is difficult to find. However, given a question with a limited scope and a realistic project for collecting and analyzing data, it is possible to undertake very valuable research with support from employers (usually the public sector health providers) but without significant external funding.

Figure 2.1 Research questions

Question 1 – Is brand A psychotherapy more effective than brand B, and how does it compare with no treatment for patients with depression?

Question 2 – Is the frequency and accuracy of transference interpretations in psychodynamic psychotherapy a significant positive factor in improving outcome in 20 sessions?

Question 3 – What are the main ways that Patient A, who had a good outcome in a 20 session tape recorded therapy, changed?

The first aspect to consider is the research question itself. Consider the three broad research questions in Figure 2.1 and imagine the designs of research – for instance, the sample, scope and methodology – which would be appropriate for attempting to answer them.

Without at this stage discussing the questions in detail, it can readily be seen that the research programmes in relation to the three questions would be radically different. The first question is concerned with efficacy (whether a treatment produces a positive benefit compared to no treatment) and will necessarily involve a group design. It is likely to be expensive to mount. The second question would seem to be approachable using a small group, or even single case, design which will inevitably focus on the content of the sessions, particularly the frequency and accuracy of interpretation. The third question relates to just one patient and seems to require a fairly open-ended approach to the issue of change. This question will require a single case design. We will return to examine these questions in more detail after we have addressed some of the general issues of research design for group-based and single case studies.

Research design in group-based studies

A fundamental principle of all group-based designs is to have the maximum experimental control in order to ensure that valid comparisons between groups are being made. Within conventional efficacy research, for example, the aim is to ensure that the change which is observed in a dependent variable (for instance, outcome) is really attributable to an independent variable (for instance, a particular form of psychotherapy) rather than to other factors (for instance, spontaneous remission). There are various factors which need to be considered in order to maximize control. Attention needs to be paid to ensuring that the sample is representative of the population being considered. This requirement has increasingly led to the use of narrow diagnostic limits to set the entry threshold to a research trial. Another important aspect of conventional group design is the randomization of the allocation of subjects between the different treatment conditions. This is a way of ensuring that observable differences in outcome are the result of the treatment condition being tested rather than a bias in the allocation of subjects. In addition, a central issue to which researchers using group designs must attend is that of the overall sample size. For example, in a current project with which we are involved, 560 referrals into a psychotherapy service resulted in fewer than 100 who completed therapy and the full set of outcome instruments. This experience is echoed by McLeod (1994), who advises the researcher to assume that the number of subjects will be one-tenth of the first estimate. There is drop out at every stage of the process (referred to as 'attrition'), from referral to assessment, to start of treatment, and during treatment. Researchers need to ensure that they will end with sufficiently large groups in each of their treatment conditions to give the possibility of meaningful statistical analysis.

Control is also exercised through the standardization of the treatments, to ensure that what is being compared is what it claims to be. Early research within the Menninger Project (Wallerstein, 1989) found that psychoanalytic treatments included a significant element of support, despite a therapeutic model which does not espouse this. If we are trying to compare different treatments it is necessary to preserve what is different about them. This has increasingly led to the manualization of therapies and to process research methods being used within research trials to test for adherence to therapeutic guidelines. In the coding of material, control is exercised by ensuring that coders are blind to outcome and to the temporal sequence of extracts.

Control is needed within efficacy trials in order to give maximum *internal validity* – in other words, to give maximum confidence that the conclusions reached are justifiable and generalizable to other similar populations. It is for this reason that this kind of research is referred to as 'gold standard research' and is given higher credence by commissioning bodies. However, the problem with this kind of research is that it tends to be very artificial and consequently to have a low applicability into normal practice. For instance, randomization itself is a very artificial constraint which goes directly against the current trend for patient choice. The use of narrow diagnostic criteria – for instance, depression with no accompanying personality disorder, no concurrent treatment, and no previous depressive episode – is also highly artificial. In the real world of public sector psychotherapy provision there are practically no patients who would satisfy these conditions. The research trial condition, that of manualized therapy, is also artificial. It can be argued that therapists need to adapt their style to the client material and that strict adherence to a particular approach is not what would happen in normal good practice. The applicability into normal practice is referred to as *external validity*, which refers to the confidence with which we might feel able to generalize the findings of research trials to normal practice. Hence we have the dilemma that high internal validity leads to low external validity and *vice versa*, an issue that is discussed in detail by Roth and Fonagy (2005) and others. The conflict between internal and external validity has led some researchers to call for more naturalistic studies of psychotherapy in actual practice (Margison *et al.*, 2000), and this is the focus of most of the research discussed in this book.

Validity and reliability in group designs

Apart from the validity of the design itself, validity and reliability need to be established in the instruments and methods used. This has a clear parallel in scientific instruments. For instance, the validity of a thermometer is the extent to which it actually measures temperature, the reliability of a thermometer is how reliable it is in doing this (i.e. whether it will show the same temperature in the same conditions or with repeated application). In the case of research which uses questionnaires or coding instruments it is a central issue whether the instrument measures the phenomenon under study. This is normally established through comparisons with other instruments (concurrent or convergent validity), how the questionnaire items on the surface seem to relate to the phenomena (face validity), and how well the questionnaire demonstrates palpable change in the phenomena under study (predictive validity). The psychometric properties of an instrument are usually investigated on its launch. There are therefore clear advantages in using an established instrument rather than developing one's own. The issue of reliability in relation to instruments is whether there is demonstrable consistency in repeated use of it: either in self-report instruments administered or in the coding assigned by different raters. Researchers needing to develop their own instruments are referred to more detailed discussions of the issues involved (for instance, Hill, 1991).

Once validity and reliability have been established, the researcher needs to decide which statistical or other tests are to be applied to the results. In any hypothesis testing research, it is important to decide in advance what will be the criteria by which the results will be judged. In conventional quantitative research design the standard procedure is to set a confidence level for seeing a result as significant. For instance, in aggregated changes in clients who have undertaken a particular therapy a calculation is made (based upon the size of the change and the standard deviation of the sample) as to the chance that this could have happened randomly. This is usually calculated using a standard statistical package suitable for a PC. Normally, the confidence interval is set as the probability (of the effect happening by chance) of less than 5% or 1% (that is, $p < 0.05$ or 0.01). These respectively give a confidence of 95% and 99% that the effect is a true treatment effect rather than attributable to chance. The higher the confidence level (the lower the value of p), the less the chance of a *Type 1 error*: that is, of attributing a difference to the treatment when it really arises from chance. Using a value of p of 0.05 gives a 5% chance that a Type 1 error will occur, so clearly researchers aim to find changes which are statistically significant at the level of $p = 0.01$. The opposite error – of attributing an effect to chance when really it is due to the treatment – is referred to as a *Type 2 error*. The chance of finding a statistically significant result will decline (even where there genuinely *is* a true effect) as the sample size gets smaller: hence the need to ensure a large enough sample. The use of statistical significance as the overarching criteria for determining efficacy has been questioned by Jacobson and Truax (1991), as discussed in Chapter 1. Their criterion of clinical significance sets a higher threshold for determining efficacy.

Within pure process research simple measures of change are not usually the focus, but within process-outcome research – where the interest is which elements of process relate to observable change – it remains a key question. In pure process research the issue of whether the research hypothesis is supported or not is usually more complicated because the analysis data is often not available in a form to which statistical tests can be applied. Researchers therefore need to pay careful attention to the tests or arguments which they use to establish the validity of the result that they are claiming. This is discussed below in relation to text-based research methods.

Research design in single case studies

An alternative to the standard psychotherapy group design is that of the single case design, which aims to measure variance within a case, rather than comparisons between groups of clients or cases. This has been termed an *intensive* rather than an *extensive* research design (Chassan, 1979). Most of the early 'research' in psychoanalysis was of this form, with Freud and followers writing up a case which was illustrative of the relevance of the clinical theories which were in the process of development. The inadequacies of the traditional psychoanalytic case history as scientific method have been highlighted (see, for instance, Grunbaum, 1984, or Spence, 1993). Clinical case studies were originally (and are still) used as teaching tools within the psychoanalytic model and also subsequently within other therapeutic modalities. From the perspective of research, the problem with the traditional case study is that it lacks any kind of control to ensure that there is a reasonable basis for comparison, and any claim to objectivity. The person writing up the case is invariably the therapist, who usually relies upon notes taken from memory after sessions rather than audio recording, and who may have a particular line to pursue. The opportunities not just for *random* distortion, but for *systematic* (even if unconscious) distortion, are rife. This is not to deny the value of case histories in giving an insight into a particular theoretical model or therapeutic approach and as training aids. Also, as McLeod (1994) points out, case studies have been used as the starting points for more systematic research, either through the accumulation of competing or supporting cases, or through more systematic quantitative studies.

Despite the problems in establishing the validity of single case studies there has been some development of systematic case study research in recent years. Research methodologists such as Kiesler have moved from the position that the single case study has little place in the confirmatory aspect of scientific activity (1971), to viewing it as the most appropriate way to study change process in psychotherapy (Kiesler, 1981, 1983a). Hilliard (1993) addresses the methodological issues in relation to single case studies and argues that they are best viewed as a sub-class of intra-subject research, where the generality of findings is addressed through replication on a case by case basis. He describes three basic types of single case research: single case experiment; single case quantitative analyses; and case studies. In order to make this distinction he employs three main criteria. He defines *quantitative* as employing measures which are interval, ordinal or ratio (i.e. allowing some numerical relationship or ranking) and *qualitative* where measures are nominal. He defines *experimental* studies as those in which an independent variable is directly manipulated by the researcher, in contrast to the *passive-observational* study where this is not the case. The third aspect that he looks at is whether the study is testing a hypothesis or whether the focus is upon generating hypotheses to be tested in later research: i.e. principally exploratory.

Hilliard defines the *single case experiment* as involving quantitative data and the direct manipulation of an independent variable, usually with the aim of hypothesis testing. In principle this could involve the greater or less use of empathy or transference interpretation, but more typically it is a design used within the behavioural therapy field, where there is arguably more scope for experimental manipulation. In contrast, *single case quantitative analyses* involve passive observation rather than experimental manipulation. These include studies where quantitative techniques are used, for instance, for the analysis of temporal changes in variables. Single case quantitative analyses can be used to both to test and to generate hypotheses and Hilliard uses the terms *confirmatory* and *exploratory* to distinguish these two principal aims. The third single case study type is the *case study*, usually used for designs with text-based, qualitative data. The term 'case study' implies both qualitative data and passive observation, although in principle it could involve experimental manipulation. As with the quantitative analysis, the case study can be either confirmatory or exploratory.

While Hilliard feels that single case designs fall into these three basic categories, he does also refer to research informed case studies which are basically qualitative but in which individual cases from a traditional group comparison have been selected for comparison. This has been true of much of the process research discussed previously, where individual cases have been selected for more intensive study on the basis of good or poor outcome. He also draws attention to studies in which quantitative and qualitative data are assessed within the same case. This has been true of much of the work coming out of the Vanderbilt projects (for example, Strupp, 1990) and of research using the change event perspective (Rice and Greenberg, 1984). Most of the small scale research studies discussed in this book fall into the category of the case study – whether confirmatory designs employing coding methods, or exploratory designs using discourse methods – although some generate data which are quantifiable.

Despite attempts to systematize single case research, and considerably greater interest in recent years in this form of study, the central problem for all (except single case experiments used within behavioural treatments) remains that of internal validity. The issue is the extent to which findings can be generalized to other cases. Critics argue that while the case gives a rich description of a client or a group, this does not mean it can be applied to other populations. McLeod (1994) argues that caution must be exercised in drawing conclusions from a single case study but argues that replication is the key strategy in addressing this issue. Whereas the traditional between-groups design can use sampling to ensure that chance elements are eliminated, this is impossible in the single case design and replication is the key tool to ensure the validity of single case research. This leads us to a discussion of validity and reliability in process research.

Reliability and validity in text-based case studies

Validity

For every researcher, whether using a group or a single case design, issues of the interpretation of data are crucial to the power of the analysis. Whether following a hypothesis testing strategy, or working with textual analysis in a theory building way, the process researcher designing a single case study must pay careful attention to issues of validity from the onset of designing the study. Validity aims not at reaching objective 'truth' so much as at determining whether the findings, as interpretations of data collected and analyzed, are consistent with the observations or measurements they describe. Validity is related to the process of naming phenomena, and is accepted as having been achieved when there is close alignment of data and interpretation. Kirk and Miller (1986) give three aspects of validity, all of which depend on each other:

- *Apparent validity*: the degree to which observations are clearly related to a phenomenon. For example, correct answers to a test assessed against previously established criteria.
- *Instrumental validity*: matching of one form of observation or measurement against another demonstrates consistent outcomes. This process is sometimes called 'triangulation of data'.
- *Theoretical validity*: the underlying theory corresponds substantially with the observations or measurements. This concept is also known as 'construct validity'.

Validity, in this view, is a *process* in which all three of these aspects are interdependent. A finding may have apparent validity, but this may be illusory. It may have no grounding in instrumental or theoretical validity. It is not sufficient. Instrumental validity may back up apparent validity, by a process of triangulation, but without the support of the other condition of validity it too may prove to have been a coincidence. To gain a convincing level of validity, apparent and instrumental validity must be grounded in theoretical validity, and interpretations of the data should take into account all three aspects. The design of a study which takes into account all three elements supports the process of validity. In group research designs, the use of recognized and suitable statistical instruments underpins the validity of the findings. The data, and the process of analysis, are often concealed within the standardized statistical testing procedures. In textual analysis, by contrast, where data is used to construct images and generate concepts, validity must be demonstrated through the transparency of the data analysis, and the availability of the data for inspection, where all three components of validity come together in a convincing demonstration of theoretical validity.

Reliability

Validity would have no basis if it were not founded in reliable data. For all researchers, the selection and analysis of data, adequate to the questions being asked of it, is the basis of the quality of the findings. For the process researcher, enhancing reliability is a concrete, as well as a procedural matter (Perakyla, 1997). The accuracy of the transcript is a pre-condition for the completeness of the analysis in relation to the questions asked of the data. The criticism of the psychoanalytic case study as a means of building theory – that it uses selected data, smoothing narratives, for example (Spence, 1993) – holds for all text-based analysis. To be reliable, data must be collected within the basic framework of inquiry: research design, data collection and analysis; and documentation. At each stage of the research, questions arise which the researcher must be prepared to answer:

Is this design sufficient to the question?
What is sufficient data?
When do I stop?
Have I justified my interpretation by reference to the data?
Is the entire process documented and transparent?

It is by rigorous adherence to the basic framework of investigation that the objectivity of the findings will be tested.

For each of the general principles, there are some commonly accepted specific methods underpinning reliability and validity. They are:

- *saturation of the data*: in text-based analysis, all data subject to the initial question and design must be accounted for;
- *constant comparative analysis*: the process by which data is organized and comprehensively analyzed;
- *theoretical sampling*: data for continuing comparative analysis are selected with reference to the conceptual framework within which the analysis is being undertaken;
- *deviant case analysis*: all cases which do not fit into the developing analytic categories must be accounted for, either by revising the hypothesis, or demonstrating how their difference supports the conceptual framework;

- *inter-rater agreement*: the process by which coding decisions are validated through systematic comparison of two or more coders.

Each of these will be introduced in the discussion of specific methods and their application in the chapters which follow.

Strategies for answering the research questions

We can now return to the three research questions proposed at the outset of this chapter, and discuss in detail the research designs and methods which might be appropriate given the discussion above.

Question 1 – Is brand A psychotherapy more effective than brand B, and how does it compare with no treatment for patients with depression?

A research programme designed to tackle this question would probably follow the route that was used for two well known, large, funded studies: the NIMH Treatment of Depression Collaborative Research Programme (Elkin, 1994) and the Sheffield Psychotherapy Project (Shapiro and Firth, 1987). Patients would be randomly assigned to a no-treatment control group and to the two treatment conditions. Given that the aim is to measure outcome, the sample size would need to be large enough to ensure that sufficient numbers of patients complete their treatment to enable meaningful comparisons of outcome. There is inevitably significant attrition – patients not completing treatments or outcome measures – in any psychotherapy outcome research. The ethical dimension of assigning patients randomly rather than according to assessed need would have to be addressed, particularly into a control group which receives no treatment or a placebo (see Lepper, 2000). The definition of the sample would need to be further refined – what kind of depression, are people with concurrent or previous treatments excluded, how do you ensure that the variation in the sample is evenly distributed between the three treatment conditions? There would have to be a process element to ensure that the actual delivery of the psychotherapy conforms to the requirements of the two modalities being studied. It has become increasingly recognized in psychotherapy research that what clinicians espouse in terms of their therapeutic orientations is not necessarily what they do in the consulting room. This has led to treatment manuals becoming the norm in this kind of research. (However, this raises important issues about the comparability of manualized therapy with treatment in practice.)

Another issue which must be addressed is which outcome measures would be used and what would be seen as an indication of significant change. Decisions would also need to be made about how the instruments would be administered and when. This leads to the question of whether a follow-up measure should be used, increasing the problem of attrition but taking account of change after the completion of therapy and maintenance of gains. Finally, there would be the inevitable difficult choices to be made about which statistical tests were appropriate and how they should be interpreted. This is a decision which should be made in advance to minimize the risk of researchers applying a series of statistical tests until they come up with a significant result. In summary, this question leads to a research programme which should produce general-izable results but which is highly expensive and which raises complex ethical and methodological problems.

Question 2 – Is the frequency and accuracy of transference interpretations in psychodynamic psychotherapy a significant positive factor in improving outcome in 20 sessions?

This question would seem to be more modest with two obvious starting points. One would be as a controlled experiment where therapists deliberately either used a high or low frequency of transference interpretations. However, this kind of single case experimental design would be problematic since the change which is to be measured is likely to be too long term to respond to variations in interpretation frequency within a single therapy of 20 sessions. As a result, this approach would give a very low external validity and would not address the issue of accuracy. An attempt at this kind of design in relation to a different independent variable is found in Barkham *et al.* (1996), where a patient was given alternate treatments of cognitive behavioural and psychodynamic interpersonal therapy. A more viable design would be between groups: one randomly assigned group of patients receiving high frequency, and one receiving low frequency of transference interpretations. A process research element would be needed to check on adherence to this plan, probably through observer rating of transcripts. However, this approach would not address the issue of accuracy since this is a variable which is difficult to manipulate experimentally. We cannot imagine an ethical design where therapists were asked to give inaccurate interpretations!

The only viable route would therefore seem to be a retrospective one, using a sample of audio taped psychotherapy sessions from different therapists with patients who have completed outcome measures. This would enable treatments to be split into high frequency and low frequency transference interpretation and, so long as the sample size is sufficient, a comparison made in the outcome of the two groups. The issue of accuracy is more difficult to address. Interpretations would need to be studied in order to locate accurate and inaccurate interpretation. This would need a method to score for accuracy, and the obvious candidate would be a coding method such as the core conflictual relationship theme (CCRT) method (discussed in detail in Chapter 3). Luborsky and Crits-Christoph (1990) have published results showing a positive link between the accuracy of transference interpretations and outcome.

Considering the issues in detail makes it clear that this is a very complex question to tackle. For instance, there is an ethical problem in randomly assigning patients to high or low transference frequency treatments because this takes no account of what may be clinically appropriate to different patients. A retrospective design has fewer ethical issues since the clinical treatment is not being artificially determined by the research design. However, this then raises the problem of whether it is possible to find sufficient numbers of low and high frequency cases, and of accurate and less accurate interpretations, and whether this is principally determined by the clinical preference (or competence) of the therapist or by the clinical need of the patient. If the former then what we end up comparing may be the effectiveness of different therapists rather than the high or low transference and accurate/inaccurate interpretation condition. If the latter then the result is not generalizable over the whole group, but merely shows that some patients are more able to work with, or to tolerate, transference interpretations than others. There are also the usual problems of how to measure outcome, and how to compare results statistically, that came with the previous research question. In addition, this question raises the difficult issue of whether the treatment modality of transference-based psychotherapy is best delivered in a 20 session format. It is likely that 20 sessions is the maximum feasible length of therapy to research in this way, but many would argue that this is a sub-optimal length for this kind of therapy. In summary, this is a very complex question to tackle. For an example of attempts to do so, you are referred to the work of Malan (1976) and Piper et al. (1993) in particular.

Question 3 – What are the main ways that Patient A, who had a good outcome in a 20 session tape recorded therapy, changed?

This is a question which seems to be designed for small scale practitioner-based research. It is based upon one patient, who is already known to have had a good outcome in psychotherapy, and who can be studied by an observer or by the treating clinician. The design is necessarily retrospective, qualitative and passive-observational: thus a case study in Hilliard's (1993) terms. The evidence for good outcome needs to be demonstrated: is this in the view of the therapist, the patient, an observer (maybe the clinical supervisor) or through patient completed outcome measures? Given that these questions are satisfactorily addressed, the researcher can focus on the change process itself and this leads to consideration of the possible methods of inquiry, described in detail in later chapters. We could take an open inductive approach, maybe selecting a random sample of text from the recorded sessions and undertaking a grounded theory or discourse analysis to explore any changes at the level of the therapeutic interaction. The aim of this might be to show that there are changes in the content or interactional process between the early and the late sessions. Discourse-based methods have the advantage of being exploratory approaches which do not impose a pre-conceived structure on the material. However, the downside of this strategy is that, while the resulting analysis may be detailed and interesting, it may be difficult to link to clinically significant concepts. At worst the risk is that the researcher is left hunting for a needle in a haystack without even knowing that it is a needle that is being hunted! A more structured approach which focuses on specifically clinical phenom-ena may be adopted by using a coding method which starts from a theoretical model, such as CCRT, to compare early and late sessions. Or, change in a problem area could be tracked using a method like the Assimilation Model, or one of the interpersonal process models. Each of these methods have their own strengths and weaknesses. With each of them we may reasonably expect the researcher/clinician to have some check on the categorizing or coding process to ensure consistency and objectivity in the process, which inevitably means collaboration with another researcher.

In summary, this research question is also a complex one which poses methodological challenges: what is our evidence for change, how might this be measurable, what are the appropriate techniques for demonstrat-ing it? It also needs to be recognized that the outcome of such a research project is not likely to be readily generalizable to other cases, in that we may end up with understanding of a change process which is unique to this client or to the client–therapist dyad. Generalizability is likely only to come from replication within other research projects. However, this is a research question which in principle can be undertaken without substantial funding, exhaustive data and a full team of researchers. A number of examples of this kind of research project are given within the later sections on the different methodologies.

Summary

The above research questions have been chosen because they to some extent exemplify particular approaches, ranging from the traditional randomized controlled trial methodology to qualitative single case methods. In reality many research projects will combine elements drawn from several research strategies. As discussed above, there has been a trend away from research aimed at demonstrating the efficacy of psychotherapy towards research which is aimed at explicating the change process and what leads to change. However, both endeavours have a process and an outcome element. Pure outcome research still needs to address the issue of what is actually happening in sessions – namely the psychotherapy process – in order to ensure that what is being compared is what it claims to be. Similarly, research which is mainly aimed at looking at the psychotherapy process will usually also have to ask what evidence there is for change, or for impasse, or even for deterioration. The researcher often wants to combine process research methods with the administration of outcome measures to put the findings in perspective. Our next topic is therefore the sources of such data.

The sources of data

There are various forms and sources of data that will be used by the psychotherapy process researcher. The principal of these, and the main focus of this book, are tapes and transcripts from psychotherapy sessions themselves. However, most research projects will start with a preliminary literature search to ascertain what existing published research there has been within the area. This is now very much easier because of computer and internet technology. The easiest and often the first search will be made on an internet search engine such as Google. Libraries have access to more specialized search facilities which contain archives of publication details, abstracts and sometimes full text copy of articles published within the subject, such as PsychLit within the area of Psychology and Medline within the area of Medicine. A considerable amount of initial research and reading can be done from the researcher's own computer, particularly if there is access to a university library login. This process is getting access to data of a kind; not usually the raw data, but summaries of research which has been conducted on raw data within other settings. Sometimes published articles and books will contain a sample psychotherapy session which can be used as raw data for original research (see for instance Snyder, 1963 and *Psychotherapy Research*, vols. 3 and 4, 1994). Some of the examples used in the subsequent chapters are taken from the Ulm Textbank (http://sip.medizin.uni-ulm.de), which contains a large number of session transcripts, often with associated outcome data.

The main data for a project will need to be collected by the researcher, either through his or her own service, personal clinical work, or in collaboration with other providers. In outcome research, the normal method is to collect data through the administration of questionnaires to patients, and sometimes to therapists, typically before, during and after therapy. In its simplest form this could include a questionnaire collected at the start of therapy and on completion, with the results compared between the two time points. This kind of data collection is often in use for everyday audit conducted within public sector psychotherapy or counselling providers. However, basic audit data provide little information about the psychotherapy process. Instruments which focus on the psychotherapy process can include questionnaires collected at the end of therapy asking for the perceptions of clients as to the process of therapy and the relationship with the therapist, or even instruments completed at the end of each session. This can be backed up with an interview and even a replay of parts of the tape of the session, as in the interpersonal process recall (IPR) method (Elliott, 1986). It can be argued that the more intensive this process, and the closer in time to the actual session, the fresher will be the data generated as a result. However, this has the disadvantage of intruding in to the therapy process itself, and of creating a rather artificial situation which might be problematic as the basis for generalization to normal practice.

The main focus of this book is on data which is generated directly from the session itself. This will normally entail tape or video recording of psychotherapy sessions and the subsequent transcription of the content of some or all of the sessions. An alternative is to use clinician process notes, which are detailed notes written up very soon after the sessions. It is difficult to find reliable information on how process notes, which some claim to be virtually verbatim, differ from taped transcripts. However, it has been our experience in using tape recording of psychotherapists in training that transcripts of tapes are very much longer than even the most detailed process notes. Clearly a lot of material is left out in the process of remembering. This would arguably not be too much of a problem if there was a random forgetting of material, but the strong likelihood is that this forgetting is not random and that what happens is effectively a distortion of the material according to preconception, theoretical model and counter-transference factors. This can therefore be seen as an occurrence in the micro focus of what Spence (1993) has described as a weakness of psychoanalytic case presentations generally: that is, that they cannot provide reliable data on the clinical process. Therefore the use of process notes for textual research may tell us more about the clinician than about the client or the process of therapy.

The process of tape recording is not as difficult as it sometimes seems at first to clinicians. Clients rarely refuse to give consent for tape recording and there is little evidence that after the first few sessions there is any awareness of the process. It has been our experience, and that of most of our trainees and clients, that tape recording is not intrusive to the process. Video recording adds a level of intrusiveness, requiring more equipment, but minimum intrusion can be achieved with fixed cameras and recording equipment that is kept in a separate room. Family therapists have long used the technique of the two-way mirror and video taping without problems. However, given the emphasis of most of the psychotherapy research methods discussed in this volume (with the possible exception of SASB), audio recording is likely to be sufficient. This enables an easy and cheap collection of process material, although the process of transcription is time consuming: about 5–7 hours for a competent transcriber for each session. The task of transcription is made more complicated by the need to record the timing of silences, the incidence of ums and ahs, or grunts, coughs etc. All of these non-verbal communications can have a bearing on the interpretation of the material. Transcription of a video is even more complicated and time consuming. Where videos are used it is the normal practice to code direct from the tape rather than from transcripts.

It is unlikely that researchers will want to transcribe all available sessions and it is more common to sample the text using a procedure with a clear rationale. The sample may be taken systematically as way of ensuring that the extracts chosen are a random representative sample of the material. For example, segments of text from the same part of a session or, in a larger project, sessions from the same part of several therapies, might be chosen. Or samples may be chosen from significant sessions or parts of sessions which were identified by the therapist or patient through a method such as interpersonal process recall (IPR). The sampling strategy chosen will depend on the methodology being used. For instance, CCRT (see Chapter 3) uses a random sampling method by advising the use of two randomly chosen early and two late sessions to locate relationship episodes and compare change between early and late therapy. The Assimilation Model (see Chapter 4) advises the immersion of clinicians or third party observers in the themes of the sessions in order to locate episodes for coding. This resembles the 'theoretical sampling' strategy used in grounded theory analysis (see Chapter 6). The researcher needs to be explicit about the sampling strategy used and the rationale for it. In order to minimize the unnecessary recording or transcription of material, decisions about sampling need to be made early in the research process.

Ethical issues

In the early years of psychotherapy research, it was relatively easy to gather data. Today, there is intense focus on the ethics of research. This is a good thing from the point of view of ensuring the protection of the clients' interests. However, concerns about ethics are increasingly making it difficult to undertake research projects, and research designs using transcriptions are subject to particularly intense scrutiny by research ethics committees. Arguably it is unethical *not* to research treatments, or to hinder forms of research which do not fall within a conventional medical model research protocol. The latter has sometimes been the case with qualitative designs, although these are now becoming better understood within the research community.

The ethical issues in relation to practice and research need to be addressed early in the research process. There are some ethical issues which enter at the design stage of any research. For instance, is it ethical to withhold treatment through the use of randomization in a control group? Is it ethical to artificially constrain treatment, through the use of manuals or experimental manipulation? Within the drug metaphor that prevails in medical research ethics there is the assumption that we are testing a new drug and comparing it to 'normal' treatment by randomizing patients between the new drug and the control. In these terms it can be argued that the research is ethical because it is not yet known for sure if the new drug is efficacious. (This is obviously subject to the normal pre-clinical trial checks, usually on non-human subjects, of basic drug safety.) However, this paradigm does not readily apply to psychotherapy, even in a conventional treatment versus control design. In particular, the design of the 'control', non-treatment or minimal treatment, group is problematic. It means that a treatment (psychotherapy) which has already been demonstrated to be generally efficacious is being withheld from people who could benefit from it. There is also considerable difference between the administration of a drug and the conduct of a psychotherapy. Much of the research evidence points to the need for therapists to be flexible and responsive in order to be effective. This goes against the kind of control needed to ensure that the treatment under test does not use other methods which might be seen as belonging to other treatments: for instance, cognitive behavioural methods by psychodynamic practitioners, or transference interpretation by behavioural therapists. The design of our research may therefore require therapists to deliver their treatment in a more rigid, less effective, way. This is clearly not ethical.

The normal minimal ethical requirement for research involving human subjects is the practice of informed consent. Clients must give permission for the administration of questionnaires or other measures, and for the recording and transcription of session material. They need to be given full information on the use of this material and particularly on its reproduction in any form of publication. It is common practice for clinicians to use clinical examples in their publications – usually within traditional case presentations – but this raises difficult issues in relation to the amount of detail given and the possible identification of the client. It is normal practice to change names, proper nouns, and demographic details of the material in order to protect the identity of the client. However, the most elaborate disguising of session material will not normally prevent the client (and maybe friends and colleagues who know about their therapy) from identifying themselves if their therapist is the author. The issue of confidentiality is not so complex if session or case study material is not reproduced, or if what is being presented is a summary of questionnaire data. However, the identity and interests of the client need to be carefully protected in any form of reproduction.

The assumption in requiring informed consent from participants is that this consent is voluntary. However, this is not entirely straightforward. Lepper (2001) concludes that it is probably not possible to be absolutely sure that consent is entirely voluntary and given in a fully informed way in the widest sense. One issue which needs to be clarified is whether consent is a condition of treatment. It is normal practice within public sector psychotherapy services for it to be made clear that treatment will not be withheld if consent is not given by the client. However, the recording of sessions and the administration of questionnaires may need to be a condition of treatment. For instance, in our training of psychotherapists we require sessions to be recorded in the early stages of training in order to ensure the adequate supervision and training of candidates. Within a public sector psychotherapy department, outcome questionnaires may be required for the audit of the service (although there is no way that clients can be made to complete them). One way around this is to separate the consent for taping or the use of questionnaires for clinical governance from the consent for the use of the material within research or publication. We require clients to provide two-stage consent. The first consent is for the use of tapes and questionnaires for clinical audit purposes, which is a condition of treatment. The second consent is for the use of taped material and questionnaires for research, which is not a condition of treatment.

Most research projects using human subjects will require the researcher to present the research design plan in some detail to a research ethics committee. The research committees exist to review projects of all sizes, and their systems are often complex and highly bureaucratic. They inevitably create delay and complication in the research process, and often some frustration amongst researchers. This has undoubtedly been an obstacle and prevented a lot of small scale research within the public sector. However, it is important to remember that research ethics committees exist for the protection of the client, and that it is essential that ethical issues are addressed in a rigorous manner. Research ethics procedures vary in different countries. Within the UK National Health Service (NHS), each area has a Local Research Ethics Committee (LREC) which is required to consider all research using NHS client data. Where data is taken from more than one area the research project needs to be considered by a Multi-Centre Research Ethics Committee (MREC). In addition, university-based research will usually need to be considered by a university-based research ethics committee, although this may be a rubber-stamping operation where projects have received ethical approval by the health services provider. Whatever the local or national requirements for research ethics approval, researchers are advised to check these early in the process of designing a project, and to allow ample time to go through the process of gaining approval. In particular, attention needs to be given to the procedure for informing clients and gaining their consent to participation in the project.

Choosing a research method

One of the objectives of this book is to help researchers to find a method which is appropriate for their research project. In later chapters these have been divided into discourse-based methods, which are generally more appropriate for the exploratory, inductive style of research; and coding methods, which usually start from a particular theoretical perspective and focus on specific features of the process in order to test clinical hypotheses. Clearly both approaches have their own strengths, as do the particular methods included within these broad categories, and it is for the researcher to decide which methods are appropriate to tackle their research questions. The reader is referred to the detailed discussion of the methods for a better understanding of the available options and which would be most appropriate for their intended study.

Another choice to be made is whether to use one method, or to employ a mixed model strategy, which can have great strengths. One way might be to start with a more exploratory approach, for example, grounded theory, in order to tease out some of the underlying structures within the therapy discourse. This might then be combined with a content analysis, such as Mergenthaler's Therapeutic Cycles Model (discussed in Chapter 9), or be used to identify a problem area, possibly in its pre-conscious manifestation, that can then be analyzed using a method such as the Assimilation Model (discussed in Chapter 4). One method may be used to identify an area of clinical interest in a text, and another to conduct a detailed analysis of the selected text (an example of this strategy can be found in Part IV). Alternatively, transcripts can be explored using different methodologies and then the findings compared. This strategy has been employed in several recent international meetings of the Society for Psychotherapy Research, where an international group of researchers has focused on a single transcript or set of transcripts. The potential for such collaboration is enormous.

Some research begins with a burning question in the mind of the investigator, which might be based on an observation, or a clinical hunch. Other questions emerge from the process of the research itself. The research design is to a large extent a pragmatic process of matching question to method. For the deductive, or theory testing, methods, the research question will take the form of a hypothesis, and the methods chosen will be designed to confirm or disconfirm the hypothesis. The discourse methods lend themselves to a theory-building strategy, capable of addressing more open, exploratory questions. In either case, the development of a question will depend on the data available to the investigator, and the resources (including time and money) available for data collection and management. The tasks of data collection and management will depend upon issues of sampling – how much data need to be collected, and how they are structured – and the methods which are being used. Attention needs to be paid to the issues of validity and reliability at each stage of the process: in the overall design, the collection of data, and, finally, in the course of the analysis. In the chapters in Parts II and III, we turn to the specific methods which we propose to introduce in some detail, demonstrating how a question can be matched to a method and how the research design can be constructed. Finally, in Part IV, we turn to the process of integrating the data analysis, and presenting the findings in the form of a research report. The management of large quantities of text can be a daunting task. In Chapter 10, we introduce some of the IT methods which can be used to aid the research process. Finally, in Chapter 11, we present a complete student research report to illustrate the final documentation of a small scale project.

SUGGESTIONS FOR FURTHER READING

Hill, C.E. and Lambert, M.J. (2003) 'Methodological issues in studying psychotherapy processes and outcomes', in M.J. Lambert (ed.), *Bergin and Garfield's Handbook of Psychotherapy and Behaviour Change*, 5th edn. New York: Wiley.

McLeod, J. (1994) *Doing Counselling Research*. London: Sage.

McLeod, J. (1999) *Practitioner Research in Counselling*. London: Sage.

Spence, D.P. (1993) 'Traditional case studies and prescriptions for improving them', in N.E. Miller, L. Luborsky, J.P. Barber and J.P. Dochehty, *Psychodynamic Treatment Research*. New York: Basic Books.

The coding approaches

Introduction

Part II is concerned with coding methods in common use in psychotherapy process research. In broad terms these are the methods which were identified in the introduction to Part I as following the naturalistic tradition which is prevalent in academic psychology. They start from a theoretical model which defines to a large extent the focus of the inquiry. For instance, the core conflictual relationship theme (CCRT) method starts from Freud's transference hypotheses and then uses transcripts of psychotherapy sessions to test these. The CCRT researchers assume that transference elements will be locatable from relationship episodes and have designed a specific coding system based around the structure of wish, response from other and response from self. Clearly using the CCRT enables the researcher to focus upon this area, but this also constrains the identification of material which is thought to be relevant. Any coding method must start with a view of what should be coded and how to structure that coding process. This is different from methods such as grounded theory (discussed in Part III), which aim to generate the conceptual framework directly from the text. For further discussion of the underpinnings of the discourse approaches you are referred to the introduction to Part III.

In common with all methods which we will discuss, any coding method must be concerned with the issue of sampling. In the naturalistic tradition great emphasis is placed upon the process of random sampling. This is to ensure that the sample is representative of the population as a whole. For instance, in election polling researchers have to ensure that they use a random sampling methodology and a large enough sample to justify generalizations about voting intentions in the population at large. Within conventional psychotherapy outcome studies (randomized controlled trials), emphasis has been placed upon randomization of treatment groups between the test conditions – that is, particular brands of psychotherapy –

and no-treatment groups. This is in order to avoid any bias in the sampling of the two groups and to justify the generalizations made about the efficacy of psychotherapies. The same kinds of considerations come into coding research: how many and how much of the available psychotherapy transcripts need to be coded; and how sessions or extracts are selected. The approach to this issue has varied amongst coding researchers. For instance, in CCRT it is often advised that two early (but not the first) and two late (but not the last) sessions are selected at random to identify relationship episodes for coding. The first and the last sessions are usually excluded because they are thought to be unrepresentative of the therapy as a whole. In the structural analysis of social behaviour (SASB) model researchers have argued the 'pond water' theory to justify the assumption that randomly selected parts of the psychotherapy session will be representative of the interaction as a whole. Researchers using the Assimilation Model have emphasized the importance of researchers becoming immersed in as much of the material as possible to enable the identification of relevant problem areas. Other researchers have used specially developed instruments, such as interpersonal process recall (IPR) to identify parts of the session on which they should focus (see, for instance, Elliott, 1986).

When employing a coding strategy, the process researcher uses pre-determined categories, or 'scales', derived from a theoretical construct – such as 'assimilation' – in order to sample segments of the text for comparison. The data are usually audio or video recordings or written transcripts. Given the unreliability of recall, process notes – notes compiled by the therapist after the session – are not usually considered adequate for coding methods. Process notes arguably tell us more about the therapist, and maybe about the relationship, than about the patient. While this may be very interesting in itself, as data it lacks any external verification of the actual interaction. Coding methods which examine verbal content only, without the need for non-verbal information, can be applied to the written transcript which is usually transcribed from an audio tape, often by the therapist. Transcripts vary in the amount of non-verbal information they include. Most coding systems will benefit from having access to some non-verbal information – for example, the length of pauses, non-verbal utterances such as grunts, marked rise and fall in the volume of the voices etc. Generally transcribers are asked to make a note of as much non-verbal process as is reliably possible. Those coding methods which are primarily concerned with the interactional process often need to go beyond the purely verbal as represented in the written transcript. These will generally require reliable methods for coding non-verbal process which can become very complex.

There has been a rich history of psychotherapy process research which uses coding methods to analyze process. Some have used questionnaire or interview methods, asking patient and therapist about the process after the session. Since these do not use the material (verbal and/or non-verbal) from the session itself, they are outside the scope of this book. In the following chapters, we will introduce the coding methods which have a clear and well validated methodology, and which have a proven track record in terms of use within research publications. It has been impossible to cover all coding systems, and new ones continue to be developed. For instance, recently two coding systems specific to the identification of cognitive processes have been developed at the Centre for Cognitive Psychotherapy in Rome (Semerari *et al.*, 2003a, 2003b). Using verbatim transcripts of sessions, the 'Grid of Problematic States' analyzes patient narratives to identify problematic states such as rage, negative self-efficacy, competition, compulsion and mistrust; and the 'Metacognition Assessment Scale' identifies the capacity for monitoring the mental states of others. There has also been a plethora of instruments developed in the attachment theory area. Since most of these to date have used structured interviews such as the adult attachment interview (AAI) rather than psychotherapy sessions they have not been included. Those who are interested in the field of attachment theory research are referred to specialist texts such as Cassidy and Shaver (2002).

The three methods that we have chosen to focus on in detail have all been established for over ten years and all are being used in current research programmes, regularly presented at Society for Psychotherapy Research conferences and in recent publications. We have used them with psychotherapy students, who have applied them (with greater or lesser success) within their small scale research projects. They range in methodology from the core conflictual relationship theme (CCRT) model, which focuses primarily upon the content of client verbal material, specifically narrated relationship episodes, to the structural analysis of social behaviour (SASB), which focuses on the interactional process. The Assimilation Model comes somewhere in between, in that it, like CCRT, has a primary focus upon the content of client material, but is also concerned with the relationship and specifically how therapist interventions promote assimilation. Whereas CCRT can be applied using traditional empirical methodology (random selection of sessions, blind and independent coding of extracts, separating out of the various coding operations), the Assimilation Model is applied through coding by consensus. Although access to the audio tape is very useful in the Assimilation Model, both it and the CCRT can be coded from written transcripts. An analysis using SASB requires audio recording as a minimum, and video taped material adds substantially to its power. Reliability in coding is obtainable in less time with CCRT and the Assimilation Model than it is with SASB.

Each of the coding methods under consideration starts from a particular theoretical model with a particular focus that has advantages and disadvantages for the researcher. Each is well documented and tested, and in frequent use. The discussion of each method in the following chapters is intended to give enough information to enable the small scale researcher to get a flavour of the method and to try it out on some clinical material. A more serious and sustained application of any of the methods will need extra reading, and we have provided suggestions at the end of each chapter.

CHAPTER 3

Transference-related methods

Introduction

A fundamental concept within any psychodynamic model of personality is that of repeating relationship patterns. The expectation is that some aspects of early relationships with parents and siblings, possibly linked to trauma but more likely to a consistent failure in interpersonal relating by caregivers, become reproduced through a kind of template which is then imposed upon later relationships. Furthermore, it is expected that the greater the level of pathology the more fixed and problematic such patterns become. The well adjusted person is expected to adopt a wide range of interpersonal styles in an appropriate way, whereas maladjusted individuals are expected to have a limited interpersonal repertoire and to replicate dysfunctional relation patterns.

Psychodynamic theorists expect this pattern or core conflict to emerge in the transference relationship where it can be analyzed, allowing insight to bring about change. Many of the features of classical analysis (ego deprivation, frequency, no eye contact etc.) were rationalized as a means to induce the transference relationship since this was seen as the essence of treatment. While non-psychoanalytic approaches such as cognitive behavioural therapy and the humanistic therapies do not explicitly adopt techniques designed to bring the transference into play, there is also a recognition that pathology usually involves a repeating pattern of behaviour which is maladaptive in some sense. These may be explained, as in cognitive theory, through the notion of internal schema, or in attachment theory through internal working models. What differs in the various therapeutic modalities is not so much the idea of repeating patterns itself as the developmental theories used to explain the origins of these repeating patterns: for instance, whether they develop primarily in early attachment relationships, or in problems in learning and adapting behaviour.

Methods which aim to identify and analyze these repeating patterns are the topic of this chapter. We will review these psychotherapy process coding methods, which have been described as 'transference-based'. We will introduce the rationale for the methods and then briefly describe three of them for comparative purposes. The most common of the methods, the core conflictual relationship theme (CCRT) will be described in detail with worked examples. We will then outline published research using CCRT and give an example of a small scale process research project which uses CCRT to investigate some of the aspects of a therapy.

Transference-related methods

Methods which focus on the commonly observed repeating patterns of relationships have been coined 'transference-related methods' by Luborsky *et al.* (1994) in their introduction to an issue of the journal *Psychotherapy Research* devoted to seven methods applied to a single therapeutic interview. However, the use of the term *transference* in the title is perhaps a little misleading, in that these methodologies focus upon patient accounts of relationship episodes within therapy rather than upon the patient's relationship specifically with the therapist. They have also been referred to as 'central relationship pattern' methodologies (Barber *et al.*, 2002), which is arguably more appropriate. Luborsky justifies the use of 'transference-related' through their expectation that these repeating patterns of relationship will be shown to have a strong link to the relationship with the therapist. This is, indeed, the expectation of psychodynamic theorists who will often read the patient's account of outside relationships as communicating about the transference relationship in a disguised way. It calls for a broader understanding of transference in order to see this as the phenomenon whereby the individual transfers his or her experiences and expectations into all new situations and relationships, including the therapeutic one. It should be noted, however, that while the concept of repeating relationship patterns originates in psychoanalytic theory, it has become more broadly applied through the cognitive behavioural concept of 'schema'. For this reason the methods described in this section are not limited to a purely psychodynamic view of psychological process.

What makes transference-related measures so compelling for the psychotherapy process researcher is that they provide the key to examining systematically a very central clinical concept within theories of psychotherapy. This is in contrast to the elusiveness of many key concepts – such as psychic defence, aetiology, resistance – to systematic analysis. The most well established transference-based method – Luborsky's core conflictual relationship theme (CCRT) method – has been used extensively by researchers in the United States and in Europe, and has also been adopted to develop a new method of brief psychotherapy (Book, 1997). While most methods which target the repeating relationship patterns of core relationship complexes employ the same basic psychodynamic concept, the actual techniques employed vary in emphasis and in detail. This can result in some considerable confusion to the casual reader. This chapter will try to clarify this by first introducing some of the principles, and then going into greater detail with an outline and some worked examples based on the first and the most popular of the methods, the CCRT.

The development of methods designed to identify the central relationship pattern followed from the emerging realization in the psychoanalytic world that the traditional method, which relied on therapist recall and case study as the main methodology for analyzing therapeutic process, was not a consistent or reliable way of collecting data. Evidence of the lack of agreement amongst clinicians was provided by Seitz (1966) and the issue of the unreliability of case study methodology has been discussed as a major problem in psychoanalytic research by Spence (1993). The alternative, of client completed self-report measures, was not attractive to psychotherapy researchers because of the presumed hidden or unconscious element in repeating patterns. The development by cognitive researchers of the concept of schemas, and the strong relationship of this concept to that of repetitive relationship scripts, has enabled some integration between cognitive and psychoanalytic models and has encouraged a more systematic approach to studying these patterns. A number of methods designed to be used on taped psychotherapy transcripts were developed through the 1970s and 1980s.

The core conflictual relationship theme (CCRT) method, which claims to be the best validated transference-related measure and is certainly the most actively used transference-based research method, is discussed in detail below. However, at least ten clinician-rated measures of central relationship patterns have been developed, some of these designed to provide a better focus for interpretation in brief psychotherapy. Descriptions and comparisons of the various methods have been provided by Barber and Crits-Christoph (1993), Henry *et al.* (1994) and Luborsky *et al.* (1994a). The last of these articles looked in detail at the results of seven of the methods applied to a single interview and concluded that, despite starting from varying theoretical perspectives and adopting widely differing methodologies, 'they all turn out to be moderately similar' (p. 277) in their analysis of the test case. Luborsky (1994a) concludes that all of the methods reviewed have important clinical applications, including helping to make reliable formulations, enabling more accurate interventions, and providing a context for care planning. However, the issue of the economy of application is a considerable one and some of the methods which require large teams of coders are too ambitious to be applied in practitioner-based research.

In order to provide a context and an awareness of possible alternative approaches, we will briefly introduce three of these alternatives to CCRT: consensual response method (Horowitz and Rosenberg, 1994); plan formulation method (Curtis *et al.*, 1994); and FRAMES (Dahl and Teller, 1994; Siegel *et al.*, 2002).

Consensual response psychodynamic formulation method

The consensual response method (CRM) aims to be relatively theory neutral. It approaches formulation from the standpoint of averaging the clinical diagnoses of groups of clinicians and is therefore in principle useful from a variety of theoretical standpoints. Horowitz and Rosenberg (1994) point out that, while psychodynamic formulation is recognized as important for research and for focusing clinical practice, there are no methods for generating a formulation which are standardizable, reliable and valid. Indeed, where different sets of clinicians have generated formulations for the same set of clients, they have often produced quite dissimilar results (DeWitt *et al.*, 1983). The CRM deals with this problem by collating judgements and presenting these as *quantitative* ratings indicating the level of agreement between judges. Obviously the larger the number of judges the greater the level of reliability attained by the method. Since it is difficult to render words into quantitative data, the method requires clinicians to make formulations which are then broken down into thought units by a separate team of raters, who have to make a judgement about consensus. The frequency of each coded idea is then counted in order to provide a numerical indication of consensus. If, for instance, the idea 'she isolates her affect' (or something that is deemed to equate to it) is judged to occur in all of the formulations, it is shown as 1.0. A lower level of agreement is indicated by a lower score, between 0 and 1. The final formulation thus indicates through the numerical codes which are the most commonly occurring (or *consensual*) ideas and excludes thought units which are coded by fewer than three out of eight judges, thus eliminating idiosyncratic ideas. This contrasts with the conventional case study method where a single judge (the therapist) selects items to justify judgements about the formulation.

Since reliability is established on a consensual basis through the use of multiple judges it is difficult to assess this aspect of the method. However, good reliability was demonstrated for the process of thought-unit extraction. Using a panel of five graduate students as judges of a single case showed 81% of thought units appearing in the first formulation present in the replication (Horowitz *et al.*, 1989). Horowitz and Rosenberg (1994) also provided some evidence of the validity of their approach by using the Inventory of Interpersonal Problems (Horowitz *et al.*, 1988) to demonstrate that the interpersonal items derived consensually did form the focus of subsequent psychotherapy. They further found that patients whose formulations had a high interpersonal content tended to have positive outcome scores. The main drawback with the method, as with many process research tools, is that it is labour intensive. It requires a significant number of original formulations and a separate set of judges to break the formulations into thought units and to assess consensus. This is perhaps the reason that the method does not appear to have become well established, as reflected in the absence of recent reports in the research literature.

Plan formulation method

The plan formulation method aims to produce formulations that identify both patient problems and stated and unstated goals for psychotherapy. The authors claim that it 'has proven to be reliable, easily teachable, and applicable to different forms of psychoanalytic and non-psychoanalytic psychotherapies' (Curtis *et al.*, 1994). It is based upon control-mastery therapy (derived from both cognitive and psychoanalytic theory) developed by Weiss *et al.* (1986), which posits that psychopathology arises from pathogenic beliefs which are frightening or constricting. These might include irrational beliefs in the power to damage others or expectations of being overwhelmed by feelings, or suffering retaliation, which are based within early experience and progress through developmental stages. The patient is seen as motivated to challenge and disconfirm these beliefs within therapy and the plan diagnosis specifies the pathogenic beliefs and the plan for testing and disconfirming these.

Formulations have four component parts:

- *goals* for therapy;
- *obstructions* (pathogenic beliefs) that prevent the patient from achieving goals;
- *insights* that help the achievement of the goals;
- *tests*, the way in which the patient can use the therapy to overcome the obstacles.

The plan diagnosis is extracted by judges from therapy transcripts (often the first three), with the judges first making a formulation using the four elements identified above and listing the various elements. These master lists are then combined anonymously and judges are asked to rate each of the items on the master list on a scale of 0 to 4 ('not relevant' to 'very highly relevant'). The items which receive a low mean score of relevance are dropped, leaving those items on which there is good consensus. The authors claim that this method can be applied reliably and that it provides a valuable method of developing accurate formulations which can be used as a focus for effective psychotherapy. However, it clearly suffers from the same problem as the CRM in that it is time consuming to apply, using in some cases eight judges to increase reliability.

It seems that the authors have demonstrated acceptable reliability for the plan formulation method, with high inter-judge agreement on the items included in the master lists for the four components of the plan diagnosis. However, the authors report better reliability for research conducted in-house and attribute this to the lack of experience of the model amongst some of the judges used by other projects (Curtis et al., 1994). Henry et al. (1994) refer to a high level of agreement being reached 'with difficulty and required judges to specify a theoretical framework' (p. 492). This implies that the method may be difficult to apply reliably by clinicians without specific induction and training. The case for the validity of the method has been argued through the link between the adherence of interpretations to the plan formulation and subsequent patient progress. However, the possible problem of reliable scoring, combined with the cost of applying the method, may explain why the plan formulation method has not been adopted as widely as CCRT.

Fundamental, repetitive, and maladaptive emotion structures (FRAMES)

FRAMES, which stands for Fundamental, Repetitive, and Maladaptive Emotion Structures, is a method which aims to explore recurring patterns of maladaptive interpersonal behaviour within patient narratives. It attempts to avoid the 'top-down' methodology of imposing an assumed structure onto the data. Rather than starting from a set of pre-defined categories which define the structure of narratives – such as the 'wish', 'response from other', 'response from self' coding categories of the CCRT – FRAME structures are sequenced according to the plot of the manifest narrative of the patient. Siegel et al. (2002) point out that the FRAMES method has been well received as a clinically rich method, although it has also been perceived as complex and labour intensive to apply. This encapsulates a dilemma for many process research tools, in that the closer the method comes to a full idiographic and rich description of the patient, the more time consuming it becomes and the more difficult to assess reliability.

It is acknowledged by Siegel *et al.* (2002) that FRAMES as originally presented was problematic because of the difficulty of establishing reliability. The modifications in the later paper aim to solve this through the introduction of a standardized categorization of emotions into eight groups, enabling comparison of coding. The five step procedure for finding FRAMES starts with coders constructing an 'object' map which locates sections of text according to a particular object focus. The identified sections are then coded independently by two raters for the occurrence of emotions using the eight basic categories, including labels such as *negative emotion directed at someone (anger/criticism)* or *emotion to turn away from someone (fear, horror)*. The emotion codes in the larger narrative segments are listed in the order they manifestly occur, retaining the temporal structure of the original data. Emotion code sequences which are agreed by both raters and which recur with the same or different objects form the FRAMES. An example of a FRAMES structure given by Siegel *et al.* (2002) is: feels uncomfortable/bad > will be attacked > scared/ wants to avoid > tries to reassure. The authors argue that this method retains the 'bottom up' emphasis of the original FRAMES methodology while enabling reasonable reliability to be established.

In the Luborsky *et al.* (1994) review, FRAMES was found to be quite close to CRM and CCRT, but at that stage a weakness in the method was the difficulty in establishing reliability. As mentioned earlier, the authors have paid some attention to this weakness and produced a new version using the eight emotion classification (Siegel *et al.*, 2002). The eight emotion classification scheme was validated by a study using 58 judges who were able reliably to assign 400 emotion words in terms of the basic dimensions of the scheme. The adoption of the emotion classification scheme has enabled the authors to test the reliability of the emotion coding sequence in FRAMES and to report an acceptable reliability. Sequencing reliability has been a persistent obstacle for researchers because FRAMES researchers 'do not derive personality patterns from an a priori structure of thematic content but rather from sequencing thematic content according to the logic of an individual's unique story' (pp. 73–4). It is thus a significant achievement that reliability can be demonstrated. The researchers have also replicated the findings of other studies that it is possible to achieve a high level of agreement on the narrative segmentation of psychotherapy transcripts. Arguably FRAMES has the advantage of maintaining the individuality and uniqueness of the client while achieving acceptable reliability, albeit at the cost of a fairly labour intensive method.

The core conflictual relationship theme method

Introduction

The CCRT was developed by Luborsky from his work within the Menninger Project, in which he studied taped psychotherapy and psychoanalytic sessions in detail. He observed that he tended to draw most of his inferences from narratives of interactions. This led him to define the 'relationship episode' as the basic unit of analysis. He also observed that he tended to focus on the recurrent aspects of these interactions (Luborsky *et al.*, 1994b): 'He realized that his formulation of the central relationship pattern contained *three components of relationship narratives:* What the patient wanted from the other people, how the other people reacted, and how the patient reacted to their reactions' (p. 172).

This was formulated into the three components of CCRT – the wish (W), the response from other (RO) and the response from self (RS). It can be seen that in viewing the underlying motivating force as the *wish*, this model is rooted more explicitly within a Freudian drive-based model than the other methods considered. Luborsky's manual for applying this method – *Understanding Transference* – was first published in 1990 and subsequently reprinted in 1998 (Luborsky and Crits-Christoph, 1990, 1998). This volume describes the approach in detail and discusses the use of tailor-made classifications and the various standard categories to classify the main components. Luborsky places great emphasis upon the relationship of the CCRT to Freud's observations about transference and has made a comparison between the findings of CCRT research and Freud's original assumptions, some of which are discussed below.

Relationship episodes

The relationship episode is the basic unit of analysis within the CCRT system and the first stage in an analysis is to extract these episodes from a session transcript. Normally psychotherapy sessions provide the data – usually several sessions taken from various stages of a full psychotherapy – although an interview designed specifically to elicit relationship accounts has been developed, called the relationship anecdote paradigm (RAP) interview (Luborsky and Crits-Christoph, 1998). The RAP interview has the advantage of enabling a CCRT analysis to be done at assessment and hence for data to be collected more economically and in advance of treatment. Research into the RAP interview has established that good reliability in coding can be achieved and that there is a strong similarity between the narratives derived from RAP and from normal sessions

(Barber *et al.*, 1995). Relationship episodes (REs), including those derived from naturally occurring narratives within therapy sessions, have been found by CCRT researchers to be extractable with good reliability. Luborsky and his co-researchers have managed to achieve a high level of agreement amongst appropriately trained coders over what constitutes a relationship episode. One of the reasons for this is that narratives tend to have a beginning, middle and end and are 'often signalled by conventional signs such as a pause, a transition to a new topic, or a direct introductory statement of a change in topic' (Luborsky *et al.*, 1994b, p. 175). An example of a relationship episode taken from a psychotherapy session analysed within a student research project is given in Figure 3.1.

Figure 3.1   A relationship episode – patient talking about partner

The other night I wanted to just have a quiet evening in with him. I don't believe I was particularly rejected, I don't know I can't remember, then I was really quite surprised when he stood up said I will be off now thank you very much in a kind of formal manner that it threw me and I really felt offended, I felt quite offended. I felt like that the way he said it was very distant. It wasn't a cuddle and I am off or anything it was a leave taking of a very formal nature. and that it had been so off and one I just thought God here we go again. He is off again, he's off, he is turned off, um … It just pissed me off.

The coders of relationship episodes also need to decide the level of completeness of the episode – whether it has sufficient content to enable coding into the main components, which is done on a scale of 1 to 5. If the level of completeness is 1.0 the relationship episode is deemed to enable coding of no CCRT components: the example given in the manual is 'I met Joe and we talked'. A completeness rating of 5.0 indicates that all three components can be assessed accurately from the relationship episode. The cut off for inclusion is usually set at 2.5. Luborsky's example of completeness ratings given for sample texts is shown in Figure 3.2.

The relationship episode coders are also required to specify who is the main focus of the relationship episode: often other people from the current or past life, but also including the therapist (through a narrative or through a behavioural enactment), and the self. Luborsky and Crits-Christoph (1994) report acceptable reliability using trained coders for extracting relationship episodes and for assigning the main focus and completeness score.

Figure 3.2 Completeness ratings on hypothetical relationship episodes

Rating	Essence of the Relationship Episode
1.0	I met Joe and we talked. (No CCRT components.)
1.5	I met Joe and we talked and he said little. (A fairly vague response from other.)
2.0	I met Joe, we talked and he said little. He's an old friend from school who I like. (More vague components, a hint of a wish and a response from self.)
2.5	I met Joe, we talked, he said little. He's an old friend from school who I like. I was disappointed he said so little about the event we went through together. (Enough information to score a wish, response from other, and response of self.)
3.0	(Beyond the 2.5 level, the completeness ratings are based on how much the patient elaborates on the story and how detailed the information for each of the components is.)
4.0	I met Joe, we talked, he said little. He's an old friend from school who I like. I was disappointed he said so little about the event we went through together. I was kind of trying to relive those days and get back the feeling of that event we shared, but Joe seemed distracted. I suggested we meet for lunch next week and he agreed. (All three components are more detailed and more explicit.)
5.0	(Like the 4.0 description above, but with more detail.)

Reprinted with permission from L. Luborsky.

Extraction of the main CCRT components

The extraction of relationship episodes is a preliminary stage which can be done by different coders than those who do the classification of the main components. Using separate coders arguably has the advantage that the main component coders are not influenced by exposure to the complete session transcript. Whether this is methodologically desirable or not depends on the philosophical perspective of the researcher: a more holistic approach would argue for immersion into the world of the client to enable a fuller understanding of the context of the episodes. Alternatively, breaking down the coding tasks can be seen as giving the advantage of maximizing the objectivity of coders, particularly in comparative studies where the relationship episodes from a number of different clients can be coded without the coder knowing which episode belongs to which client.

The coding task of CCRT is to extract the elements within the relationship episodes which relate to the three main components defined by Luborsky. Often it is *response from other* (RO) which is the most explicit of these, followed by the *response from self* (RS), whereas the underlying *wish* (W) often has to be inferred from the material. Luborsky advises dividing the relationship episode into smaller 'thought units' and then coding each of these for one of the three elements. The RO and RS coding should further be categorized as *Positive* or *Negative*, maintaining Freud's division of transference into positive and negative, and indicate whether the responses involve compliance or interference with the satisfaction of the wish.

Taking our earlier example given in Figure 3.1, the reader may like to try to identify the three main components. The researcher's coding of this episode is given in Figure 3.3.

Figure 3.3   Coded relationship episode

The other night I wanted to just have a quiet evening in with him *(Wish – to be close to others)*. I don't believe I was particularly rejected, I don't know I can't remember, then I was really quite surprised *(Negative responses of self – don't understand, feel unloved)* when he stood up said I will be off now thank you very much in a kind of formal manner *(Negative responses from others – are distant, dislike me)*... that... it threw me and I really felt offended, I felt quite offended *(Negative responses of self – don't understand, feel unloved)*. I felt like that the way he said it was very distant. It wasn't a cuddle and I am off or anything it was a leave taking of a very formal nature ... and that ... it had been so off and one I just thought God here we go again *(Negative responses from others – are distant, dislike me)*. He is off again, he's off, he is turned off, um ... It just pissed me off. *(Negative responses of self – feel angry, feel disappointed)*.

This episode occurred naturally in a psychotherapy session and, although the CCRT coding may not seem to add much to an immediate reading of the extract, it does give the possibility of looking at repeating relationship configurations in a quite structured way.

Tailor-made versus standard categories

The method as originally devised needed the researcher to find the most accurate description of each of the elements using their own words, which Luborsky and Crits-Christoph (1990) have termed assigning 'tailor-made categories'. This has the advantage of finding a best fit but has the disadvantage of making comparison between coders, or between clients, virtually impossible without a further stage of assigning judges to decide if the tailor-made categories equate. In the interests of monitoring the reliability of coding, a number of standard category tables for CCRT have been devised for classifying the coded components. Coders are advised first to develop their own tailor-made classification of the main components and, as a next stage, classify them according to one of the sets of standard categories. Given the frequently encountered difficulty of finding an exact match, coders are instructed to give the best and the next best match. Examples of standard categories for wishes are: to assert self; to oppose others; to be close; to be loved etc. Readers are referred to *Understanding Transference* (Luborsky and Crits-Christoph, 1998) for the various alternatives. The standard category clusters version, which reduces the categories to eight empirically derived categories for each of the main components is reproduced in Figure 3.4. However, it should be pointed out that what might be regarded as appropriate standard categories, and the methodology for devising these, goes rather beyond the application of CCRT as a method for finding relationship themes. Researchers can approach the building of standard categories from an *empirical* standpoint (for instance, through applying a statistical analysis of the assigned tailor-made categories for a number of patients to find clusters or factors), or from a theoretical perspective. In principle, any over-arching inter-personal model can be used to define a set of standard categories. An obvious candidate for this is the Structural Analysis of Social Behaviour or SASB (Benjamin, 1974), which is discussed in Chapter 5. An attempt to combine the CCRT and SASB systems has already been made by Crits-Christoph *et al.* (1994).

Figure 3.4 CCRT standard category clusters

Wishes – 1. To assert self and be independent; 2. To oppose, hurt and control others; 3. To be controlled, hurt and not responsible; 4. To be distant and avoid conflicts; 5. To be close and accepting; 6. To be loved and understood; 7. To feel good and comfortable; 8. To achieve and help others

Responses from other – 1. Strong; 2. Controlling; 3. Upset; 4. Bad; 5. Rejecting and opposing; 6. Helpful; 7. Likes me; 8. Understanding

Responses of self – 1. Helpful; 2. Unreceptive; 3. Respected and accepted; 4. Oppose and hurt others; 5. Self-controlled and self-confident; 6. Helpless; 7. Disappointed and depressed; 8. Anxious and ashamed

Reproduced by permission from L. Luborsky.

Derivation of the single theme

This brings us to the issue of how a single CCRT – the main relationship theme which is assumed to encapsulate the patient's core conflict – is derived from the method. Essential to any of the transference-related measures is the belief that it is possible to sample data sufficiently to provide insight into the core theme. Given the time consuming nature of the coding process this is a key issue for researchers. Luborsky maintains that it is usually sufficient to sample two early and two late sessions in order to locate about ten early and ten late relationship episodes. This enables a comparison to be made between the content and the frequency of the CCRT in early and late sessions in a psychotherapy. This gives the opportunity to use a process measure to give an indication of progress and outcome in psychotherapy. Typically a twenty minute segment is taken from each session, each of which might contain four to six relationship episodes. Clearly this can vary from patient to patient, and between different phases of therapy and it is sometimes difficult to obtain sufficient usable relationship episodes from this kind of sample: a compelling reason for the increasing use by researchers of the custom-built RAP interview.

A more controversial decision in the CCRT method was to use a simple majority basis for deciding the core theme. This is done by including all of the judgements of wishes, responses from other and from self, compiling these into a table and amalgamating the most frequent of each of these categories to form a theme. An example of such a theme might be that the patient wishes for closeness with others, then experiences their response as rejection, and feels bad about him/herself. Luborsky justifies the decision to use simple majority on the basis that frequency is a good indicator of importance and that the main theme tends to form the core of a complex of related sub-themes. While other measures, such as intensity or duration, could be used to define the main theme, he maintains that the findings of CCRT have tended to vindicate the use of frequency, given the high association of CCRT-based results with clinical-based observations about the transference. The use of frequency to some extent avoids the need for some overall judgement to be made on the theme based upon clinician interpretation or intuition, thus avoiding one of the criticisms of conventional psychoanalytic case discussion methodology as being too subjective or theory-based. However, it needs to be remembered that judgements are still being made at the level of scoring the components of the relationship episodes, although arguably the smaller the unit used for the judgement the better the chance of specificity and objectivity.

Findings of CCRT research

Following the original successful efforts to demonstrate the reliability of CCRT (Crits-Christoph *et al.*, 1988b), much of the research using CCRT has followed the agenda set out by Luborsky to test Freud's observations relating to transference (Freud, 1912). In particular, we would expect to find one main pattern dominating. Luborsky (1986) found in a sample of eight patients that the most frequent wish was much more frequent than the next most frequent wish, and claims this as evidence to support the original observation (and also of evidence of the appropriateness of the CCRT method). However, later researchers have found more mixed results. For instance Albani *et al.* (2001), using RAP interviews with 70 female patients, found consistency in the relationship theme between parents but little consistency between the CCRT for parents and that for other relationships of the same gender. Barber *et al.* (2002) studied 93 patients with some diagnosed personality disorder and found substantial variability in themes across and within relationships. There has also been little evidence presented showing that early life relationships have more impact than later ones, despite this being an important clinical assumption.

Other researchers have looked for evidence of the expected parallel between the patterns of relating to others and the pattern of relating with the therapist. Some evidence of this correspondence has been found using 35 patients from the Penn Psychotherapy Project (Fried *et al.*, 1992). A link between accurate CCRT formulation and therapeutic relationship has also been found. Crits-Christoph *et al.* (1988a) found a link between outcome and accurate interpretation, and Crits-Christoph *et al.* (1993) between accurate interpretation early in therapy and stronger therapeutic alliance. Given the well established link between therapeutic alliance and outcome this is a significant finding. Crits-Christoph and Luborsky (1990) found a significant change from negative to positive responses of other and self between early and late psychotherapy sessions, and no change in wishes. This is consistent with the expectation and the observation that underlying wishes do not change but the ability to realize these increase with successful therapy. Bressi *et al.* (2000) also found CCRT to be a useful measure of psychodynamic change in patients assigned to crisis intervention, brief psychotherapy or drug therapy. It is therefore argued that CCRT can be used as a richer measure of outcome than that provided by self report questionnaires or unstructured clinical judgement.

Attempts to demonstrate that patients with higher levels of pathology display a greater *pervasiveness* of CCRT theme (that is, that they should more rigidly apply a relationship template onto all relationships) have been disappointing to date. While Crits-Christoph and Luborsky (1990) have reported a reduction in pervasiveness during therapy, and Cierpka *et al.* (1998) linked pervasiveness with severity of pathology, there has been no clear demonstration of the link between particular CCRT patterns and DSM diagnoses. This was explored by Wilczek *et al.* (2000), who found that patients with different DSM-III-R diagnoses did not differ in their CCRTs extracted from the RAP interview, and that pervasiveness was not associated with psychiatric symptoms. Chance *et al.* (2000) also failed to find a CCRT distinction between BPD patients who attempted suicide and those who didn't, although it could be argued that the two groups were not sufficiently distinct to enable differences to emerge.

Example of a practitioner project using CCRT

This section will look at a small scale project completed by a student. The CCRT can be used easily for practitioner-based research projects, and lends itself to the therapist using their own session tapes and transcripts to analyze the repeating themes. Because the focus of the coding is on the narrative account of a relationship – the relationship episode – which usually is not the therapy itself, the analysis is not confounded by counter-transference or enmeshment in the therapeutic dyad. The therapist/researcher is able to code in a fairly objective way, focusing closely upon the patient's actual words describing their relationships. The method has thus been used successfully by our students, and most researchers have used their own clinical material as data. This has the added advantage that there can be considerable clinical gain from their detailed and rigorous analysis of their transcripts. The other advantage of CCRT for small scale research is that it is a method which is easily learnt and there is not a long lead time into the actual coding process. So easily applicable is the method that there has been a brief therapy based upon it (Book, 1997), where the therapist identifies CCRT themes as the therapy progresses and uses this understanding to inform the process of focusing interpretations onto the core relational issues.

The aim of this project, which was completed by an advanced psychoanalytic psychotherapy trainee, was to examine whether there was CCRT evidence of a change in content or pervasiveness in the relationship episodes. The psychotherapy was a one year, weekly therapy which had been tape recorded as part of the training requirement. In the view of the patient, therapist and supervisor this was a case with a good outcome, which was supported by outcome questionnaire data.

Transcripts from an early and a late session – numbers 3 and 35 – were selected for analysis. The selection of these sessions was not based on any particular event or evaluation of these sessions, and was therefore random within the constraint that an early and a late session was required. It should be noted that this sample of sessions is below that recommended by Luborsky and Crits-Christoph (1990), who recommend at least two sessions from early therapy and two from later. However, arguably it is acceptable for a small scale practitioner-based project which is not intended for publication.

The coding process was done by two coders: the therapist and a colleague. There was no separation of the process of locating relationship episodes, but there was independent coding of the CCRT elements. Since only one of the coders had been trained in the method it was decided to agree the identification of the REs and the CCRT coding through discussion. This can have the advantage of producing a more considered and consensual coding, but does have the disadvantage that there is no opportunity to provide a kappa score for the inter-rater reliability (Cohen, 1968). As advised by Luborsky and Crits-Christoph (1990) the CCRT elements were scored first using the tailor-made system. The coders then independently matched these to the standard category system and again settled differences through discussion. The final stage was the aggregation of the codings into a summary score sheet which was then used as the basis for a discussion of the evidence for the changes that occurred in the process of therapy. An example of a relationship episode from this project with the therapist as the focus is given in Figure 3.5.

Figure 3.5 An example of a relationship episode

I find that there are moments when I walk out of here and think that was really interesting you know, the fact, you know, the notion of all that going on. Do you know what I mean, it is kind of what, it is like what does therapy provide at the end of the day, and when it, when it is mostly my uh, my how can I put it so, it is coming from me you are maybe saying that is interesting. And maybe, uh, thinking 'what's he going on about?' really. But still leaving me with some nuggets. What I want from therapy is when I pull those nuggets out I would just love somebody to say why don't you try next time doing this or that, some kind of practical advice. Yes I would love it. I would love for you to say, well listen __, I would like you to summarise something and to say it is the last class, the last whatever, we have talked about a lot of things, these to me seem to be the key issues.

The patient had felt that as a result of treatment she had been better able to articulate her needs in relationships and to feel more connected to others. The therapist and supervisor felt that the patient had gained insight into her relationships and was able to engage more effectively as a result. Overall the results of the CCRT analysis gave support to these views of the change that had occurred. There were small but observable changes between the two sessions in how the patient viewed the responses of others and the patient's own responses to situations. The responses of others showed a shift in the intensity of the patient seeing other people as unhelpful, distant and not understanding. It also showed an increase in the number of times that the patient related feeling accepted by others. The responses of self showed a small shift in the pervasiveness of negative responses, such as anger, sadness and feelings of being unloved. Both of these responses showed an overall shift from negative towards positive responses. The expressed wishes also seemed to show some shifts. The wish 'to be helped' increased in frequency, but 'to be opened up to' and 'to be understood' did not appear in the last session. They were replaced with 'to be accepted ', 'to feel comfortable'. However, it is difficult to evaluate the significance of this shift because of the small scope of this study.

The study thus seemed to support the observed therapeutic outcome and to concord with the observation of CCRT researchers that the main shifts in a successful therapy are in the RO and RS categories. The research project had clear limitations which were acknowledged by the researcher. The researcher reports on difficulties in reaching agreement both on the identification of REs and in the CCRT coding process. This is attributed to the lack of training and experience of the coders in the system. The limitation of taking only two sessions as the basis of the analysis is also acknowledged, in that only a small number of REs were available for analysis. They found four REs for each of the sessions. This inevitably limits the confidence with which the results can be taken. The researcher/therapist also reports a problem in selecting sessions. While there was a desire to take a random session, it was not thought desirable to choose one next to a break or at the very end of the therapy because of the effect this may have on the material available for analysis.

While these are all limitations in terms of claiming generalizations from the research project, this is almost always the case in practitioner-based research. However, what is gained by the researcher/therapist is a richer understanding of the clinical material and the ability to view it from a fresh perspective. This study therefore provides an example of a modest research project which is not aiming to produce generalizable results but which has acceptable validity and reliability and clear clinical benefit.

Conclusion

While CCRT researchers have not been able to find unequivocal evidence for all of Freud's transference predictions, there has been a prolific and rigorous set of research findings presented since the method was originally outlined by Luborsky. Two weaknesses of the method are arguably its basis within a Freudian perspective and its failing to adopt a more two-person or interpersonal model, but it is difficult to argue with the rigour with which it has been applied and the findings that have been reported. Although some of the alternative methods outlined have the advantage of being less located within a particular theoretical perspective, or of less rigidly imposing a pre-set theoretical perspective on the data, they have not been as successful as CCRT in establishing a body of research. It is difficult to know whether this is because of problems in applying the methods – for instance, the difficulty of finding large teams of coders – or merely because of the vagaries of the funding of research. It is clear that once a certain momentum and critical mass in a research programme has been achieved this itself attracts additional interest and funding.

Whatever the transference-based method used, they generally have provided support for the hypothesis that people adopt fairly stable relationship configurations which are imposed upon new relationship experiences, including that with the therapist. There are encouraging indications that therapeutic progress can be reliably measured through changes in CCRT configuration between early and late sessions, although some other anticipated features, such as the link between pervasiveness and diagnosed pathology, have been difficult to establish. Given that there is the expected change in CCRT over time, the aim of psychotherapy can be seen as being to expose relationship rigidity, although whether you see the cure as arising from insight or from the new relational experience depends on the model of therapeutic change which you adopt.

The advantages of the CCRT system as a coding method for psychotherapy process are clear. It has been specifically designed to focus on repeating relational themes, including those with the therapist, and it therefore has clarity of aim. It is an instrument which is clearly based within a theoretical model and which is not difficult to understand. It is not too time consuming to learn or to apply, although like any coding system the researchers need to practise in order to improve reliability. It has a clear method for summarizing the findings of the coding, although the use of a majority method is not entirely convincing. Clearly as with any coding system it benefits from an expansion of its dataset. In the practitioner research project discussed there were not sufficient REs to provide a convincing analysis, and researchers have sometimes reported a difficulty in finding the necessary number of REs within some sessions. For this reason the RAP interview has advantages, although it has the disadvantage that it departs from naturally occurring material from actual psychotherapy sessions. Maybe the most convincing case for CCRT is that it has been used by psychotherapy researchers over a long period of time and that it still appears regularly within published research. The fact that there is still an active CCRT research programme, not just based within one school, is testament to its utility.

SUGGESTIONS FOR FURTHER READING

Curtis, J.T., Silberschatz, G., Sampson, H. and Weiss, J. (1994) 'The plan formulation method', *Psychotherapy Research*, 4: 197–207.

Horowitz, L.M. and Rosenberg, S.E. (1994) 'The consensual response psychodynamic formulation: Part 1. Method and research results', *Psychotherapy Research*, 4: 222–33.

Luborsky, L. and Barber, J.P. (1994) 'Perspectives on seven transference-related measures applied to the interview with Ms Smithfield', *Psychotherapy Research*, 4: 152–4.

Luborsky, L. and Crits-Christoph, P. (1998) *Understanding Transference*, New York: Basic Books.

Siegel, P.F., Sammons, M. and Dahl, H. (2002) 'FRAMES: The method in action and the assessment of its reliability', *Psychotherapy Research*, 12(1): 59–77.

CHAPTER 4

The Assimilation Model

Introduction

The Assimilation Model was developed by William Stiles as a way of tracking the process of change in psychotherapy. As such, it seeks to form a link between outcome and process research, developing the notion of *change process* research developed by Greenberg and others (Greenberg, 1986; Rice and Greenberg, 1984). Change process research aims to study the processes that produce change. Elliott *et al.* (2001) review the various strategies for doing this and point out that in the past most change process research has been essentially quantitative and hypothesis testing. Studies have taken the form of *process-outcome* studies, where session processes are measured, in some cases manipulated experimentally, and linked to outcome. Elliott *et al.* point out that results have been disappointing when researchers have attempted to move beyond global indicators (such as the quality of the therapeutic alliance) to more clinically useful processes (such as the type of therapist intervention). For instance, early claims that transference interpretation could be linked positively to outcome (Malan, 1976) have been challenged by later researchers using more sophisticated methodology (e.g. Piper *et al.*, 1993).

It can be argued that merely linking measurable features of the therapy process with outcome in a quantitative way is a very crude approach. Instead, we should attempt to look not just at *why* therapy works but *how* that change takes place. Most of the research which has attempted to do so uses psychotherapy transcripts as the data source, although other data collection methods have been used such as the change interview, helpful aspects of therapy (HAT) form, and tape-assisted recall methods such as Brief Structured Recall (described in Elliott *et al.*, 2001). Since these are not directly based on analysis of the text of the session itself, they are outside the scope of this book. The methodologies used to analyze textual data also include some of the discourse-based qualitative methods for dealing with text, such as conversation analysis, discourse analysis, grounded theory, which are outlined in Part III. It is a feature of all of these methods that they are time consuming and demanding with a focus at the micro level, and therefore limited as the basis of wider generalizations about psychotherapy process. In contrast, the Assimilation Model adopts a coding methodology to look at change and at therapy interaction which makes it more approachable for the researcher with limited time and resources.

One of the key aims of the Assimilation Model is to challenge the implicit *drug metaphor* assumptions in attempts to link psychotherapy process variables to outcome. For instance, in the early work of Malan (1976) the hypothesis being tested was that transference interpretation would improve outcome, explored through a process of classifying and counting interpretations and linking to outcome measures. This has an implicit assumption that more of a good thing is better (maybe up to a limit). This is a simplification which ignores the quality of the relationship and the moment by moment interaction. Perhaps transference interpretations can have a positive benefit in some relationships and not others, or at some times but not others. Piper *et al.* (1993), while still adhering to the quantitative methodology, found that additional factors, such as the patient's quality of internal object relations, are also determining variables in whether transference interpretations are effective. Stiles *et al.* (1995) go further in arguing for a method which evaluates an intervention in context, maybe for its adherence to a theoretical model and its observable impact on the client as demonstrated within the transcript. Within the Assimilation Model there is no possibility of a simple quantitative matching of process features with outcome. This also produces a shift in focus from therapist *technique* and *intention* to client *experience*.

The Assimilation Model

Pre-cursors

The foundations and antecedents of the Assimilation Model are in the work of Elliott (1985), McConnaughy *et al.* (1989) and Rice and Greenberg (1984). Rice and Greenberg saw successful psychotherapy as resolving a series of affective tasks and outlined the beginnings of a method for looking at the raw material of the session to focus on these change processes. This used a measure of the client vocal style, classifying into 'focused', 'externalizing', 'limited' and 'emotional'. Another process measure they introduced was designed to code perceptual processing levels using cognitive theory. In *Patterns of Change*, they give examples of the emergence of a problematic experience into therapy and the way that this can be worked on through the interaction with the therapist to bring some resolution. In their conclusion they called for 'the intensive analysis of different classes of recurrent change episodes in order to discover the client mechanisms that make these changes possible' (Rice and Greenberg, 1984, p. 289). Rice and Greenberg asked important questions and embarked on the journey, but they lacked an over-arching model which could chart therapeutic change.

Elliott (1985) points out that most research designed to find process elements which are linked with good outcome starts with counsellor action or intention and that results have generally been disappointing. Instead he focuses upon 'immediate therapeutic impact' and uses client descriptions of helpful counsellor responses to form an empirical taxonomy of change events in therapy. He finds that helpful events form two main clusters – *task* and *interpersonal*. The dominant factors within these are, respectively, new perspective (related to psychodynamic and cognitive insight models of change) and understanding (related to client-centred empathy models of change). Non-helpful events included misperception (or misunderstanding) and negative counsellor reactions. These findings are very interesting, particularly in the light of the support for the various change models of different approaches. They also tend to support the subsequent findings of the importance of negative process; for instance, in research using the structural analysis of social behaviour or SASB (Benjamin, 1974; Henry *et al.*, 1990). However, Elliott does not develop a model that can be used to track the actual stage in the change process.

McConnaughy *et al.* (1989) built on their earlier study (1983) using a new clinical sample of 327 adult psychotherapy patients and a 32 item instrument to categorize the stage of change of clients at the start of treatment. They devised five global stages. These were:

- *precontemplation* – clients seeing change as need in others or the outside world rather than themselves;
- *contemplation* – aware of distressing life situation and interested in exploring resolution;
- *decision-making* – attempted to make a resolution of the parameters of the problem and made commitment to change;
- *action* – begun to work on change and seeking help to implement strategies;
- *maintenance* – already made changes in problem areas and seeking treatment to consolidate gains.

There are clear links between this model and that of Stiles outlined below. However, McConnaughy *et al.*'s approach is to devise a self-report instrument-based model which attempts to classify clients onto a single global position. Although they did point out that there was evidence that clients might be involved in several change processes simultaneously, the method does not allow for this more complex picture to emerge. The model therefore lacks the flexibility of the Assimilation Model, both in terms of its inability to provide a classification based upon a particular problem domain and its use of questionnaire-based data rather than psychotherapy process material.

The theoretical basis of the Assimilation Model

The aim of Stiles and his co-researchers in developing the Assimilation Model was to produce an 'integrative model of a central aspect of change in psychotherapy' (Stiles *et al.*, 1990). According to the model, clients in successful psychotherapies proceed along a sequence of stages in dealing with their problematic experiences. The perspective is integrative in that it is seen as happening within all successful psychotherapies, whatever the therapeutic technique or model of change. The Assimilation Model draws heavily on the cognitive model of change, particularly the theory of schema and the notions of assimilation and accommodation. However, it also draws on concepts from psychodynamic, experiential and personal construct theories. The relationship of the model to therapeutic modalities, such as psychoanalytic, experiential, personal construct, gestalt, and cognitive behavioural therapy is outlined in detail by Stiles *et al.* (1990). The model is a way of analyzing change that actually occurs rather than a framework of what kinds of therapeutic intervention may produce change. However, it does have some implications for appropriate technique at particular stages, which are discussed below.

The principal theoretical components of the model are:

- schema;
- problematic experience;
- the complimentary process of assimilation and accommodation.

The idea of schema was developed as part of cognitive theory, but is now well understood by other modalities. It bears a strong relationship to the idea of transference configuration in the psychodynamic model, as discussed by Luborsky and others (1994a). It refers to a familiar pattern of ideas or way of thinking in which new experiences need to become assimilated. Stiles *et al.* use it in a broad and inclusive way as a generic term 'that may refer to a tightly organized theory, a metaphor, a narrative or script, or a more loosely organized network of associations, incorporating both mental content and patterns of action' (1990, p. 412). In psychotherapy, therapists and clients are seen as developing dialogue with words and phrases which evoke concepts and memories which relate to the client's schemata. The schema is obviously derived from the client's personal experience and psychotherapy can be seen as promoting subtle changes, or accommodations, to the schema to enable new experiences or insights to be integrated rather than to remain split off.

The problematic experience is defined as a 'perception, intention, impulse, attitude, wish, fantasy, or idea that causes psychological discomfort when brought to awareness or put into action' (Stiles *et al.*, 1990, p. 412). Life is a continual process of new experiences and those which readily fit into existing schemata are not problematic. Those which are not easily contained by existing schemata, and cannot therefore be readily assimilated, can be ignored (disavowed) or can create a kind of cognitive dissonance or incongruence. They cause distress and confusion and can lead to the mobilization of psychological defences, which might cope with the problematic experience in some way but be damaging in another. Indications of a client's difficulty in assimilating some experiences may be given by statements like 'that was not like me'. For instance, if a client has a self perception of not being angry or aggressive to others and yet starts experiencing violent fantasies this can cause considerable distress. Although these ideas fit readily into the cognitive model, they also bear a close relationship to psychodynamic ideas of warded-off repressed unconscious material, or split off (dissociated) experiences.

The complementary processes of assimilation and accommodation are taken from developmental cognitive theory. Within this model the schema is seen as taking in a new experience: a process of integration and incorporation. Experiences which cannot be assimilated are denied or repressed. In the Freudian model much of the material of the unconscious can thus be seen as unassimilated, and not available to conscious thought or memory. Partially assimilated experiences can be distorted or vague: within psychodynamic theory this gives an important role to the defence mechanisms. Alongside the process of assimilation is the process of accommodation, which is the modification of the schema and the experience necessary for the process of assimilation. The process of psychotherapy can be seen as facilitating the exploration of problematic partially assimilated experiences (from the present but often from the childhood past) to enable accommodation and assimilation to take place. As a result schema come to consist partly of understandings achieved during therapy. Stiles proposes that this process or assimilation can be coded in relation to particular problematic experiences discussed in psychotherapy through the analysis of the session transcripts.

The assimilation of problematic experiences scale (APES)

The central coding frame for the Assimilation Model has been developed partly from the research of other writers discussed above. The APES scale began with Elliott's list of therapeutic impacts which he developed from his analysis of helpful and unhelpful events in therapy (Elliott, 1985). It also has a strong resemblance to the stages of change model developed by McConnaughy *et al.* (1989). The APES scale in a recent version, which incorporates the voice formulation discussed below, is shown in Figure 4.1 (overleaf).

Figure 4.1 describes stages of assimilation which have been labelled: warded off; unwanted thoughts; vague awareness, problem statement; understanding or insight; application or working through; problem solution; and mastery. Within a successful psychotherapy a problematic experience will work through these stages of assimilation over the course of the therapy. Far more common is that an experience is voiced at one level and then progresses a few stages. It is argued that different therapeutic modalities focus on different ends of this scale (Stiles *et al.*,1990; Barkham *et al.*, 1996). Psychodynamic psychotherapists might be expected to focus upon problematic experiences which are warded off (APES 0) or avoided (APES 1) with a view to bringing these into awareness (APES 2) and exploring the conflicts that surround them (APES 3) and developing insight (APES 4). A cognitive behavioural approach emphasizes looking at problems which are already in awareness and helping clients to apply new understanding (APES 5), problem solution (APES 6) and eventual mastery of them (APES 7). Of course, it is not quite as simple as this and our expectation would be that these different levels of focus would be used within most psychotherapies. However, it does raise the interesting research question of whether the focus of interpretation to some extent determines the kinds of problematic experiences which may emerge within different types of therapy.

The voices formulation of the Assimilation Model

Several complementary interpretations of the Assimilation Model have been developed. The first of these was the formulation by Stiles *et al.* (1990) which is described above. The main emphasis of this formulation is therapeutic change as facilitating the assimilation of problematic experiences into the client's schema. A more recent formulation (Honos-Webb and Stiles, 1998; Stiles, 1999) conceptualizes assimilation as the process of integration of problematic and split off internal voices. They follow Rice and Greenberg (1984) in using the terms 'topdog' and 'underdog' to characterize the voices as those which are already assimilated into the schema (topdog) and those which are seen as disparate or split off (underdog). In successful therapy the problematic, or underdog, voices are gradually assimilated into the dominant community

Figure 4.1 Assimilation of problematic experiences scale (APES)

0. Warded off
Content is unformed. Client is unaware of the problem; the problematic voice is silent. An experience is considered warded off if there is evidence of actively avoiding emotionally disturbing topics (e.g. immediately changing subject raised by the therapist). Affect may be minimal, reflecting successful avoidance. Vague negative affect (especially anxiety) is associated with levels 0.1 to 0.9.

1. Unwanted thoughts
Content reflects emergence of thoughts associated with discomfort. Client prefers not to think about the experience. Problematic voices emerge in response to therapist interventions or external circumstances and are suppressed or avoided. Affect is often more salient than the content and involves strong negative feelings – anxiety, fear, anger, sadness. Despite the feelings' intensity, their connection with the content may be unclear. Levels 1.1 to 1.9 reflect increasingly stronger affect and less successful avoidance.

2. Vague awareness/emergence
Client acknowledges the existence of a problematic experience, and describes uncomfortable associated thoughts, but cannot formulate the problem clearly. Problematic voice emerges into sustained awareness. Affect includes acute psychological pain or panic associated with the problematic thoughts and experiences. Levels 2.1 to 2.9 reflect increasing clarity of expression by the problematic voice and decreasing intensity and diffusion of affect.

3. Problem statement/clarification
Content includes a clear statement of a problem – something that could be worked on. Opposing voices are differentiated and can talk about each other. Affect is negative but manageable, not panicky. Levels 3.1 to 3.9 reflect active, focused working toward understanding the problematic experience or negotiation between the opposing voices.

Reproduced with permission from William Stiles.

of voices that constitute the self. The established community of voices initially comprise the clear and dominant voices, while the underdog voice starts as weak or even unheard (warded off). This formulation has been used as the basis for the development of a coding manual based on 'markers' (Honos-Webb *et al.*, 1998b) discussed below.

The relationship of the voices formulation to the Jungian ideas of archetype and complex, and to the object relations idea of split off internal

4. Understanding/insight

The problematic experience is formulated and understood in some way. Voices reach an understanding with each other (a meaning bridge). Affect may be mixed, with some unpleasant recognition, but with curiosity or even pleasant surprise of the 'aha' sort. Levels 4.1 to 4.9 reflect progressively greater clarity or generality of the understanding, usually associated with increasingly positive (or decreasingly negative) affect.

5. Application/working through

The understanding is used to work on a problem. Voices work together to address problems of living; there is reference to specific problem-solving efforts, though without complete success. Client may describe considering alternatives or systematically selecting courses of action. Affective tone is positive, businesslike, optimistic. Levels 5.1 to 5.9 reflect tangible progress toward solutions of problems in daily living.

6. Problem solution

Client achieves a successful solution for a specific problem, representing flexible integration of multiple voices. Affect is positive, satisfied, proud of accomplishment. Levels 6.1 to 6.9 reflect generalizing the solution to other problems and building the solutions into usual or habitual patterns of behaviour. As the problem recedes, affect becomes more neutral.

7. Mastery

Client automatically generalizes solutions. Voices are integrated, serving as resources in new situations. Transitions between voices are smooth. Affect is positive or neutral (i.e. this is no longer something to get excited about), interpersonal process in which two people initially oppose each other, begin to communicate with each other, and ultimately reconcile their differences.

objects, is fairly clear. It also corresponds closely to concepts such as automatic thoughts in cognitive theory, reciprocal roles in cognitive analytic therapy, and the Gestalt therapy 'two chair' technique. As such the voices formulation continues to emphasize the integrative nature of the Assimilation Model. Stiles and Angus (2001) see these two formulations of the model as describing the same underlying structures, but viewed from a different perspective. They also refer to a third formulation of the model which draws explicitly on cognitive science, seeing assimilation in its early stages as linking disparate memories, but this is a formulation which to date has been less developed than the other two.

Standard coding method

The most productive method of studying assimilation has been 'assimilation analysis', which begins with an 'open' coding method, similar to that used for grounded theory (fully described in Chapter 6), to identify problematic experiences and then code them according to the APES level. Open coding differs from the kind of coding used in the CCRT in that it builds codes from the text itself, rather than applying pre-existing coding categories to the data. In the second phase, topics identified in the first phase are coded onto the APES scale. The coding process can be used to track the progress of assimilation over a particular session extract, several sessions, or a whole psychotherapy. It uses transcripts and/or audiotapes of sessions. The four steps outlined by Stiles and Angus (2001) are:

- familiarization and indexing of the text;
- identification of a problematic topic;
- selection of extracts which focus on topic;
- coding of APES level.

The first step of this process requires the researcher to become familiar with the material, to take systematic notes, to start to observe possible problem topics, and to index these themes to the location. There is no doubt that this is a time consuming procedure which, in common with the discourse methods introduced in Part III, requires immersion in the text. It lends itself well to practitioner research since the therapist is in a far better position to identify problem themes, although we need to be aware of the possibility of blind spots when the therapist is the only coder. Stiles and Angus define a topic as 'an attitude or action toward an object, that is, (a) a belief or feeling or evaluation or behavior and (b) the person, thing, event, or situation toward which the attitude or action is expressed' (Stiles and Angus, 2001, p. 115). For instance, topics might be 'mixed feelings about mother's move to nursing home' or 'worry about brother's role in shared business'.

The second step is to identify and choose a topic which is discussed repeatedly and which has become a focus of the therapy. Sometimes themes can be identified merely through the frequency of occurrence, sometimes through 'aha' experiences in therapy, where there has been a clear shift in understanding. The third stage is to select extracts which deal with the chosen problematic experience: this is where the index developed in stage one becomes important. However, it is difficult to imagine how this could be done in a mechanical way because the passages chosen need to deal with the specific problematic experience rather than with some generalized, or key worded concept such as 'worry' or 'sadness'. The final stage of the assimilation analysis is to code passages according to the APES level, usually using two or more coders. Stiles and Angus (2001) emphasize the importance of doing this in the context of the passage and the temporal location within the therapy. In other words, they do not subscribe to the importance of blind coding in order to increase reliability. Instead, the process is one of immersion, understanding, discussion and eventually finding the best APES score for the passage. This method of achieving reliability is similar to that of the grounded theory method of open coding (see Chapter 6).

The marker system of coding

Another approach to coding is to develop a system of 'markers', whereby particular features of the client's style can be used to indicate the level of assimilation. Honos-Webb *et al.* (1998b) have developed a coding manual based upon markers but this is unpublished at the time of writing. The aim was to develop a marker driven rating system to assign quantitative APES rating without the full knowledge of content: i.e. obviating the need for immersion, and shortening the coding process. The system has demonstrated reasonable reliability of coding where coders are adequately trained, even with coders who have no clinical experience. The authors argue good construct validity, in particular through the demonstration of progress up the APES levels through therapy. Markers were developed initially out of the therapeutic literature and then through intensive transcript analysis.

There is more than one marker for each APES stage and they include items such as:

- somatization (APES level 0 warded off);
- observation of abrupt change of subject, and fear of loss of control (APES 1 unwanted thoughts);
- puzzlement (APES 2 vague awareness);
- reflexivity (APES 3 problem statement);
- flexible use of voices (APES 4 new understanding);
- exploring possible solutions (APES 5 working through);
- sense of pride (APES 6 problem solution).

No markers were found for APES 7 mastery. The authors comment on the lack of markers for the higher APES levels, which they feel may be due to the use of process experiential therapy (PEP) rather than CBT texts in developing the method. They also observe that levels 0–3 are primarily intra-psychic, whereas levels 5–7 concern planning and practice of new behaviour; hence the matching of those ends of the scales to exploratory and cognitive therapies respectively. The method still requires some immersion in the material by raters – they recommend starting with a 'pre-reflective' open attitude and then moving to a rational, analytic approach in deciding whether the markers are present on a 'yes/no' basis. This is then integrated into a single assimilation rating (Honos-Webb *et al.* 1998b, p. 122).

The marker system is an interesting and important innovation which has attractions from the point of view of economy. It has been trialled on the well researched case of Jan (Honos-Webb *et al.*, 1999), where it was found to correlate reasonably with APES ratings using the standard consensual method. However, it is in the early stages of development and more work needs to be done on establishing its reliability and validity. It is unclear from the work that has to date been published using this method how much time is saved by adopting markers and how reliable it is.

Overview of published research using the Assimilation Model

The Assimilation Model has been productive for researchers. Much of the early work came from the early collaboration of Stiles and others using the taped and transcribed material from the Sheffield Psychotherapy Projects (Shapiro and Firth, 1987). Assimilation analysis was also used on a case that was first transcribed and published in 1963 by Snyder (Snyder, 1963; Stiles *et al.*, 1992b). Later work includes research using the voices formulation and the marker system discussed above. In reviewing the state of research, Stiles (2001) points out that there have been many interpretive studies using assimilation analysis to identify problematic experiences and how these change over sessions. There have been fewer hypothesis testing studies, particularly examining the hypothesis that certain modalities of therapy will be more effective with clients at different levels of assimilation. To date, the research has examined the strength of the Assimilation Model itself, rather than the value of particular techniques. Stiles acknowledges that it is a limitation that most of the research using this method has been conducted by a closely associated group of researchers, although more recently other groups have started to contribute. The published research work will be reviewed in broadly chronological order to give the reader an idea of the range and potential of the method.

Establishing validity of the model

One of the objectives in using the Assimilation Model to analyze a well known good outcome case that had already been published was to demonstrate its validity in a transparent way. The case of John Jones (Stiles *et al.*, 1992b) was a 20 session therapy which had been published with full transcripts some years earlier (Snyder, 1963). In the view of both the therapist and the client there had been significant positive change in the course of therapy. The researchers started by reading each of the 20 transcripts and making a catalogue of topics, defined as the client's expressed attitude toward the object (such as 'disappointment toward father' for instance). They identified three significant insights relating to the problem topics (fear of homosexuality, dependence and passivity, and concern about work adequacy) that the client was judged to have achieved. They then identified passages and assessed the level of assimilation using the method described above to chart the growth of assimilation over the therapy. They found that these separate areas converged into a theme which they characterize as 'becoming a man' (Stiles *et al.*, 1992b, p. 99). The levels of assimilation in the topics focused on were at the lower end of the APES scale, from APES levels 0 to 4. This is as they anticipated for an exploratory therapy such as psychodynamic or experiential psychotherapy and the progress was in the expected direction: towards higher levels of assimilation. They found that therapeutic attention was focused on the less assimilated material, whereas the more practical and consolidating methods which might be found in a cognitive behavioural treatment (such as homework assignments) were not present. The evidence of progress in assimilation levels and of the focus of the therapy is taken as useful validation of the model.

Further analysis of good outcome cases was based on those drawn from the first Sheffield Psychotherapy Project. Barkham *et al.* (1996) use four cases with good outcome, the transcripts of which were then studied intensively to identify problematic experiences and to track assimilation levels over sessions. They describe the case of Jane, a 34 year old woman referred for panic attacks and depression. This case is discussed in greater detail in Stiles *et al.* (1995). Jane showed good progress in the therapy. The main problematic experience studied was her difficulty in expressing feelings, which manifested in her use of objectifying language. For instance, in the early stages of therapy she referred to herself as 'one' and appeared to be in the warded off and vague awareness stages of assimilation.

An example of how this issue presented in an early session in shown in the following extract from session 1:

> Jane: I think that's fair, yeah. which I suppose is sometimes, you know again, why one puts up the front, (Therapist: Yes.) but rants can also be equally off-putting.
> Therapist: And even now again the language: Why 'one'? You know, 'why one puts up the front'. We're dealing, you know, we're –
> Jane (over Therapist): Sorry, that's just me. (Therapist: Yes, but –) though, yeah, ok (laughs), it is important.
> (Stiles *et al.*, 1995, p. 7)

Stiles *et al.* see this passage as showing Jane moving from APES level 0 in 'sometimes ... one puts up the front' to APES level 2 with 'yeah, ok, it is important', admitting the issue into awareness.

Jane's gradually emerging awareness of this tendency is charted in the extracts that the authors provide. Her understanding of the old pattern of her defence is shown in this brief extract:

> Like, I know, and I use it frequently: I use 'one' when I mean 'me' or 'I'. Ahm. Which may sound little. But, you know, consciously trying to emphasise that it is, it is me, the person as opposed to 'one does this' and one does that'. And so you keep it over there.
> (Stiles *et al.*, 1995, p. 9)

The authors judge that Jane moves to APES level 5.5 at this stage. They also use this study to reflect on the role of the therapist in moving the patient on from lower to higher APES levels (discussed below).

The analysis of the above case used a consensual, interpretive approach to coding, with investigators immersing themselves in the transcripts and arriving at agreement after discussing transcripts. They acknowledge that this, arguably, has methodological problems because researchers can be swayed by others and because knowledge of the temporal location of passages could affect judgement.

Another research study using the Sheffield material selected a client called Marie (Shapiro *et al.*, 1992). In this case assimilation was assessed by independent groups of raters, separating out the stages of assimilation analysis. First, two raters identified a clinically prominent problem domain. The second stage of locating statements of the problematic experience was done by three independent raters. Lastly, another team of six raters agreed the assimilation levels of the passages randomly presented. 'Our intent was to develop a systematic procedure for extracting the essence of the assimilation process while reducing contextual information that might engender bias in the final rating' (Barkham *et al.*, 1996, p. 8). This is important and legitimate at the stage of establishing the validity of a method but it obviously goes beyond what is feasible within small scale practitioner research.

The main theme used to chart the progress of assimilation was Marie's 'coming to terms with feeling guilty about letting go of her mother'. Marie had considerable guilt and warded off feelings of loss around the decision to allow her mother to enter a nursing home. The study demonstrates how her level of assimilation within this problem domain progressed from around APES level 1–2 in her first session to APES level 4–6 in her seventh. This provided some good evidence for the progression of assimilation using a methodology which protected against bias.

The role of therapist intervention

Barkham *et al.* (1996) concluded from both the above Sheffield studies that there is great significance in the vague awareness/emergence stage (APES 2), which they felt was pivotal in indicating the client's readiness to pursue work on a particular topic. They conclude that this stage 'represents a transition from avoidance toward a potential for active therapeutic engagement' (Barkham *et al.*, 1996, p. 7). This suggests that attention should be focused on the interventions that help clients to move beyond this level. Clearly this is a significant stage in the formation of the therapeutic alliance at the early stages of therapy. It is also arguably likely to be pivotal in the denial/recognition of therapeutic ruptures, and their subsequent resolution and repair, which has been found to be so important in keeping clients engaged in the therapy process (Safran and Muran, 1996, 2000).

The effect of therapist technique and specific interventions were investigated in the case of Jane and in a third study from the Sheffield project. Barkham *et al.* (1996) devised an integrative eight session therapy wherein a decision to work in a cognitive behavioural (CBT) or a psychodynamic interpersonal (PI) way was made at the beginning of each session. This decision was based upon four problem themes identified at assessment and the therapist's judgement of the client's level of assimilation in relation to a particular salient theme at the start of the session. This was an attempt to examine the hypothesis that PI techniques are more appropriate at lower levels, and CBT at higher levels, of assimilation. The researchers used a client completed measure of progress based on the Assimilation Model called the therapy session topic review (TSTR) to assist in scoring of assimilation levels. The client showed good improvement in treatment and at follow-up, but we cannot help thinking that this is potentially very confusing to a patient. However, it can be argued that skilled therapists are likely to adopt this flexibility within the confines of their own model – for instance, more facilitative, open interventions are likely to be used where there is an emerging consciousness.

The expectation that PI treatments would work better with clients at lower levels of assimilation and CBT with clients at higher levels was further explored using the Sheffield data by Stiles *et al.* (1997). They grouped clients who had been randomly assigned to PI and CBT treatments on the basis of a global judgement of assimilation level at assessment interview. (This method clearly lacks the specificity and sophistication of a full assimilation analysis by problematic experience.) The researchers found some evidence that clients with well assimilated problems would do better in cognitive behavioural therapy, but no evidence that those with poorly assimilated problems did better in psychodynamic interpersonal therapy. This is a finding which needs to be tempered by the global method of coding used and the lack of specific consideration of the actual interventions employed.

The case of Jane is used to code and analyze the therapist interventions alongside the coding of assimilation level by Stiles *et al.* (1995). Here the authors used Hobson's treatment rationale (Hobson, 1985) for what is now called psychodynamic-interpersonal psychotherapy to code the therapist interventions according to Hobson's typography. Therapist tasks are coded on a five point scale which moves from building relationship and trust, promoting intense experiencing and expression, drawing attention to patterns of feeling and defence (understanding hypotheses), promoting self-understanding (linking and explanatory hypotheses), and exploring and experimenting. It can be seen that this is a progressive scale which can be related to the progress of assimilation, albeit focusing on the lower levels of assimilation as one might expect for a psychodynamic treatment method. The coding of the therapist interventions enables the authors to look at the relationship between Jane's problematic theme of objectifying language (as discussed above) and the therapist interventions which seem to facilitate the assimilation of this. They found that the therapist was active in drawing attention to her defence and in promoting her understanding of this.

This still leaves the question of whether it was the therapist interventions that enabled Jane to progress so well. The authors conclude that the evidence for this impact is good at several observable levels. At the level of the passage it was possible to see how Jane responded to the therapist's interactions, including 'grammatically finishing his sentences and going on to expand and clarify earlier remarks' (Stiles *et al.*, 1995,

p. 10). At the level of the problematic experience it is more difficult to be so sure about the impact. However, the evidence for this is good given that Jane's objectifying language noticeably changed over the course of the therapy. In terms of the global measures of progress, this is at a yet further level removed from the actual interventions and it is very difficult to draw conclusions with great confidence. However, taken with the outcome research finding of the general efficacy of psychotherapy and of the importance of the therapeutic relationship, it is legitimate to conclude that there is a generally beneficial impact from sensitive intervention.

Use of the model in different settings

A limitation of the Assimilation Model research has been the fairly narrow group of researchers who have used it. However, it has been applied successfully within other settings: in family therapy (Laitila and Aaltonen, 1998) and with intellectually disabled clients (Newman and Beail, 2002). Laitila and Aaltonen describe an experiential therapy technique using sculptures with a 10-year-old psychotic boy and his family. They use the standard coding technique, but applied to repeated family member sculptures of the problematic situation. In their study they found evidence for the feasibility of coding non-verbal material such as sculptures, and the normally reported rise in APES levels over the course of treatment. They conclude that the model is a valid method of analysis within this setting. Newman and Beail use the model to examine evidence for the efficacy of psychodynamic psychotherapy with people with intellectual disabilities. The data was taken from the first eight sessions with a 25-year-old man seen for sixteen session of psychotherapy. The methodology used was standard: identification of problem area and independent APES coding using transcripts of psychotherapy settings. They report good inter-rater reliability and evidence of client change in the main problematic area of being an adult and separating from mother, moving between APES levels 0 and 4. They conclude that the Assimilation Model is a valid and reliable method for studying this group, but are unable to draw conclusions on whether intellectually disabled clients are able to attain higher levels of assimilation.

Examples of practitioner projects using the Assimilation Model

The Assimilation Model lends itself to small scale practitioner projects. The therapist is in an ideal position to identify relevant problematic experiences for their clients and to locate passages where these themes are covered. The emphasis within the method on the importance of immersion, rather than on the need for blind coding, means that the therapist is uniquely situated to identify and code episodes. A number of students within our *Psychotherapy Process Research* course at the University of Kent have used assimilation analysis to track therapeutic change and to provide better understanding of their own work with clients. Sometimes this has focused on the interaction and the interpretations; sometimes it has merely focused on progression over the course of a therapy.

The fact that the model is not attempting to say anything global about a therapy means that it can be used in quite a confined, but highly clinically relevant, way. For instance, in one project the therapist focused upon a problematic experience of a patient who had a friend working

Figure 4.2   Example of APES progress within a psychotherapy session

P201	No – because I intend – there's a er – woman a woman who's em at work who can do the typing and that – and then there's just to write up their estimates. I've got Angela doing more and more estimates now in the week so I don't have to do on Saturday's so much.
T202	I mean more if it breaks down – if the trouble comes along and you know – if they do work sort of erratically – both of them working erratically.
P203	No. I hadn't thought of that. I mean it doesn't mean that it wasn't going on in my head.
T204	Hmm. And that somehow – I just had the feeling then – you know – you going off to University – with all the connotations of going off to University.
P205	They are going to have that anyway.
T206	But they are going to be left in their chaos. You know – are you laughing – you know – are you up there at University kind of well there you are down there – it serves you right – I'm here you know. (Pause)
P207	I hadn't thought of that. (Pause) But we are in a position now where we've picked up an awful large amount of work. I mean a position or we are – where we have to employ another person. We are in that position. (pause) I have another choice. I have a friend who is saying she'll work for us full time or I can go out on the open market and look for somebody. (pause) Now there is my choices. Really. (pause) I have a definite struggle with this really. (pause) Not a massive one. Not as big as it could have been for me thank God but it's em somat I have got to deal with and think through. That's why I must have given myself this space. I've got to deal with it. (pause).

within her business. Her difficulties realizing, voicing and expressing her anger in respect of the friend's emerging pattern of fiddling the business became an important theme in the therapy. The therapist took a single extract relating to this theme and, with three other coders, scored the APES level of each of ten patient turns against a coding for level of therapist confrontation in the therapist turns. The extract is given in Figure 4.2.

It is difficult to assign an APES score reliably from a short extract without contextual knowledge, but the reader may wish to reflect on the level of assimilation indicated in this example.

The coders found evidence of a progression from APES level 2.5 to 4 within the extract. It is possible within the last patient turn (P207) to practically hear her, through the pauses, bringing about some kind of internal processing. The therapist was able to use this extract from the one year therapy to reflect upon his own role in enabling the patient to progress. This provided a useful discussion of how the therapist's interventions may at appropriate stages in therapy move on the process of assimilation. He tentatively concluded that there was support for the hypothesis that an appropriately confrontative style at this point in the therapy contributed to this process.

Another student project used a taped one year therapy and had the advantage of a co-supervisee to help locate relevant problematic themes. The theme chosen was the patient's understanding of her acting out, or 'tantrums', in relation to situations where she did not feel special to significant others. For instance, in the first session the patient acknowledges the existence of a problematic experience and describes uncomfortable associated thoughts, but does not have a clearly understanding of the problem as illustrated in the following extract:

> Everybody gets on with things and copes. Why don't I? It's just not understanding myself sometimes. Not knowing why I'm doing things sometimes. Not knowing why I'm doing things or getting upset or getting annoyed. Having to storm out ... getting upset. Having to release things in tears or shouting, rather than just working through them. (APES level 2)

The therapist/researcher identified five extracts from sessions between the first and the 21st to see the progress of assimilation in relation to this problem. Four raters were used and they were able to achieve moderate reliability in independent coding. The final APES level was agreed by discussion. After the initial session the patient showed a steady increase in assimilation level to APES 5 in Session 21. Figure 4.3 shows a brief extract from that session.

Figure 4.3 Extract from session 21

P5 It was a change because sometimes in the past when I've tried to explain whether it be how I feel or what, they'd get the wrong end of the stick or I'd not say it right. And then it just blows things out of proportion. Yesterday it didn't, ok, but it hurt X. But there was no, it doesn't turn into an argument, but there were no harsh words. Or anything like that... I feel guilty for hurting X but I was pleased we spoke about it.

T5 You were pleased.

P6 Definitely because it just came naturally. You know I didn't even know how we got there. It was very honest I suppose ... And relaxed to feel they could say what they wanted to say, and I couldn't say what I wanted to say, without it being taken the wrong way.

T6 It's almost that in the last few weeks here you've opened your eyes and allowed yourself to see what has been going on within you ... and with that felt safe enough to tell X.

P7 It just didn't seem so silly ... Maybe because I understand it a bit more.

APES level 5

While it is impossible to adjudicate the APES scoring process from these brief extracts we hope that it gives the reader an idea of what is involved in this process. The difficulty of coding from short extracts reinforces the need for raters to have an understanding of the context for the particular patient and to discuss and agree with other raters. However, it can be seen that the methodology has the potential for a detailed focus upon particular problem areas and upon the content of sessions. In terms of clinical usefulness, the therapist/researcher concluded that the process enhanced her understanding of the patient material and the development of this over the course of the therapy. She felt that there was no progress beyond APES 5 throughout the duration of the therapy in relation to this theme, which is consistent with the contention of Assimilation Model researchers that psychodynamic therapy focuses upon the lower levels of assimilation.

Conclusion

The Assimilation Model has established an impressive body of research to provide validation. It has a clear methodology for coding which can be applied with reliability and with some greater economy than many of the process research methods described in this book. It has a proven track record for small scale practitioner research and we have found that trainees are able to produce credible projects based on it. Generally speaking their experience has been that using the Assimilation Model on their own clinical work has the ability to contribute to their understanding of the process. The Assimilation Model also has the facility to focus upon therapist–patient interaction and to provide a more specific understanding of the process of changing insight. It is useful in recommending intervention styles relevant at specific APES levels and this can provide a useful clinical tool.

However, it needs to be acknowledged that the model is limited in focusing only upon specific problem areas identified in the sessions rather than the broader scope of the therapy. This does not leave much room for looking at what is happening beneath the surface. Like CCRT, its focus is primarily the patient material rather than the inter-subjective space. There is little ability to look at the real process happening in the session between client and patient. This has been acknowledged by Assimilation Model researchers and recently Stiles has used Vygotsky's concept of zone of proximal development (Leiman and Stiles, 2001; Vygotsky, 1978) to rectify this. The standard method of assimilation analysis remains somewhat limited in its scope: based primarily within transcripts rather than direct process coding, with its focus on patient narratives, it lies somewhere between CCRT, which almost entirely focuses on patient narratives (i.e. 'out there' rather than 'in here') and SASB, which almost entirely focuses upon interpersonal process rather than the content of narratives. Its main strength is in the contextual understanding of emerging and resolving problem areas as discussed in therapies rather than the testing of general hypotheses about the change process.

SUGGESTIONS FOR FURTHER READING

Honos-Webb, L. and Stiles, W.B. (1998) 'Reformulation of assimilation analysis in terms of voices', *Psychotherapy*, 35: 23–33.

Stiles, W.B. (2002) 'Assimilation of problematic experiences', in J.C. Norcross, *Psychotherapy Relationships that Work. Therapist contributions and responsiveness to patients*. New York: Oxford.

Stiles, W.B., Elliott, R., Llewelyn, S.P., Firth-Cozens, J.A., Margison, F.R., Shapiro, D.A. and Hardy, G. (1990) 'Assimilation of problematic experiences by clients in psychotherapy', *Psychotherapy*, 27: 411–20.

CHAPTER 5

Interpersonal theory approaches

Introduction

In looking at interpersonal approaches to the psychotherapy session we are moving to methods which have a central focus on two person interaction, rather than the mainly one person perspectives of CCRT and the Assimilation Model. Although the transference-based models such as CCRT do have provision for some interactional coding, they focus mainly on the relationship episodes: the patient's accounts of relationships outside of the session. The Assimilation Model moves towards a two person model in that it turns its attention to the role of the therapist in the encounter, but its main focus is still the problematic situation 'out there' as described by the patient. Interpersonal theory approaches (particularly SASB, the coding method which is described in detail in this chapter) tend to focus on the actual encounter in the room. It can be argued that due to this researchers end up with a much richer, and more complex, understanding of the process of psychotherapy. The inevitable price that has to be paid for this is the time consuming nature of the coding process.

This chapter will review the antecedents and development of interpersonal theory. It will then focus on the only well established observational coding system which has been based upon interpersonal theory, the structural analysis of social behaviour or SASB (Benjamin, 1974). The SASB model will be described and the basics of the SASB observational coding system will be outlined. This will be followed by a summary of the research using SASB and a more detailed discussion of a medium scale doctoral research project which used the SASB observational coding system.

Interpersonal theory

There is a long tradition of research into interpersonal theory, a model based upon Sullivan's interpersonal psychology (Sullivan, 1940, 1953). Sullivan rejected Freud's drive-based model and put environmental and cultural factors squarely back into prominence. Sullivan's 'needs' were unlike the Freudian drives in that they were not seen as biologically derived from physical urges originating within the infant's own body, but instead were intrinsically inseparable from relationships. The role of the interpersonal was also central to Sullivan's model: 'the field of Psychiatry is the field of interpersonal relations – a personality can never be isolated from the complex of interpersonal relations in which the person lives and has his being' (Sullivan, 1940, p. 10).

The infant has a need for contact which is reciprocated by the mother – a reciprocation which Sullivan referred to as a complementary need. In stressing the need for contact, or closeness, Sullivan laid the ground for the development of the two axis model which is described below. The roots of these relationship needs (in coping with anxiety arising from actual interpersonal experiences in the past) places Sullivan's theory close in basics, if not in language, to those psychoanalytical models which developed after Freud and stressed the importance of early relationships to later pathology, particularly the object relations and self psychology schools (see Greenberg and Mitchell (1984) for a full discussion).

Sullivan thus started a school of psychology which came to be known as interpersonal theory, and was the source of the 'Interpersonal Circle' (IPC) which was later developed by Freedman *et al.* (1951), Leary (1957) and others. The underlying basis of interpersonal theory was an understanding that relating can be placed on two dimensions: a vertical axis relating to 'affiliation', or friendliness/hostility, and a horizontal axis relating to 'control', or dominance/submission. It could be argued that these dimensions were implicit in Freud's later drive model itself – with the duality between Thanatos and Eros. The correspondence is less clear within the early biological drive-based model. It was only later psychoanalytic writers who came to stress relationships over drives.

It was the achievement of Leary in *Interpersonal Diagnosis of Personality* (Leary, 1957) to develop these theories into a system for classifying interpersonal behaviour into a two dimensional model that became known as the Interpersonal Circle. While acknowledging that inter-personal behaviour is a small part of human activity, he believed this 'to be the area of psychology which is most crucial and functionally important to human happiness and human survival' (Leary, 1957, p. 6). Drawing on the work of Sullivan, Fromm, Horney and Erikson, Leary saw the main motivation for characterological interpersonal patterns as being the avoidance or minimization of anxiety. Anxiety arose from the fear of rejection, social disapproval and loss of self-esteem deriving from the basic fears of abandonment and death. Leary also drew upon Jungian theory to argue for normal and pathological interpersonal behaviour to be seen on a continuum, the latter being indicated by excessive rigidity and high intensity. He argued against the predominant symptom-based classification of psychiatric disorder, seeing symptoms as 'external signs' of unsuccessful adaptation, and felt that the use of direct interpersonal terms would come to be more important. This has to some extent been realised in the DSM-IV Axis II definitions (American Psychiatric Association, 1994).

Along with the consideration of *intensity* and *rigidity* as indicators of maladjustment, Leary added *stability* and *accuracy* or *appropriateness* as indicators of psychological health. Given the desire for an integrated model that can see behaviour within any of the predominant categories as normal or pathological depending on these quantitative factors, Leary was concerned to find neutral descriptors of the positions within the interpersonal circle: not an easy task given the limitations of language. For instance:

> It was, however, a tedious task to get three or four commonly used words for the concept of adjustive, socially approved hostility. Considerable dictionary, thesaurus, and literary research uncovered a few such words – *frank, blunt, critical* – but it appears that the English language, and the implicit folk conceptions of human nature that underly it, pay little attention to the theme of appropriate expression of disaffiliative interpersonal behaviour (Leary 1957, p. 29).

Similar problems were encountered in trying to find terms for extreme, rigid maladjustive affectionate behaviour: the language did not accommodate the concept of being *too loving*.

A richness of Leary's model that is sometimes forgotten is that he talked of five levels of classification, all of which would have appropriate instruments to provide measurement. He saw these as being:

Level I   Public communication – overt behaviour rated by others;
Level II   Conscious descriptions – of himself and others, derived from a variety of sources including questionnaires;
Level III   Private symbolization – derived from fantasy material, dreams, projective tests;
Level IV   Unexpressed unconscious – defined by 'interpersonal themes which are systematically and compulsively avoided';
Level V   Values – subject's system of moral judgements, ego ideal.

It is clear from this typology that a full 'diagnosis' could give considerable complexity and sophistication, allowing for internal conflict and seemingly contradictory behaviours. Leary developed suggestions for the classification within each of the levels except that of Level IV, which he felt needed further development, possibly enabled by the use of statistical techniques and the analysis of taped material. It should be borne in mind that the questionnaire-based research which forms the basis of most psychotherapy outcome studies, focuses on Level II and therefore lack the richness of Leary's full model. The observational coding of psychotherapy encounters has the potential to measure on all of the Leary levels.

The interpersonal circle

The interpersonal circle (IPC) was developed empirically using data from 'several scores of individuals . . . brought into interpersonal relationships in small groups' (Leary 1957, p. 62). Leary and his colleagues found that by placing 'dominate' and 'submit' at either ends of the vertical dimension; 'love' and 'hate' were at either end of the horizontal axis, a two dimensional space was provided which enabled all interaction to be placed. This then enabled a subdivision into 16 segments in the two dimensional space and the description of personality traits within these segments. The model was used to categorize both 'normal' and pathological behaviour: the latter being a more extreme form of the former (the concept of *intensity*). In conformity with the notion of rigidity, one would expect a well adjusted person to move between different positions in different relationships while more pathological forms of behaviour are often stuck in a particular mould.

There have been various elaborations of the Leary's circle, which are reviewed by Birtchnell (1993) and Wiggins (1982). Although the underlying dimensions have been successively relabelled and particular descriptions have been moved between segments by various writers (see, for instance, Benjamin, 1974; Strong *et al.*, 1988; Wiggins, 1982), there has continued to be a high level of consensus that the underlying dimensions themselves are theoretically and empirically justified. The model developed by Benjamin (1974) had an interactional focus, with separate 'surfaces' for transitive (described as *parentlike*) and intransitive (described as *childlike*) behaviours and for 'introjected attitudes from significant others'. This is the structural analysis of social behaviour (SASB) model which is described in detail below.

An interactional model was also developed by Kiesler (1983a), who aimed to apply it in a more clinically useful way. He argued that the full power of interpersonal theory in the clinical field had not been demonstrated because 'researchers have directed the bulk of their energies to the area of personality, with considerably less theoretical or empirical attention being devoted to issues of psychopathology and psychotherapy' (Kiesler, 1983a, p. 185). One key to this desirable development, Kiesler felt, was the further elaboration of the issue of interpersonal *complementarity*: the link between behaviour and the response from others. The

'1982 Interpersonal Circle' developed by Kiesler claimed to address some of the problems of previous models and was supported by a comprehensive list of traits within 16 segments of the circle. The aim was that the circle should reveal a circumplex ordering, with adjacent segments positively correlated and opposite segments negatively correlated. It thus assumed a bipolar structure, with, for instance, hostile behaviour not normally expected to be found alongside friendly behaviour. While the clinical relevance of this is clear, it has not been extended into a process coding method using psychotherapy transcripts or tapes.

It is the notion of complementarity which is particularly interesting from the point of view of psychotherapy. Kiesler (1983a, 1992) argues that if we define complementary behaviours we should be able to use this within the psychotherapy session to promote change in pathological interpersonal relating patterns. He develops a basic model of complementarity which had been suggested by Sullivan (1953) in his 'theorem of reciprocal emotion'. This was observed but not developed in Leary's (1957) original model, and explicit in later writings by Carson (1969) and others:

> Generally speaking, complementarity occurs on the basis of reciprocity in respect to the dominance–submission axis (dominance tends to induce submission, and vice versa), and on the basis of correspondence in respect to the hate–love axis (hate induces hate, and love induces love). (p. 112)

Kiesler claims empirical validation of this theory and develops a series of propositions relating to what he termed *complementary, acomplementary* and *anticomplementary* reciprocation. Acomplementary interaction occurs where there is complementarity on one axis but not the other: for instance, where dominant love is met by dominant love (complementary on the hate–love axis, but not on the dominance–submission one). Anticomplementary interaction is where there is no complementarity on either axis: for instance where dominant love is met by dominant hate. He argues that, within psychotherapy, complementarity may be important to build the therapeutic alliance (hence in the early stage of therapy) but that later stages of therapy would confront entrenched behavioural patterns by challenging through reciprocations of an acomplementary or anticomplementary kind (Kiesler, 1992). For instance, the therapist might respond to dominant attack from the patient with the acomplementary dominant love. The transference relationship can be understood as an attempt by the patient to duplicate previous (pathological) patterns of interpersonal complementarity: it is the job of the therapist *not* to reciprocate these patterns in the middle phase of therapy:

A transactional prediction might be that the patient and therapist will move from rigid and extreme complementary transaction early in therapy, to non-complementary positions in the change-oriented middle phases of therapy, to a later transactional pattern that exhibits mild and flexible complementarity. In contrast, within unsuccessful therapy, the patient–therapist relationship will remain bogged down in various degrees of complementarity throughout the entire therapy course. (Kiesler, 1992, p. 92)

While not systematized to this extent, the notion that the therapist should behave in such a way as not to reinforce pathological relationship patterns is a common one within psychodynamic therapy: 'the task of a psychodynamic therapist, in part, is to modify these interactional patterns within the patient–therapist relationship and help the patient produce similar change outside of treatment' (Horowitz *et al.*, 1993, p. 550). The success of therapy, according to Kiesler, should therefore also be shown in that 'patient transactions with significant others outside therapy should demonstrate movement from pre-therapy rigid and extreme patterns to post-therapy mild and flexible patterns' (Kiesler, 1992, p. 92). This is a change which should presumably show up in instruments which focus on interpersonal relating.

Kiesler's propositions with regard to complementarity have been challenged by others, both in respect of general relating and specifically in the psychotherapy relationship. While there is some evidence that 'goodness of fit' between therapist and patient is significant in contributing to psychotherapy outcome, it is difficult to understand this in terms of Kiesler's complementarity rules. Safran (1992) points out that Kiesler speculates that greater complementarity should be associated with a better therapeutic alliance, but is not convinced by some of the implications of this: for instance, that matching a hostile client with hostile therapist will build the therapeutic alliance. Safran argues that the model would need to be extended to the intra-psychic sphere to take on real meaning.

Kiesler's claims of empirical validation are disputed by Orford (1986), who argues that while friendly-dominant and friendly-submissive behaviours are often found to be complementary (as required by Kiesler's model) there is also evidence that hostile-submissive behaviour is often met by friendly-dominance and that hostile-dominance is reciprocated (neither predicted by the model). Orford argues for a more complex model which can take account of factors such as 'group membership, role, status, and setting' (p. 376). This is a particularly important point if we are to attempt to apply this model to the artificiality of the psychotherapy setting. Strong *et al.* (1988) also argue that interpersonal behaviour has multiple determinants and concludes:

> Clearly, how one person behaves toward another profoundly influences how the other behaves toward that person. However, a specific interpersonal behavior does not impel a specific response from the other. Rather, the person's behavior biases the other's responses in a particular direction, a direction that is evident in the other's overall pattern of response but may not be apparent in specific responses. (Strong *et al.*, 1988, p. 808).

All of these points would argue against the rather simplistic model of therapy phases outlined by Kiesler (1992).

The interpersonal octagon

A variant of interpersonal theory is provided by Birtchnell's interpersonal octagon (Birtchnell, 1994). Birtchnell accepts that the interpersonal circle has been the basis of useful research but feels that it started with fundamental deficiencies. A fundamental weakness is the nodal points, since they are not general enough and don't allow for constructive as well as pathological relating: which is essential if the model is to be securely based within evolutionary theory. The interpersonal circle thus has a built in bias: for instance, hating is clearly negative, and submitting is usually thought also to be negative. Birtchnell (1993, p. 514) also argues that the interpersonal circle becomes unmanageable beyond eight segments and that the assumption of bipolarity (as required for a circumplex model) is not useful. In addition to these weaknesses, Birtchnell argues that there needs to be a distinction between adaptive and maladaptive behaviour that is qualitative and not quantitative. In other words, the concept of *intensity* – of seeing pathological positions as more extreme forms of 'normal' ones – is not acceptable. Birtchnell describes three forms of maladaptive relating: egocentric, insecure, and avoidant (1994).

Birtchnell (1993) claims to correct these deficiencies by building a model based on two axes of relating: the 'power' one with the nodal points of 'upper' and 'lower' and a proximity dimension with the nodal points of 'closeness' and 'distance'. Although different in conceptualization, these new axes clearly correspond to the IPC ones of dominate–submit and love–hate. Birtchnell draws on evolution theorists to point out that the issues of distancing in relation to others and in seeking or accepting power are fundamental for any living species. Unlike the interpersonal circle the dimensions do not have a built in bias: distant behaviour is often associated with creativity, achievement and personal space; lower behaviour with being nurtured, taught, accepting rational authority etc. Birtchnell argues that well adapted humans move between different 'states of relatedness' freely depending on their different roles, life stages and tasks. He points out that:

> the (good) states of relatedness associated with each of the four positions are equally desirable and equally pleasurable. In terms of relating skills or competencies, the good relater needs to be as skilful or as competent in one direction of an axis as s/he is in another. Conversely, the bad relater may be equally bad in both directions on a particular axis (p. 42).

It can be seen that this model is more able to explain the fact that more severe patients tend to score highly over a broad range of interpersonal problems. This fits in with the co-morbidity, or breadth of pathology, observation (Dolan *et al.*, 1995) that personality disordered patients usually exhibit more than one Axis II DSM diagnosis.

Birtchnell blends each of the nodal positions with that of its neighbours to produce an octagon with eight positions labelled upper neutral (UN), upper close (UC), neutral close (NC) etc., and describes each of the octant positions in more detail for both adaptive and maladaptive relationship patterns (Birtchnell, 1993). He has some reservations about producing an octant, in particular because he feels that the two axes may not be completely orthogonal – 'It may be that upper people are more inclined to be distant and lower people are more inclined to be close' (p. 215). This model is used as the basis for a 'new approach to psychotherapy' (Birtchnell, 1999) which requires the therapist to be aware of the repetitive pathological relating patterns and to encourage the patient to try out and become confident in new ways of interrelating.

Summary

The above interpersonal models have the potential to provide interesting process research perspectives. A number of instruments have been built upon the models, particularly Kiesler's Impact Message Inventory (IMI) (Kiesler, 1996; Schmidt *et al.*, 1999) and Birtchnell's PROQ and CREOQ questionnaires (Birtchnell, 1999). In addition a well established empirically-based interpersonal instrument – the Inventory of Interpersonal Problems (IIP) (Horowitz *et al.*, 1988) – has been used to build instruments based on the IPC (Alden *et al.*, 1990) and the octant (Riding and Cartwright, 1999). However, the only model which has been used as the basis for a coherent and comprehensive coding system for psychotherapy process is SASB.

The structural analysis of social behaviour (SASB)

Benjamin started from the basic two dimension structure of interpersonal theory, which she felt had been well validated theoretically and empirically. However, she changed it significantly to produce the SASB model. This results in a conceptually richer model which has the capability, Benjamin (1996a) claims, of measuring on all of Leary's five levels, as detailed above. In particular, it attempts to include unconscious process and incorporates the notion of introject (or internal object). This makes it far more compatible with psychoanalytic object relations theories. It also departs from a view of pathology as just being to do with 'intensity', as in Leary's original and Kiesler's subsequent models. Benjamin defines normality as qualitatively distinct from pathology. As such, it rectifies one of the weaknesses of the interpersonal circle that Birtchnell (1994) criticized. The conceptual relationship between the SASB approach and that of the IPC has been characterized by Pincus et al. (1998). They refer to the IPC as an *individual-differences* approach because it attempts to attribute to individuals particular overall personality traits based upon measurement of interpersonal relating. SASB, in contrast, is seen as a *dyadic* approach because it focuses on interpersonal behaviour in particular dyads, deriving from Schaefer's work with the mother–child dyad (Schaefer, 1971). It is for this reason that SASB lends itself more readily to process coding.

However, much of the application of SASB has been in elucidating pathological personality traits – deeply entrenched repetitive tendencies in interpersonal functioning, as in personality disorder (Benjamin, 1996a). The INTREX questionnaires have been developed to measure these (Benjamin, 1988), comprising questions about particular relationships at best and at worst, specifically: significant other; mother; father; yourself. Although the INTREX questionnaires have the usual limitations of self-report measures, they do go further than most relating questionnaires in focusing on specific relationships rather than attempting to generalize to all relationships. In this respect they are similar to Birtchnell's CREOQ questionnaires (Birtchnell, 1999) which focus specifically on the couple relationship. However, they do not provide a method of analyzing the psychotherapy process. For this reason, of more interest to us is the observational coding system that Benjamin has developed to analyze relationship processes (Benjamin and Cushing, 2000). This has been successfully used in psychotherapy process research. It has also been convincingly applied to relationships portrayed in films and soaps as an illustration of the method (Benjamin, 1996b; Paddock et al., 2001).

The SASB surfaces

SASB adopts the two orthogonal axes of the interpersonal circle, which are defined as love–hate and dominate–submit, but presents interpersonal behaviour in relational terms by producing three focuses. These comprise:

- *transitive* – focus directed towards the other (e.g. I control her);
- *intransitive* – focus on the self in relation to the other (e.g. I submit to him);
- *introject* – focus directed at the self (e.g. I control myself).

The transitive focus is described as typically parentlike, whereas the intransitive focus is typically childlike. The introject focus clearly relates to our relationship to ourselves, or our internal objects.

These focuses can be depicted as three surfaces. The three surfaces have been produced in two forms: the full form with 36 points on each surface and the simplified cluster form, which has eight points on each surface. The full form provides too great a level of discrimination for process coding so the simplified cluster form is all that we need to concentrate on. Figure 5.1 shows the simplified cluster form with the three surfaces conflated into one two dimensional space. Although the simplified cluster

Figure 5.1   The SASB simplified cluster model

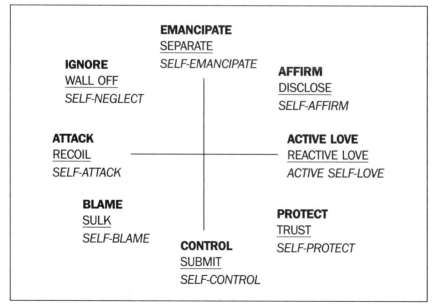

Reprinted with permission from Guilford Press.

model has been given in various forms we will use the labels in Figure 5.1 throughout this discussion. We will also follow the convention of showing the transitive focus in **bold**, the intransitive with <u>underline</u> and the introject in *italics*.

It can be seen that within this model the normal opposition of control–submit and love–hate within the IPC has been replaced by control–submit going between the first two surfaces. Transitive **control** is seen as accompanying intransitive <u>submit</u>. The opposite of **control** on the transitive surface is **emancipate**, whereas the opposite of <u>separate</u> on the intransitive surface is <u>submit</u>. The introject surface can be harder to observe since it is only in certain situations (including therapy) where people are encouraged to talk about their relationship to their inner self/ selves. A statement such as 'I was so stupid' can readily be seen as *self-blame*, but often these self directed statements need to be inferred from the material. However, in principle this system enables any interpersonal act or communication to be analyzed in terms of the three surfaces, giving a much richer picture than is possible with the two dimensional IPC or the octagon.

Benjamin acknowledges the influence of Schaefer's circumplex model of parenting behaviour (Benjamin, 1974; Schaefer, 1971). However, Benjamin saw dominance and emancipation as opposites, with dominance and submission as complementary: hence the need for a separate surface for intransitive behaviour. Emancipation had not been accommodated in previous interpersonal circle models, and Mahler's observational work on separation individuation in toddlers is seen as an important influence (Florsheim and Benjamin, 2001; Mahler, 1968). Underlying the notion of the introject surface is Sullivan's idea that actual interpersonal relationships are internalized to form the intrapsychic world. It is also consistent with the object relations idea that our relationship with ourselves or with our internal world will largely be governed by the relationship of significant others to us in childhood. Thus people who exhibit self-blaming could be expected to have been in situations where they were continually blamed by (usually) parents.

Benjamin describes predictive principles based upon this model (Benjamin, 1996b; Florsheim and Benjamin, 2001). Complementarity is akin to Kiesler's concept (Kiesler, 1992, 1996), although seen differently because of the use of three surfaces. It is the predicted normal course of interaction, whereby for instance, protecting behaviour by a caregiver is reciprocated by a trusting response from the child (**protect** and <u>trust</u>). In time this would be expected to establish the introject (or internal object) of *self-protect*. However, complementarity may also be negative. For instance, **attack** prompts the response of <u>recoil</u>. Continual attack of children by parents in childhood can produce the introject of *self-attack*, sometimes leading to deeply embedded pathology as in self harming. One of the challenges for therapists is to bring about a change so that patients can overcome these tendencies. In its simplest form, the acceptance and emancipating responses of therapists, even under extreme pressure as is often the case for instance with borderline patients, may be thought eventually to bring about some more positive introjects in the patient. It is for this reason that researchers in the SASB model have been concerned to look at unintended controlling, critical or contradictory behaviours by therapists and how this might relate to negative outcome (see below).

Where complementarity is located at the bottom of the vertical pole (**control** submit) it is described as enmeshed. Where it is located at the top (**emancipate** separate) it is described as differentiated. It can be seen that there is some notion of normality/pathology built into this, in that enmeshed complementarity is clearly more pathological than differentiated complementarity. Actually Benjamin argues that normality (or healthy relating) is defined by behaviours which are friendly and moderately enmeshed or moderately differentiated. These are **affirm**/ disclose, **active-love**/reactive-love and **protect**/trust with their accompanying introjects, and are known as the 'attachment group' (Benjamin, 1996b; Henry, 1996). Behaviours which are hostile and moderately enmeshed or differentiated are characteristic of personality disorder, and hence seen as pathological. While personality disordered patients do display attachment group behaviour at times, they have excesses of interpersonal submission, distance and hostility. In accord with the psychodynamic model of aetiology, this is seen as largely determined by the early relationship with parents. Pathology is thus defined more by the horizontal axis, although it is acknowledged that hostile behaviours can be normal in specific contexts.

The replication of the way that a person has been treated by another is described as concordance or similarity. This can form the core of conflict in relations, for instance where one partner's attack is reciprocated by attack (**attack** leading to **attack**). It can also be the source of the defence of identification with the aggressor, as conceptualized by Anna Freud (1938). Within clinical populations the conversion of excessive abusing and bullying behaviour in childhood by a parent (**attack**) into the introject *self attack* and/or the transitive behaviour of aggression to others is commonly observed. However, 'oppositional' behaviour is also commonly observed, for instance where bad treatment in childhood leads to the adult deliberately adopting the opposite behaviour of their own parent by attempting to become a good parent. While it is arguably predictable that the introject will show complementarity (e.g., **attack** leading to *self* *attack*), the conversion into the transitive focus in relation to others is more difficult to predict.

This leaves anticomplementarity or .antithesis, which is seen as occurring in unstable relationships. This is where a transitive behaviour is reciprocated by a response which is the opposite. A common example of this is in adolescent rebellion where the parent may attempt to **control** but the adolescent responds with separate. This is clearly not a stable situation and usually marks a transition from one form of relationship to another, for instance a teenager becoming an adult, or a partner becoming a ex-partner.

The SASB coding system

Benjamin and her co-workers sound a warning to researchers thinking of using the coding system:

> it is difficult and time consuming to become a reliable SASB coder . . . it may require up to 100 hours of training to achieve inter-rater reliability. Relative to most coding schemes on the market, the SASB model is more complicated and more difficult to learn, requiring a high degree of patience and persistence. Moreover, we recommend against self-instruction, and strongly suggest that novice SASB researchers receive instruction from someone who has already achieved reliability (Florsheim and Benjamin, 2001, p. 140).

However, a more optimistic estimate is given in the coding manual update (Benjamin and Cushing, 2000) where they advise that 30–50 hours is needed to get coders to an acceptable level for family transactions; less for patient–therapist transactions. In addition, they point out that the tasks of coding, processing and analyzing are themselves time consuming, advising that a 10 minute family interaction may take 2–3 hours to microcode and process. In relation to the latter there is now a data processing software package called SASBWorks to provide assistance, but the main task still obviously lies in listening to (and observing) interactions and assigning codes in relation to the three surfaces. Readers are advised to obtain the coding manual and investigate the possibility of training if they intend to undertake any large scale research using SASB. The coding manual is available at the time of writing, along with the SASB software package, on the SASB website at the University of Utah: www.psych.utah.edu/benjamin/sasb.

The raw data for SASB coding of psychotherapy process is usually a recorded extract of a session. Since so much of the emphasis in SASB is upon the interaction between therapist and patient, video taped material is preferable to sound only recordings. Verbal transcripts without sound are very difficult to code because the nuances of the interaction are virtually impossible to detect in a purely verbal presentation. As is the case with CCRT, SASB researchers claim 'pond water theory' (Benjamin and Cushing, 2000) validity for using only a sample, on the basis that the sample will be representative of interpersonal patterns throughout the data. Sometimes these will be set up artificially, for instance where a family is asked to re-enact a current conflict on video. In the case of psychotherapy it is more common to select sessions at critical points or to locate key moments using patient and therapist process recall methods. It is quite legitimate, particularly for the purpose of small scale practitioner-based research, for the therapist to locate points in the therapy where meaningful or difficult interpersonal transactions are occurring, maybe in impasse or at termination. Benjamin advises that materials selected should be of at least 10 minutes in real time because of the importance of context for coding (Benjamin and Cushing, 2000).

Stages of SASB coding

The stages of SASB coding are described in the following steps:

- *Initial overview of the sample*, maybe watching or listening alongside a written transcript.
- *Division of transcripts into elements and units.* The aim of dividing into elements is to capture a complete thought, often expressed with subject, object and verb. Elements need to be small enough to ensure that coders can focus on the same concept. Units are typically defined by change of speaker, but sometimes turns are divided into more than one unit if they are long.
- *Designation of whether the coding relates to process or content.* Process codings relate to here and now transactions between therapist and patient, whereas content coding relates to a transaction which is being talked about. Where SASB differs from the other coding methods discussed is that the emphasis is upon process rather than content coding. Whereas there will always be a process coding for any element, there will often not be a content coding.
- *Assignment of referents*, where these are either those participating in the interaction (i.e. patient and therapist) and/or third parties who are spoken about. Referents can include abstract constructs ('life'), collectives or organizations ('society', 'work'), or internal drivers ('desires') etc. Two referents must be identified for each entry, with a speaker and a target. This obviously becomes complex where coding is being attempted beyond the dyad, as in family interactions.

- *Defining the focus in relation to the three SASB surfaces,* where the first two (transitive and intransitive) are interpersonal and the third surface (the introject) is intrapsychic. For instance, a patient saying to a therapist 'I always feel so guilty' is making an interpersonal transaction, in confiding to the therapist, which has a focus upon herself. A patient saying 'You seem to be angry' is making an interpersonal transaction with a focus on the therapist.
- *Scoring for affiliation (horizontal axis) and interdependence (vertical axis).* Benjamin and Cushing (2000) advise that scores are assigned −9 (hostile) to +9 (friendly) on the former and −9 (controlling) to +9 (autonomy giving) on the latter. This enables each transaction to be located on a grid and assigned the appropriate SASB code from the simplified cluster model.
- *Application of a 'final clinical test'* by comparing the SASB code with the material to see if it makes clinical sense.

This coding method is clearly intensive and detailed with a focus upon the micro process as observed through video or audio tapes. An alternative to this micro-analytic coding system is the composite system, whereby coders are asked to produce summary scores for each 2 minute extract of interaction based on tallies of SASB codes. The aim of this is to enable researchers to get results more quickly. However, it obviously produces a more impressionistic coding, with the problem of obtaining such good reliability.

One interesting aspect of the coding process is that of complex communications, and this has been the topic for some of the research using SASB. These are instances where a transaction can be taken as meaning two things or giving two messages; or where 'the literal meaning of the words spoken seem at odds with the tone in which they are conveyed, as in sarcastic, sardonic, or otherwise confusing communications' (Florsheim and Benjamin, 2001, p. 138). For instance, 'take care of yourself' can be seen as protecting, but also can have a strong element of controlling. A communication like 'I hope you're not going to get cold again' can combine protection and criticism. These complex communications are common in families and relationships and can be seen as leading to double binds and various other subtle forms of control and hostility. An entrenched and persistent pattern of complex communication within the parent–child relationship can be seen as leading to later pathology. The importance of *how* a communication is made – the tone of voice, emphasis and delivery, rather than the explicit verbal content – reinforces the need for audio or video data in SASB coding.

Reliability and validity of the SASB coding system

We need to separate the issue of the validity of SASB as a theoretical construct and the validity and reliability of the coding system. It can be argued that the underlying two dimensional structure deriving from Sullivan and Leary is well established and supported by the findings from much empirical research (see Wiggins, 1996). The issue of the validity of the SASB variant is addressed by Florsheim and Benjamin (2001), who draw attention to research using the INTREX questionnaires (Benjamin, 1988). They assert that the construct validity and internal consistency of the instrument, and by extension the model, has been demonstrated (Benjamin, 1994; Pincus *et al.*, 1998). Pincus *et al.* do raise questions in relation to the model, both about the circumplex form and the parsimony of introducing extra dimensions. They acknowledge that self-report questionnaires are not the most reliable data source and call for the use of transactional or observational data in future research.

Evidence for the validity of the coding system itself comes from the work of Benjamin and co-workers and from empirical research on psychotherapy process using the coding method. The work of Henry and colleagues (Henry *et al.*, 1986, 1990; Hilliard *et al.*, 2000) has demonstrated that the relationship between patient/therapist process and outcome is in the direction that is predicted by the model. The utility of the SASB observational coding system to differentiate between diagnostic groups has been demonstrated by Humphrey (1989). An application of the SASB model into the clinical sphere, through the diagnosis and treatment of DSM Axis II disorders is discussed in detail by Benjamin (1996a).

The issue of reliability is inextricably linked to the issue of the training of coders. As mentioned above, it is recommended that SASB coders receive extensive training of between 50 and 100 hours using clinical extracts (Florsheim and Benjamin, 2001). They further recommend that coders who do not at an early stage display the necessary level of interpersonal sensitivity and 'a slightly obsessive temperament' (p. 142) are weeded out of the training process. This enables researchers to report acceptable weighted kappa scores of 0.6 or better (Cohen, 1968) on quite complex family interactions where the coders are blind to clinical status. While Benjamin and her co-workers have demonstrated acceptable coding reliability, it has to be reiterated that the time consuming nature of the training and the guideline times given for the achievement of reliability are a deterrent to clinicians wishing to undertake small scale research.

Research using SASB

The most significant applications of the SASB observational coding system within the field of psychotherapy process research have been in the areas of dyadic therapy and in family therapy. It has also been used to focus upon psychotherapy assessment and diagnosis. In particular it has been applied successfully to focus upon eating disorders. Humphrey (1989) used a total of 74 family triads (mother, father, daughter) coded using a 10 minute video taped discussion of the daughter's separation from the family. She was able to show that the SASB coding differentiated normal from clinical families and that there were differences in the eating disorder sub-types. For instance, parents of anorexics communicated nurturant affection combined with neglect of the daughter's needs for expression. The daughters were more submissive in turn towards their parents. Bulimics and their mothers showed more hostile enmeshment, with a higher percentage of mutual belittling and blaming, as well as more sulking and appeasing than was found in the control group. She also found that the families of eating disordered girls showed a higher proportion of complex messages: i.e. seemingly contradictory SASB stances contained within the same communication. This research gives impressive evidence of the descriptive power of SASB applied within this setting. Florsheim *et al.* (1996) used 5–10 minute videotaped extracts of boys with caregivers to focus upon antisocial behaviour. Their findings showed ethnic differences in how much assertiveness and autonomy was encouraged. However, they found that 'straightforward adolescent assertiveness' was not related to antisocial behaviour, whereas assertive-ness in combination with sulky defensive behaviour was linked to high risk. This seems to support the finding of Humphrey and also of Henry and colleagues (below) that it is complex and contradictory interpersonal communication that tends to cause problems.

The most impressive applications of SASB coding to the therapy dyad has been conducted by Henry and associates (Henry *et al.*, 1986, 1990; Henry, 1996; Hilliard *et al.*, 2000) using the Vanderbilt databases of psychodynamic psychotherapies. Using audiotapes and transcripts of sessions to code samples of therapy process Henry *et al.* (1986) divided good and poor outcome cases to compare the predominant SASB codes. Overall, only 1% of therapists' communications were judged to be hostile in good outcome cases, against about 20% in poor outcome cases. They found greater levels of affiliative behaviour (**protect, affirm**), and lower levels of **blame**, in good outcome cases. Patient behaviours of disclose were more frequently observed in good outcome cases. They found higher disaffiliative levels in poor outcome cases, particularly walling-off, although there were also higher levels of trust, which is not seen as a negative response. It is interesting to note that, while this and previous studies did not show a difference in the overall level of complementarity in good and poor cases, there was a significantly higher level of *negative* complementarity in poor outcome cases.

Henry and colleagues also observed that there was a higher level of multiple, or complex, communication in the poor outcome cases. They give the following example from a discussion about how a patient had been rudely rejected for a date, where the therapist had encouraged him to confront the girl about her behaviour:

> Patient: (in a petulant tone of voice) – Well, what good is it going to do to say something to her?
> Therapist: (in a critical manner) – It's not a question to me of whether it's going to do you any good or not, it's a question to me of whether you somehow have already told her it's all right to treat you that [rude] way.   (Henry *et al.*, 1986, p. 30)

Henry and colleagues see this as a query from the patient (trust) but in a tone of voice that also communicates another code (sulk) in response to a previous therapist statement. Similarly, the therapist's response communicates both **protect** and **blame**. They feel that these kinds of complex message are unhelpful to the therapy process and their findings provide support for this hypothesis.

This work is extended further in Henry *et al.* (1990) where the observational coding scheme is used in conjunction with the SASB INTREX questionnaires to look at change in the patient's introject. Therapeutic dyads were again split into good and poor outcome cases, but this time based upon change in the patient introject. The previous result – the link between affiliative communications and outcome – was replicated. In addition they found that there was a strong correlation between hostile and controlling therapist statements and patient statements which were self-blaming and critical: i.e. *self-attack* and *self-blame* on the introject surface. They also found that patients and therapists in the low introject change group showed significantly higher numbers of complex communications. Interestingly, they also observed that patients in the poor outcome group spoke less than those in the good outcome group, suggesting a sulky withdrawal or passive compliance. Since the INTREX questionnaire was also completed by therapists, they were able to show a link between the therapist's introject and hostile communications in the therapy: namely therapists with hostile introjects showed greater hostility to their patients. They conclude that 'even well-trained professional therapists are surprisingly vulnerable to engaging in potentially destructive interpersonal process' (*ibid*, p. 773).

This research inspected a central tenet of the psychodynamic model – that early parental relations will influence later relationships and have an effect (transference) on psychotherapy process through the operation of the introjects (termed *internal objects* by object relations theorists) of both the patient and the therapist. It is further examined in Henry (1996) and Hilliard *et al.* (2000). They find support for the hypothesized links between therapist introject and therapist process, patient introject and patient process, and outcome. They develop a 'generic interpersonal model of psychotherapy' (Henry, 1996, p. 1263) based upon the research using the SASB system. They see interpersonal process in the therapy as being the therapeutic alliance (which has proved the most robust common factor in therapy outcome research) and argue that positive process depends on both patient and therapist having certain qualities. The therapist needs to establish and maintain the facilitating conditions of a good parent and to 'provide an affiliative balance of enmeshment and differentiation' (Henry, 1996, p. 1272). This entails communicating in a straightforward manner which is free of disaffiliative or complex messages. The link between this ability and the therapist's own introject deriving from his/her own early parental relationship has been established. In addition, the patient needs the capacity to form an affectional bond, and will do so if the therapeutic base is facilitative. There is a need for the therapist to attend to the inevitable process of rupture and repair to maintain therapeutic work.

While the main body of research on the dyad has been conducted by Henry and co-workers, there is some support also from Jorgensen *et al.* (2000) of the importance of interpersonal process in predicting treatment outcome. They used 20 minute video taped extracts from assessment interviews and of the fourth and seventeenth therapy session to assign SASB codes. They found that interpersonal process in the assessment interview correlated significantly with that coded early in therapy and that this was able to predict outcome. This was compared to the Dynamic Assessment Interview (DAI), and SASB was found to provide a far more reliable prediction of outcome.

Further support for the importance of negative interpersonal process in therapy outcome is provided by the work of Safran and Muran (1996, 2000), who used SASB along with other measures (including CCRT) to focus upon the rupture and repair of the therapeutic alliance. Given the importance of the therapeutic alliance established by many research studies, these researchers decided to look in detail at the process of alliance breakdown and how to bring about resolution. To this end they used the SASB observational coding scheme to look at instances of alliance rupture in therapies where there appeared to be a resolution compared to those where there had been no resolution. They concluded that in a typical rupture process the patient will move through feelings of anger and hurt over having been failed by the therapist (maybe not understood or responded to), to feelings of vulnerability and the wish to be nurtured. These are followed by avoidant behaviours, arising from the fear of being too aggressive to the therapist or too vulnerable, and expectations of retaliation or rejection. Safran *et al.* (2002) observe that there is evidence that poor outcome cases are characterized by 'a pattern of patient–therapist complementarity (vicious cycles) in which therapists respond to patients' hostile communications with hostile communications of their own' (p. 251). They advise that therapists need to be aware that patients often have negative feelings about the therapy and the relationship and that these need to be explored in an open and non-defensive way when they arise. They have developed a manualized treatment called Brief Relational Therapy (BRT) which includes interventions that have been found to be facilitative of the rupture process (Safran and Muran, 2000).

Example of a practitioner project using SASB

Unlike many of the others, this example is not drawn from the small scale projects undertaken within our *Process Research* course. The reason for this is that SASB is not practicable for very small scale projects because of the training and coding time needed to achieve reliability. It is instead taken from doctoral research conducted by Macdonald (2001) who has given permission for the reproduction of some of the material.

Macdonald had the aim of replicating some of the findings of Henry and others discussed above, particularly the effect of negative inter-personal process in psychotherapy. To these ends he used audio tapes of assessment interviews conducted at an alcohol service which had been the focus of previous research into therapeutic commitment and subsequent engagement in treatment (Cartwright *et al.*, 1996; Hyams *et al.*, 1996). These studies had found a significant link between the therapist's commitment (conceptualized as comprising role adequacy, legitimacy, knowledge, self-esteem) at the assessment interview and the subsequent therapeutic engagement of patients. The data for these studies, however, were not the therapy process but questionnaire data collected from therapists and clients. Significantly, they found that some therapists had a substantially lower engagement of clients than others. This raises the question of whether this is primarily to do with therapist skill or experience, or to do with personality characteristics deriving from therapist introjects (or a combination of both). Cartwright *et al.* (1996) observe that clients tend to perceive committed therapists as being 'warm' which would seem to imply that it is the therapist's interpersonal stance and attitude to the client, rather than a matter of mere technique, that could be the crucial factor. This would seem to support the arguments of interpersonal theorists that interpersonal process, particularly complementarity and affiliation, are what is important in engaging patients and bringing about change.

SASB process coding was used to examine whether there was a higher proportion of negative (non-affiliative) or complex process within the assessment interviews. Six assessment interviews were analyzed, comprising one engaged and one non-engaged case for each of three therapists. Macdonald hypothesized that there would be an observably higher level of negative process, negative complementarity and therapist hostile, controlling and complex communication in cases where there was a subsequent failure to engage in treatment. He received e-mail and telephone training on the SASB coding technique and used the C-I-SAID computer program to assist with the labelling and analysis of coded sequences. (C-I-SAID is discussed in some detail later in Part IV.) He coded two twenty minute extracts from each interview, taken from 5 minutes in and the final 20 minutes. Applying the 'pond water theory' argument of Benjamin, this is an ample extract to choose and one which undoubtedly led to a very demanding and time consuming coding task. It was impossible for the author to code blind to the outcomes because of his involvement in compiling the data but there was a second coder who was blind to outcome for some of the extracts. While the absence of blind coding is a limitation from the point of view of reliability, it is necessary to be realistic in evaluating practitioner or small scale research. This arises in all of the coding methods we have discussed. For instance, it is recommended that the process of locating relationship episodes in CCRT is separated from coding. While these requirements may be a necessary protection of validity and reliability in larger studies it is not possible in smaller scale research. So long as this is explicit and the necessary provisos are made about generalizability it is quite acceptable.

Macdonald compares the process in each of the six interviews, initially comparing the engage and non-engage case for each of the three therapists. He only finds significant support for his hypotheses in one of these three comparisons. Overall there was a lower level of therapist hostility than was observed in the Henry *et al.* studies (Henry *et al.*, 1986, 1990). One possible explanation of this given by Macdonald may be the tendency of researchers of a psychodynamic orientation to 'read' unconscious hostility into some therapist communications. This highlights one of the problems of coding process: however objective one tries to be there is inevitably an issue of interpretation. Macdonald also feels that the negative process in one of the interviews may have been lost in the uncoded part of the transcript. The fact is that even a small element of hostile communication from the therapist may be enough to prevent engagement and any sampling procedure runs the risk of losing this.

An example of the coding process is given by the following extract which includes a complex code. This occurs during a long turn by the therapist explaining how people use the clinic:

> but what I am saying to you is talking works. A lot of people come here to try and find the right questions. Sometimes they don't even find the right answers. (Client: Mm). But the question you have to ask yourself is what do I do. I mean I don't think you have asked the right questions yet.

Using the labelling that we have adopted up to this point (slightly different from that used by Macdonald) the last sentence is coded 1–4 **protect**, 1–6 **blame** and 2–2 disclose. As such it has a disaffiliative code and is a complex communication: both associated with poor outcome by the Henry studies.

In his comparison over all six interviews Macdonald concludes that there was no unequivocal support for the incidence of more negative process in the non-engaged cases, except in the area of increasing therapist influence and decreased client autonomy. He found that therapist hostility may have been an important factor in the failure of one of the cases to engage but that there was little or no evidence of it in the other non-engaging cases. With regard to negative complementarity he found a slightly higher level in the engaging cases, which runs counter to the hypotheses. Macdonald points out that the external factors are relevant to engagement and that these were evident in some of the cases. This is supported by Lambert's argument that the research evidence points to extratherapeutic change and expectancy (placebo) being responsible for 55% of outcome (Asay and Lambert, 2000). He also feels that it may be difficult to observe negative process at such an early stage in therapy – arguing that it may need time to develop – and that sampling of an assessment session may be particularly problematic because of the shifts in content and process in the assessment setting. In addition to the limitations that Macdonald identifies it is maybe worth pointing out that the use of audio tapes for SASB coding does limit the opportunity to observe subtle negative process. Unfortunately, video tapes are rarely available for psychotherapy process research but in the case of SASB they do give a better prospect of picking up complex communications. Overall it is difficult therefore to draw clear conclusions from this study. However, it provides a useful example of well conducted small scale research which raises interesting questions both in relation to the role of hostile or complex communications in therapeutic engagement and in the process of coding and researching such material.

Conclusion

Interpersonal theory provides a good conceptual framework for the study of the psychotherapy process which has been well validated over time. While interpersonal theory does not use a language which is particularly familiar to the main therapeutic modalities, it can be readily accommodated into most psychotherapy models without being entirely limited by a uni-dimensional focus (as in the case of CCRT). The main applications of SASB research have been in psychodynamic and process experiential therapies, but there is no reason in principle why it cannot be more broadly applied. The development of the SASB coding system has given researchers a powerful tool to look at the detailed interactional processes within the psychotherapy session. This has been supported by some impressive research by Henry and others which provides a powerful and convincing analysis of the therapeutic relationship and the link to early childhood experience. An advantage of the SASB coding system is the complexity and richness of the material it produces. A disadvantage – inextricably linked to this point – is the time consuming nature of the training and coding tasks. This has been a disincentive to smaller scale researchers and maybe explains why SASB is not better known within practitioner research.

SUGGESTIONS FOR FURTHER READING

Benjamin, L.S. (1974) 'Structural analysis of social behaviour', *Psychological Review*, 81: 392–425.

Benjamin, L.S. (1996) *Interpersonal Diagnosis and Treatment of Personality Disorders*. New York: Guilford.

Benjamin, L.S. (1996) 'A clinician-friendly version of the interpersonal circumplex: Structural analysis of social behaviour', *Journal of Personality Assessment*, 66(2): 248–66.

Birtchnell, J. (1993) *How Humans Relate. A new interpersonal theory*. Westport, CT: Praeger.

PART III

The discourse approaches

Introduction

In the introduction to Part I, two different traditions in scientific inquiry were identified. The first, called 'naturalism', presumes an objective external world, independent of our perceptions, which can be observed and studied either directly, or indirectly through the application of instruments (a microscope, for example). In the second tradition of inquiry – that of hermeneutics – the investigator seeks to understand the world as it is known to us as perceiving and thinking subjects. In Part II, we introduced a number of methods that have been developed by psychotherapy researchers as 'instruments' for the study of the psychotherapy process, in the tradition of naturalism. In Part III, we will consider a second way of addressing the psychotherapy session transcript.

The following three chapters are placed under the general heading of 'discourse approaches'. The term 'discourse' is used despite, or perhaps because of, its ambiguities to bring together disparate methods, both 'qualitative' and 'quantitative', which have a common focus on language and interaction as their core object of study. 'Discourse' is defined for the purpose of this discussion as: 'A connected series of utterances, forming a unit for analysis' (Oxford English Dictionary). All the methods described in the following chapters take discourse as the focus of their inquiry. Each, however, starts from a different set of premises, and different conceptual origins. The following is a brief overview of some of those differences, and their origins, which will give some context for understanding the logic, similarities and differences of the methods.

In the early development of the human sciences, the methods and assumptions of natural science dominated the way in which investigations within the new disciplines of psychology, sociology, anthropology and linguistics were conducted. However, very soon, social scientists began to experience limitations in the standard methods of natural sciences. They recognized that there is a profound difference between the study of natural processes, and that of social processes: the social world is a product of human activity, mediated by language. Early social researchers noticed that the social structures and forms of grand theory didn't seem to represent what they observed in the naturally occurring social environment of the 'shop floor'. They realized that their own social preconceptions affected how they perceived what they saw. The 'neutral observer' as social scientist gave way to the recognition that the investigator of the social world is an engaged observer. In sociology, anthropology, and ethnography, this recognition generated new methodological concepts, as well as new objects of study. A radical new approach, which took language as the basis of human social and psychological life, began to inform the study of social life as a process embedded in human actions.

The contemporary discipline of discourse analysis takes a variety of forms. It may take as its data written texts, transcripts of spoken interaction, or audio/video recordings from 'naturally occurring' settings; or it may take as its data 'representations', such as film, art, or theatre. All methods of discourse analysis, on the other hand, share one assumption: that social reality is created, or 'constructed' through the actions of subjects. *How* that reality is created is its object of study. Contemporary discourse analysis is a wide and rapidly developing field. Three strands of discourse analysis that have relevance for the study of the psychotherapy process are outlined below.

Discourse analysis and psychology

In the last two decades, the influence of the movement within social science towards the study of human action and interaction has made inroads into psychology, and generated a vigorous critique of mainstream cognitive science, with its 'information processing' model of mind, and its focus on the structures and processes of the individual subject. Jonathan Potter and Margaret Wetherell (1987) reviewed the new developments that were taking place within social psychology, and the transfer of attention to naturally occurring talk and text. Although the focus of this new discipline is on text, quantification is not excluded in principle. Rather, it is the sorts of 'operationalizations' that typically underpin quantification in psychology, and the sorts of theoretical concerns that they mask, that are challenged (Edwards and Potter, 1992). More recently, Derek Edwards (1997b) has brought the existing findings of discursive psychology together with the empirical methods of conversation analysis (see Chapter 7) to build a critique of, and offer an alternative method for, conceptualizing and researching the psychological subject. Discourse analysis, applied to the traditional domains of psychology –

cognition, emotion, perception and conceptualization – shifts attention from the inner experiences of the individual, to the inter-subjective domain of acting subjects. From the perspective of a discursive psychology, for example, emotion is not something the individual subject 'has', but is rather understood as an action on the part of the subject, who communicates about his or her state, and regulates his or her affective relation to others through the use of emotion actions and metaphors. Discursive psychology criticizes the traditional psychological model of 'shared knowledge as a matter of matching up speakers' and hearers' knowledge states in a process of communicating information between minds'. In its place, 'shared knowledge is analyzed as ... *a way of talking*' (Edwards, 1997b, p. 21). Many discourse analysts in the social sciences disregard altogether the psychological – the relationship between the interacting subject and the experiencing subject. Edwards provides a conceptual bridge between the study of cognition and the study of discourse. This study is in its very early stages.

Critical discourse analysis

A second strand of discourse analysis relevant to the study of psychotherapy is the study of 'social discourses'. These studies take as their focus of attention the way in which human interaction is shaped by the social, political and cultural context in which it takes place. A major figure in this form of discourse analysis is Foucault (1973, 1990), among whose seminal texts is a critical analysis of the historical development of contemporary medical and psychological practice. Studies of this kind range from analysis of psychotherapy and counselling discourses as a cultural phenomenon (McNamee and Gergen, 1992; Parker, 1992), to detailed empirical analysis of the way in which social practices shape specific interactional forms in the context of the psychotherapy process (Siegfield, 1995). A recent example of this kind of study is Kogan's analysis of an exemplar couple 'session' (1998). This study is based on a 'demonstration' video recording of a session in which a 'distinguished' therapist demonstrates best practice in solution-focused therapy. Kogan uses detailed turn by turn analysis to identify three specific communicative strategies used by the therapist. He then widens the analysis to identify a 'discursive technology' (Foucault) by means of which the therapist enables some communications, and constrains others, thereby producing a shared narrative to which both partners agree. Finally, he attempts to place these communicative strategies within a wider critical analysis of the way in which therapeutic practices can be seen to reinforce social expectations of white heterosexual marriage.

Another body of empirical discourse studies of particular interest to psychotherapy researchers is research on 'medical discourses': how do the social practices of health care shape the way in which patients present themselves – their subjective experience, and their bodies – to those who a society designates as health care providers (from medical doctors to witch doctors)? This inquiry can be transferred to psychotherapy research, in the form of questions like these:

> Do the practices of the different modalities of psychotherapy shape the way in which 'problems' are presented?
> Do different clinical practices, based as they are on theoretical premises, result in different presentations of 'problems' and how are their 'outcomes' defined?
> How do those from other conceptual systems of health 'knowledge' understand and respond to clinical practices created for, and by, Western health services?

Several of the discourse analytic methods to be discussed in the following chapters can be applied to questions like these.

Critical discourse analysis deconstructs psychotherapy theory and practice, taking it as a social and cultural activity like any other, asking questions and proposing findings that may not always be welcome to clinicians. Discussion of its methods, assumptions and findings is beyond the scope of this book. However, awareness of the implications of following a path of critical analysis of psychotherapy interaction, and its implications for practice, is an important dimension to be considered by psychotherapy researchers who are thinking of using the discourse methods. Finally, we turn to the empirical practice of discourse analysis, which will form the substance of the chapters which follow.

Discourse analysis as empirical method

As interest in the study of human meaning-making activity has grown, new empirical methods have been developed to extend the ways in which human scientists can gather data, analyze their findings and generate new theories which can take into account the activities of speaking subjects. One of these – the 'grounded theory' method – developed as a reaction to the way that meaning can be imposed on data through the theoretical pre-conceptions of the investigator. It seeks to ground analysis of meaning in the words of the subjects or texts being studied. At about the same time, in the field of linguistics, theory-driven attention to the structure and form of language gave way to an interest in the study of everyday talk, and new methods and objects of study were developed. In the 1950s, linguist Basil

Bernstein used the new technology of the tape recorder to study 'dialect' – until that time, thought of as a 'debased' form of the standard language. He collected examples of everyday talk, and demonstrated that dialect speakers have all the grammatical and semantic sophistication of standard language speakers. Soon after that, William Labov (Labov and Waletsky, 1967) applied the same strategy to the study of spoken narratives, which do not have the formal clarity of written narrative. He demonstrated that ordinary story telling is as highly structured as formal narrative. Both Bernstein and Labov used semi-experimental methods, gathering data in the formal context of a research study. Harvey Sacks (1972, 1992), exploiting the technological advantages of the newly developed portable tape recorder, began to study all kinds of naturally occurring conversation. He used tape recordings of a variety of conversations in natural settings, in order to build a theory of conversational interaction. His goal was to develop a natural observational science of social life. Conversation analysis and narrative analysis now constitute major domains of study in the social sciences, and in the last decade, have become methods of interest to psychotherapy researchers.

Discourse analysis and psychotherapy research

In the context of the growing interest in interpersonal factors in the psychotherapy process (whatever modality is practised) and the growing research evidence linking the quality of therapeutic alliance with good outcomes (Norcross, 2002), discourse methods offer an important tool for researchers of the psychotherapy process. There were some notable studies of psychotherapeutic interaction undertaken in the early years of developments in discourse analysis. Psychoanalyst Merton Gill and collaborators first studied the psychiatric interview as a discourse event (Gill *et al.*, 1954). Another group of collaborators then studied the first five minutes of the Gill data intensively, looking at the non-verbal aspects of the interchange (Pittenger *et al.*, 1960). A third study, inspired by the work of Gregory Bateson, addressed the topic of communicative actions and their relationship to behavioural disorders (Watzlawick *et al.*, 1968). This primarily theoretical study began to address the question of the relationship between the rules of communicative action and the break-down of communication in psychopathology, using the play *Who's afraid of Virginia Woolf* as 'case material'. A dense empirical study of a family therapy interview, which analyzed social and behavioural markers from a systemic perspective, followed a few years later (Scheflen, 1973). The first study to integrate content and communicative actions in psychotherapy discourse was undertaken by Labov and Fanshel (1977).

The development of interest in the application of discourse methods specifically to psychotherapy process research is more recent. In an early review of the developing field of psychotherapy process research (Toukmanian and Rennie, 1992), the authors review the mode of inquiry used in each of the contributing studies. All make use of self-report and coding systems. The perspective of the research includes various combinations of client, therapist and observer. In an early contribution to a discourse approach to process research, Rennie (1992b) introduces grounded theory as a method for analyzing the client's experience of therapy. In the methods that will be introduced in the following chapters, elements of coding will be found, as will a variety of approaches to textual analysis. All share a basic methodological commitment to the primary definition of discourse: they take as their object of study 'a connected series of utterances, forming a unit for analysis, rather than a participant perspective'.

The methods of grounded theory, conversation analysis and narrative analysis grew out of social science research, and have been imported into psychotherapy research. They will be introduced in the following three chapters. A fourth method, quite unlike these, but also taking 'a connected series of utterances' as its unit of analysis, is the therapeutic cycles model (TCM), a computerized content analysis method developed specifically for the study of psychotherapy sessions by Erhard Mergentha-ler. The TCM is introduced in Chapter 9.

Summary

From this very brief introduction to the developing field of discourse analysis, it is apparent that discourse analysis comes in a variety of forms, and cannot be considered as one, unitary field of inquiry. On the contrary, it embeds some very different basic assumptions concerning the relationship of the individual speaker to the process of meaning construction. For example, critical discourse analysis tends to work from context to utterance, demonstrating the constraints placed upon individual utterances by the cultural or social context in which they are spoken. The focus is on hidden, or embedded, contextual features that shape the specific interaction. Applied to the field of psychotherapy, such studies might examine the way in which theoretical orientation creates the context for meaning-making in the actual therapeutic interaction. More empirically oriented methods, such as conversation analysis, work from utterance to context. The claim is that it is clinical processes that can be explored through micro-analysis of specific interactions. The following chapters will concentrate primarily on the empirical discourse methods, and their application to psychotherapy process research. This perspective was well expressed by Labov and Fanshel in their pioneering discourse analysis of psychotherapy process:

> The central problem of discourse analysis is to discover the connections between utterances. We know that they are present when we participate in a conversation, and we can respond intuitively to coherence or lack of coherence in a tape-recorded conversation ... Although ... rules play an important part in our analysis of conversational interaction, they are basically ways of making explicit the intuitive analysis of speech acts that we all perform automatically (1977, p. 69–70).

SUGGESTIONS FOR FURTHER READING

Toukmanian, S.G. and Rennie, D.L. (1992) *Psychotherapy Process Research: Paradigmatic and narrative approaches.* Newbury Park: Sage.

CHAPTER 6

Grounded theory

Introduction

The method of grounded theory was developed in the social sciences, in response to the dominance of the 'grand theory' paradigm of research, which is characterized by high level theoretical concepts, logico-deductive strategy and statistical analysis in the search for verification of theory. Grounded theory was developed as a systematic process of discovery, grounded in the phenomena it seeks to represent. Its originators, Glaser and Strauss (1967), proposed that 'generating a theory from data means that most hypotheses and concepts not only come from the data, but are systematically worked out in relation to the data during the course of the research. *Generating a theory involves a process of research*' (p. 6).

In the first part of this book, a variety of coding strategies were studied. Each of these methods is characterized by the definition of a conceptual framework, based on a theoretical model of psychological functioning. The categories, or scales, which define the coding system are based on that conceptual framework. The process of coding a text involves placing identified text within one of the scales, and building a model of a particular piece of data which fits onto the conceptual framework. The logic of coding methods is primarily *deductive*, and it is particularly suited to hypothesis testing.

The strategy of grounded theory is the opposite of this method. It was developed in order to study systematically the emergence of naturally occurring categories in data – the categories through which subjects organize their experienced world. Its logic is to use naturally occurring data to generate theories and hypotheses about a particular setting, rather than to test theories or hypotheses in a general sort of way by reference to data. It is primarily an *inductive* method, less concerned with verification than with discovery: 'discovery gives us a theory that "fits or works" in a substantial formal area (though further testing, clarification or reformulation is still necessary) since the theory has been derived from the data, not deduced from logical assumptions' (1967, pp. 30–1). The objective of grounded theory is not verification, but theory building. Glaser and Strauss did not see grounded theory replacing verification, but rather as supplementing the scientific process with a specific and systematic method of developing theory from an empirical, rather than a conceptual, base. It was offered as a means of empirical generalization which could be grounded formally in systematically sampled data, in contrast to the arbitrary sampling frequently found, and criticized, in the narrative case study approach often employed in social inquiry (and psychotherapy studies).

Grounded theory is based on the principle of *comparative analysis*: the principle by which the generation of *conceptual categories* can be derived empirically through analysis of the data which then leads to generalized relations between the categories and their properties. It is a method for generating *empirical generalizations*, rather than universal facts. Glaser and Strauss emphasized that in developing their strategy of comparative analysis, they remain within the mainstream traditions of scientific inquiry, in which the principle of systematic comparison informs the basis of experimentation, statistical analysis and verification, as well as theory building.

With its focus on process, rather than concepts and structures, the grounded theory method is an important potential methodological tool for the psychotherapy process researcher. In this chapter, the core principles of the method will be introduced, with applications which will demonstrate how grounded theory can be used to develop theories of psychotherapy process and change.

The application of constant comparative analysis in theory building

The principle of comparative analysis is the basic foundation of grounded theory method. The process involves an iterative process, by means of which the researcher converts observations of phenomena into a substantive map of the processes being observed. The data may be naturalistic observations recorded in a diary form, interviews, recorded talk, textual data, images, or any combination of these. Selection of data is dictated by the context of the study, the potential for access to different kinds of data, and by the kind of question which is being asked. The researcher may be a participant observer using observational methods and recording, or an external observer (even an unseen observer) using textual data, images or recordings made in the course of the process under study. In either case, the researcher is inevitably a part of the process, and his or own process of discovery must be recorded in the form of notes, memos, or diagrams, kept at every stage of the inquiry, and included as part of the data analysis.

First the researcher studies and immerses him or herself in the data. Through the analytic process of comparing and contrasting phenomena, categories begin to emerge. Some initial categories which emerge might be, for example, 'frightened', 'excited', 'angry'. The emergent category concept must then be named. The researcher might name this emergent category, 'feelings'. As a named category, it will be more abstract than the sub-categories of which it is composed. The researcher will then return to the dataset, with a view to identifying further sub-categories of the category concept 'feelings', until the entire dataset has been searched and no further sub-categories, or properties, of the category concept 'feelings' remain. At the same time, another set of initial categories might emerge from the data – for example, 'mother', 'husband', 'children', and these will be tentatively placed within a higher order category concept – say 'family'. Further investigation of the data may reveal that a larger collection of categories within the more general category concept might emerge – for example, 'aunt', 'grandparent', 'step father', etc. In the process of exploring the data, the researcher may find that two separate category-concepts represent the data more fully and accurately – say, 'family of origin', and 'marriage'. Perhaps these two higher order categories represent two distinctive characteristics of the data under study. The investigator will adjust his or her categories and sub-categories as appropriate, using them to develop a growing understanding of the dataset as a whole and to guide these decisions. Through this process, which Glaser and Strauss called 'coding', a collection of concept categories with their constitutive sub-categories (or properties) emerges, which provides an initial substantive map of the data. The analysis aims to answer the question: what is going on here? Here, collaboration with others increases the confidence with which the research process can be shown reliably to represent the data.

Theoretical sampling

As the iterative process of coding begins to yield higher order categories, or category-concepts, the researcher begins to build a substantive picture of the concepts and their properties. At this point in the process, the researcher is faced with the question: what is the relationship between the emerging concepts? At each stage of a grounded theory analysis, he or she will then want to widen the analysis by turning to further data. This is the principle of the constant comparative method. It is at this point that the issue of 'sampling' becomes crucial.

Glaser and Strauss observed two characteristic solutions to this problem. In hypothetico-deductive research, the comparison groups will be selected for their sameness – they should provide invariance, so that variant elements can be compared. On the other hand are the naturalistic case study methods, which follow a trail dictated by theoretical interest, without regard for systematic data collection. Grounded theory forges a path between the two with the principle of theoretical sampling. In theoretical sampling, the researcher combines the evidence of the emerging categories with theoretically relevant concepts to select the focus for the next phase of the analytic process, and to identify relevant data. Sampling and analysis proceed in tandem, with each stage of the analysis guiding the subsequent process of sampling. Decisions about the next steps of the analysis are grounded in the emerging analysis, rather than in the preconceived intention of the researcher. The decision-making process at each stage is documented: the analytic process is part of the theory building.

Theoretical sensitivity

Because grounded theory is a principled, inductive method of theory building, Glaser and Strauss emphasized that an important component of the analytic process is theoretical sensitivity. By this, they meant the process by which the investigator approaches the data systematically, but with an open mind as to what may emerge from his or her engagement with the process. Theory does not precede the coding process, but guides the sampling and analytic choices which are made during the course of the analysis. The most powerful tool available to the investigator are basic questions: Who? When? Where? What? How? How much? Why? (Strauss and Corbin, 1990, p. 77). At each stage of the analysis, these questions yield empirical discoveries, which are only then linked to theoretical concepts, and developed in a systematic step by step process into a hypothesis which guides the next phase of the data analysis process.

Saturation of the data

When does the analysis stop? The iterative process comes to an end, at each stage of the analysis, when the search through the data to hand ceases to yield new categories, with their associated properties. No new categories can be identified which do not fit into the framework which has emerged from the data analysis. The data is found to be saturated. It is at this point that hypothesis formation begins. What is the meaning of this discovery? How can it be related to existing knowledge? What new discovery may be embedded here? What direction should the next step of the analysis take? Asking these questions of the data, and answering them, leads to theory building.

Theory building

The aim of comparative analysis is theory building and the grounded theory process can generate two kinds of theory:

- *Substantive theory:* theory which represents a specific domain of inquiry, addressing questions like: How does this service work? How does this treatment method work in practice? What is clients' subjective experience of therapy?
- *Formal theory:* theory which addresses general principles in a field of inquiry, e.g., its working hypotheses or concepts. Formal theory emerges from the concept categories identified in the discovery of substantive theory, and is built through a further phase of iterative, comparative analysis of the emergent concepts. Formal theory seeks to provide a general theory of the emergent data at a higher level of abstraction which is more parsimonious, and yet covers a wider range of phenomena. It might seek to build more general theories, for example, about how services are shaped by different funding contexts, or how different treatment methods affect client experience.

Depending on the setting, the circumstances of the researcher, the resources available, the development of theory may stop at the level of substantive theory: it may provide some valuable findings for the question to hand. For example, a study of assessment practices in a clinic may generate information of immediate use to the clinicians involved, and may be more generally useful to clinicians in similar clinics. A substantive theory may be sufficient in itself. However, a substantive finding may prove so powerful that the researcher process moves on to the stage of developing a formal theory, through a process of wider data collection, based on theoretical sampling, and a further stage of iterative analysis. Perhaps the original project began with a question like, 'What are the assessment and diagnostic practices in this outpatient clinic?'. In the course of this substantive analysis, the emerging categories are then used to widen the analysis by exploring the assessment practices in other clinics in the district. Differences between them emerge, and the researcher, seeking to link the findings to a theoretical domain, discovers a substantive relationship between the clinical practices and the setting, expressed in terms of category concepts embedded in the data. This discovery could then be extended to explore the wider, more formal question, 'How are assessment practices influenced by different systems of health care?'. Substantive theory is sufficient unto itself, providing a grounded theory relevant to the immediate context. It may take the form of a single case study. It may also provide the basis for a wider analysis, which yields a more general, formal theory, grounded in the emergent analytic process.

Recent developments in grounded theory

The original collaboration between Glaser and Strauss produced a lively method which became an important contributor to social science during the 1970s and 1980s. They came from different traditions, and over the first period of development of the method, some differences in their approach began to emerge. In a later collaboration, Strauss and Corbin (1990, 1998) further developed and elaborated the grounded theory method into a more structured method, which consists of a series of discrete stages of analysis, distinguishing different kinds of coding, and sampling strategies. In this elaboration of the method, two kinds of coding are distinguished: *open coding*; and *axial coding*.

Open coding

For both Glaser and for Strauss and Corbin, identification of categories proceeds through an iterative process, known as 'open coding', until the data are saturated – i.e., until further analysis yields no new categories. Open coding involves the primary exploration of the data, through a process of *making comparisons* and *asking questions*, in order to identify categories, concepts and properties.

For Strauss and Corbin, a firmer analytic frame is proposed. According to their elaboration of the original method, all the properties, or attributes, of a category which emerge through this continuing process of systematic comparing and contrasting generates dimensionality of the emerging category concepts: they represent the location of a property along a continuum (Strauss and Corbin, 1990, p. 69). Grouping categories in their context involves developing a map of their relationship to each other in terms of their dimensionality. The emerging map thus yields levels of specificity. Here is an example, using the emergent category 'feeling', adapted from the model proposed by Strauss and Corbin (1990, p. 72):

Open coding		
Category	Properties	Dimensional range (applied to each instance)
feeling	happy	often . . . . never
	hurt	overwhelming . . . . blocked
		warm . . . . cold

Starting the process of open coding involves micro-analysis of a segment of data, examining the specifics of the data, asking both specific and general questions of the data, and allowing the emergence of categories which underpin the conceptual model of the analysis (1998, pp. 65–6). When analyzing textual data, the process will probably start with a thorough reading of the data, to get a sense of the categories in use in the text. If observational data are being used, there will be notes to work from. These too will have generated categories – the observations are expressed in words. In either case, the investigator will be making a notation of his or her findings. If using handwritten notes or text, the process will begin by hand. If the notes or text have been transcribed into word-processed form, the 'search and find' option in a word-processing package can help with the mechanics of the coding process. Using this aid may speed up the process of analysis, and will add to the capacity to saturate the text and to find every instance of a category. Nevertheless, there is no short cut for an intimate engagement with the primary text as the investigator searches for qualities. In a large study, the researcher may decide to use a qualitative research package to handle larger quantities of data (see Part IV).

Notes must be kept of the coding process, in order to underpin the evidence of the findings. Notes may be written initially onto the data sample – field notes, a text, a questionnaire, whatever it may be. They may then be transferred into a separate document, which describes the process of generating categories, with their sub-categories and attributes or properties, and defining the dimensional range of each category as it emerges. The resulting narratives, maps or diagrams will become part the final presentation of findings.

Axial coding

Strauss and Corbin (1990) define axial coding as the second part of the process by which the categories generated by open coding are reassembled to generate a new picture of the data, which reflects the conditions, contexts and actions which emerge from the dataset through the iterative process of open coding. With axial coding, the analysis moves beyond a descriptive account of the dataset, and begins to develop a mapping of the connections between the categories and their sub-categories.

In this process, the analysis deepens to include:

- the conditions which give rise to the emergence of a category;
- specification of the phenomenon at which the set of actions or interactions is directed;

- the context (i.e. the circumstances in which the phenomenon is embedded);
- the actions and interactions, or strategies, by which it is enacted in the experienced world;
- the consequences (outcomes, results) of those strategies.

Through axial coding, a dynamic mapping of the experienced world represented by the dataset is generated.

> Open coding fractures the data and allows one to identify some categories, their properties and dimensional locations. Axial coding puts those data back together in new ways by *making connections between a category and its sub categories.* (Strauss and Corbin, 1990, p. 97)

For Strauss and Corbin, the extended method of coding which they propose results in a general model of the discovery process, which they define like this (1990, p. 99):

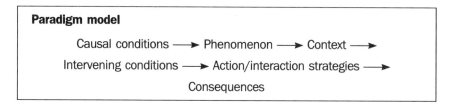

Paradigm model

Causal conditions ──► Phenomenon ──► Context ──►

Intervening conditions ──► Action/interaction strategies ──►

Consequences

The iterative coding process involves movement back and forth between open and axial coding, within the framework of the paradigm model, in order to relate the emerging categories in more and more complex ways, deepening the analysis and working towards an emerging theory which links phenomena to causes and consequences. The coding process involves a continuous movement between deductive and inductive thinking, between discovery and verification as an on-going process. Strauss and Corbin emphasize that they 'are not talking a language of cause and effect', but rather of 'a complex path of interrelationships, each in its own patterned way, that explains what is going on' (1998, p. 130).

Selective coding

The final stage of the theory building process proposed by Strauss and Corbin (1998) brings the substantive analysis into the phase of formal theory. In 'selective coding', the researcher moves from description to conceptualization, through which a core category, emergent from the grounded analysis, is systematically linked to the other emergent categories. This enables a higher, or more abstract, level of analysis.

The process is an extension of the axial coding process, from which a more general 'story line', shaped by the paradigm model, emerges. It is through this process that the core category, around which all the other categories are integrated, provides the grounded basis for the emerging theory. At this point the investigator is faced with yet more decisions: which central phenomenon is best expressed by the shaping of the core category, and its related categories. Strauss and Corbin emphasize that there is no one essential phenomenon to be discovered. The final decision is based on four criteria (discussed below) which underpin the reliability and validity of the grounded theory method.

Coding for process

In their 1998 revised edition of *Basics of Qualititative Research*, Strauss and Corbin added a chapter which extended the grounded theory method they proposed into the domain of process: 'a series of evolving sequences of action/interaction that occur over time and space, changing or sometimes remaining the same in response to the situation or context' (p. 165). Analyzing data for process is not a separate procedure, but can occur alongside the coding process. It involves an additional perspective: the purposeful attention to action and interaction, in context, as well as to the properties and dimensions of the categories and concepts. Questions asked of the data are of the kind: What is going on here? Are actions aligned, or unaligned? What happens next? Relationships between properties, dimensions, and the field of actions can then be built. This additional dimension is an important extra dimension for the analysis of psychotherapy process.

The grounded theory process is a complex process which involves the active engagement of the researcher in decision-making and developing a coding strategy which will comprehensively represent the data. The only way to master it is to practise. The following text (which will be used to illustrate several different kinds of analysis in these chapters) comes from a large study of psychodynamic psychotherapy.

Date sample 6.1

A   mm. what did you think of your mother calling G immature?

P   um, well, she never met G, so I didn't think she was misjudging her, I mean, she was, but I just thought that um she was saying something without knowing all the facts. (mumble) I, I don't, I don't really totally discount my mother's knowledge of, of people, she's very perceptive. I was in a very uncomfortable position with a girl two years ago, when I was a sophomore. the second half of the year. and uh (sigh) I had gotten in way over my head with this girl. who was not really all there, psychologically, and uh, this girl really wanted to get married. she's a year and a half older than I am, and somehow talked me into promising to marry her at some future time. and well basically, the whole thing was sexual, because uh, she was really sexually experienced and I was a virgin when I met her. and she, well, I mean it was, it was a fantastic thing for me, I felt so loved and everything, and so I, I, I was really young at the time, and uh, anyway, things were getting, were getting worse and worse, and uh at one point, I had brought her home for a weekend, and after the weekend, my mother said, 'oh, boy, look at this girl, she's not for you, she's not all there, she's uh, she's talking you into marrying her, and you don't really love her.' and everything, and I was furious with my mother. how could she dare say this to me? but in the end, she was right, one hundred percent right. and she really opened my eyes, and uh I had to break off with this girl.

A   you had to?

P   well, I had to because uh I was in no position to want to marry her.

A   and you do have a tendency to depend on people yet at the same time, while you have the tendency to depend on people, you also have a tendency to doubt whether they really know you so maybe — maybe the advice isn't so good. — it's not really ah, maybe it's you being forced to do what someone else thinks is right and not what you think is right.

P   yes. those were almost the exact same words I used um. — it was this summer. I, I, well, I'll tell you the story in a second but, I often do have the feeling, and I think I just realized recently, like this summer, that I let other people make up my mind for me. and the example, the thing was, I don't know if I told you. I travelled in Europe this summer, I was in X and I have relatives in X who I have never met but we had their address and I went to visit them, and they told me that I had other relatives in E and that they think that, they thought that, since I was in L already I should go up and uh, and meet the other relatives. well, I didn't really have much of a desire to go to, but I said, 'okay'. and it's a really long trip from, from L to E and I really didn't want to go, and I realized like the day afterwards, that the whole reason I had agreed to go was just because my other relatives thought that I should do it, and I was letting them make up my mind for me. and I called them up and said I can't go, and I was really proud of myself for doing that. but it was also, um, you know, it's not such a big thing but, it helped. it was like, what do you call it, a turning point when you realize something and, and I realized then that, uh, that I really do have this tendency.

To explore the grounded coding system devised by Strauss and Corbin, we suggest that you do a practice exercise using this text, applying the basic procedures outlined above. You will need to work through the text, asking the following questions.

- Using open coding, identify the properties and dimensions of the two narratives offered by the patient.
- Consider the axial coding framework. See if a description of the patient's experienced world of cause and effect can be derived.
- Finally, taking into account the therapist interventions, see if it is possible to identify change conditions which account for the second narrative and its categories.

First you will need to identify the two narratives, and then apply the principles of open coding, outlined above, to the narratives you identify. You may want to share this task with a colleague: the identification of properties is one of judgement (and experience) and comparisons of your interpretations of the data are vital to the validity of the method (see section below). How you choose to nominate your core categories, and their dimensions, will depend on your reading of the overall sense of the text. Having identified some properties and dimensions of the text, you may be able to establish what the 'cause and effect' logic of the patient's narratives indicates about his experienced world. You will then be in a position to see how, or whether, the therapist intervention impacts on the causal logic. As a question, it seems to query the patient's assumption. Consider the question: what is the causal logic of the second narrative, and how does it relate to the therapist's question?

Reliability and validity

Since grounded theory is primarily a method for theory building, its reliability and validity are based on a different set of criteria than those suited to theory testing and verification. Glaser and Strauss specified four characteristics of a grounded theory by means of which its validity should be assessed: fit; understanding; generality; and control (1967).

- *Fit:* the theory emerging from a grounded analysis should fit the substantive data. 'The theory should fit the data, rather than the data fit the theory' (p. 261).

- *Understanding:* the emerging theory seeks to represent the shared reality of those involved in the processes under study. Therefore it should be recognizable to those involved in the substantive area under study and enable them 'to grasp the theory in terms of their own experiences' (p. 240).
- *Generality:* the substantive grounded theory is sufficiently general to accommodate diversity, through general concepts which are 'continually subject to qualification and to being changed in direction and magnitude by new conditions' (p. 243).
- *Control:* the substantive grounded theory 'must provide a sufficient number of general concepts and their plausible interrelations' (p. 245).

The two fundamental principles of method in grounded theory support the general reliability of the emergent theory: theoretical sampling, and saturation of data. The text is exhaustively analyzed, and categories are systematically derived from the text itself. The decision-making process at each point in theoretical sampling is recorded in the researchers' notes and included in the analysis. The stages of the analysis are written into the final report, and examples from the data are used to illustrate analytic points. The final report is, thus, a transparent account of the research process and is available for critical evaluation.

Recent debates in grounded theory

The original project of grounded theory, set out in 1967 by Glaser and Strauss, was 'the discovery of theory from data systematically obtained from social research' (p. 2). They devised a powerful method for capturing processes occurring in the meaning world of interacting subjects. It enables the researcher to cross the dataset in a systematic and focused way, developing a rich mapping of its relations and connections. The original conception was to develop a research strategy which could generate theory from an empirical, rather than a conceptual, basis. The objective was theory generation. The issue of theory verification was seen to be another, and separate, process. A common critique of grounded theory was and is that it was a naïve 'Baconian' inductivism, and therefore, not scientific. A reading of the introductory chapters of *The Discovery of Grounded Theory* provides a response to those claims. Glaser (1978) continued to develop the method and to answer these questions. More recently, Miller and Fredericks (1999) argue that 'grounded theory is a type of theorizing, focused on both the context of discovery related to a plausible explanation of some phenomenon and providing an inductive argument for its plausibility' (p. 551).

As the method developed through use, some differences in its application began to appear. In 1990, Strauss and Corbin wrote a textbook, developing their application of the original method, which includes the more developed processes outlined in the previous section. While Strauss and Corbin saw this development as a way of making the analytic process easier to grasp and master, Glaser (1992) saw this development as a departure from the original method developed in collaboration with Strauss. There is some justice in this claim: the Strauss and Corbin elaboration does bring a conceptual model into the process, which is at odds with the original conception of a purely empirical data driven analysis. In particular, the introduction of the notion of axial coding is criticized by some (Cutcliffe, 2000; Melia, 1996; Stern, 1994) as introducing too much conceptualization into the process. In a useful contribution to the debate, Kendall (1999) describes her own struggle with using axial coding, and its outcome. Making a distinction between two possible research objectives – description and theory generation – she concludes that 'one grounded theory approach is not necessarily superior to another, and the decision to use a particular approach depends on the goal of the research study, description or theory generation' (p. 751).

Grounded theory rests its claim to rigour in its comprehensive treatment of data analysis and the way it enables the researcher to generate hypotheses grounded in data. Another critique of grounded theory comes from the social constructivist perspective (see introduction to Part III). These critics see the analytic approach of grounded theory as an attempt at the 'reproduction of reality' (Annells, 1996; Hall and Callery, 2001), rather than a truly reflexive process in which the actions of the investigator are as much a part of the process as those of the subjects. Another concern expressed about grounded theory is that, in its dependence on theoretical sensitivity, it may overlook aspects of cultural variance in its subjects, and rely instead on sensitivities which are culturally biased towards the researchers' frame of reference (Barnes, 1996).

In common with the other discourse methods which have evolved in the post war period as a response to the domination of 'grand theory', grounded theory has enabled social science to delve into disorderly processes of social action, and to build micro-theories of how the everyday world of human action is organized. Because of its focus on meaning in context, it has particular relevance to the study of process, and is therefore a potentially powerful method for the psychotherapy process researcher in the study of the micro-processes of therapeutic interaction and change. However, as it was developed in the context of social research, like most of the discourse methods, it requires some adaptation to the specific context of the psychotherapy process. The following section reviews some of the applications of grounded theory to psychotherapy process research, and the debates about how it is best employed.

Application of grounded theory to psychotherapy process research

Grounded theory was introduced to psychotherapy research in the first published book on process research (Toukmanian and Rennie, 1992), in a study by Rennie on the patient's experience of therapy. At the time, interest in the subjective experience of the patient was growing, and a variety of methods explored, mostly using questionnaires and interviews.

In this first grounded theory study, Rennie uses the method to explore the clients' subjective experience of therapy. The data are tape-replay-assisted recollections of the experience of the therapy hour that they have just experienced, similar to Elliott's Brief Structured Recall method (see the introduction to Part III). However, for this study, Rennie asked his subjects to recall an entire session. The resulting recollection was recorded, and analyzed using grounded theory methods.

Rennie discusses his method of gathering data, and sets out his inclination towards a constructionist approach to inquiry at an early stage of the analysis (see previous section). However, he notes that as he became a more experienced interviewer, within the terms of the study, he found himself reducing his own activity, having discovered in the process of analysis that 'spontaneous reports generally prove to be rich in meaning when it comes time to analyze them' (p. 216). It clearly took some time and experience for the investigator to become comfortable with the method and to trust it.

Rennie chose to analyze the resulting texts in terms of 'meaning units. These are passages of text that "stand out" as conveying a main concept' (p. 217). Staying close to the actual text under examination, he 'discovers' four conceptual categories which describe the data:

- The pursuit of personal meaning, with its sub-categories, such as *Scrutinizes own processes, Client's contact with feelings, Catharsis.*
- The client's perception of the relationship with the therapist, with sub-categories such as *Therapist's manner, Client's perception of the task.*
- Client' s experience of the therapist's operations, with sub-categories such as *Therapist's interpretations, Therapist's metaphor*
- Client's experience of outcomes with sub-categories such as *Impact of the therapy,* and *Impact of the inquiry.*

For each of the sub-categories, the number of instances in terms of respondents, and in terms of meaning units, is set out. It is clear that the naming of these categories, reflects theoretical concepts grounded in clinical theory, generated through the process of theoretical sampling. Finally, out of these four major categories, Rennie identified a core category: *Client's reflexivity*. He notes that the choice of this name itself involved a theoretical decision. He first chose 'agency', and notes that by changing the name to 'reflexivity', he includes both the concepts of agency and the concept of self-awareness – to encompass both the key qualities which emerged through the data analysis.

An objection to this finding might be that if the task required of the subjects is to reflect on a process they have just undergone, it might be that the results of the analysis are more indicative of the process of the inquiry than the process of the therapy. Is the emergent core category just a reflection of the inquiry process itself, rather than the therapy process under scrutiny? Rennie acknowledges this limitation of the analysis, even though his interviewing method took this factor into account in asking the interviewee, at critical points in the interview, to distinguish between the interview process and the recalled therapy session. He concludes that the analysis does generate a legitimate psychotherapy process theory: that reflexivity is central to the psychotherapy process, and that the 'challenge of therapy is to control sensitively what clients cannot control, and to work productively with the ways in which they assume control' (Rennie, 1992a, p. 231).

Rennie chose to use interview data, close to the psychotherapy process, in order to access the subjective experience of the patient, and to build a grounded theory of the clients' experience of the psychotherapy process. In subsequent research he continues to explore this theme, using a grounded theory approach to study client reports of the therapy process (1994a; 1994b; 1994c; 2000a). In later writing on grounded theory as a method in psychotherapy research, he emphasizes the hermeneutic aspect of grounded theory, as against the 'objectifying' stance of its inception, grounded in natural science (1998). This approach shows clearly in this first analysis. Rennie's implicit assumption is that the psychotherapy process is intrinsically a subjective process and, therefore, not available to observational, or objectifying investigation. In a subsequent article (2000b) he develops this thesis to make the more general case that the grounded theory method is, in fact, a disciplined hermeneutic inquiry, anchored in systematic data collection analysis. This stance, he proposes, on the one hand argues against both the common conception that method has no place in hermeneutic analysis; and on the other, challenges the objectifying assumptions of grounded theory, placing it firmly within the domain of hermeneutic inquiry.

Interview data is a common source of data for grounded theory projects, both generally and in psychotherapy research. Other psychotherapy research studies have also used interview data. In a study of mindfulness-based cognitive therapy for depression (MBCT), using a group-skills training approach, rather than individual psychotherapy, the researchers sought to capture the individual differences and commonalities in the patients' experience of the process (Mason and Hargreaves, 2001). Using questionnaires (which, as the authors acknowledged, focused on individual rather than group process factors), the research applied the Strauss and Corbin method to generate categories grounded in the patients' language (rather than their own, theoretical perspectives). Noting that patients used a language derived from psychotherapy to describe their experiences, they identified eight categories and sub-categories, of which the emerging core category was 'bringing it into the everyday'. A clearly emerging finding was that initial expectations were recognized by patients as important factors in their experience.

Another study of clients' experiences and perceptions in couple's therapy used a combination of transcript analysis, post-session questionnaires and post-therapy interviews. It was found that couples did identify significant moments as pivotal, although there was no overlap between spouses or therapist in what these moments were (in common with much research of this type). The common factor in pivotal moments was a topic closely related to the clients' presenting problem. The study concludes that client actions are central to the change process. Bolger (1999) used interviews to study a group of adult children of alcoholic parents for their experiences of emotional pain. The open-ended interviews were analyzed for meaning units, representing an idea, thought, or process, using a method devised by Angus and Rennie (1989). Three core categories with a complex set of sub-categories emerged: the 'covered self' (shameful and hidden experiences); the 'broken self' (exposure of experiences/feelings); and the 'transformed self' (acceptance of self).

More recent studies have used grounded theory to explore a variety of clinical concepts. Athern and Madill used grounded theory to investigate how therapists (1999) and clients (2002) make use of a transitional object within the psychotherapy process. This study used a comparative design to explore the varying experiences of both therapist and patient, and to investigate how a clinical concept works in practice, using post-session interviews as data. In a study of narrative processes in the patient's experience of 'helpful' and 'hindering' events, Grafanaki and McLeod (1999) used open coding to identify meaning units derived from psychotherapy transcripts, in order to identify common factors in the experience of the narrative process. Another study based on transcripts used grounded theory to focus on the phenomenon of silences in the psychotherapeutic interaction (Levitt, 2001). This analysis revealed that silences are not a homogeneous phenomenon, but rather have different functions in the clinical process, which can be monitored by clinicians in order to increase attunement to the process. Using an open coding strategy, Wacholz and Stuhr (1999) developed a taxonomy of 'ideal types' using individual case sessions, against which a larger number of cases could then be coded, with a view to linking process factors with outcomes. Using 45 follow-up interviews, they were able to build a substantive model of eight qualitative clusters, conceptual categories which describe the experienced representation of the therapist (in psychodynamic, object relations terms). These were then compared to other factors derived from quantitative measures from the dataset, in order to compare factors such as the gender of the therapist, and outcome measures to the qualitatively derived clusters.

In these studies, the focus is on the individual and his or her experience of the therapeutic process, rather than on group processes which might be part of the context of the interactions studied. Another application of grounded theory, for which it is particularly well suited in light of its origins in social science, is the study of group and institutional processes within which psychotherapy takes place. The following example of a student project takes a therapeutic community as its focus of analysis.

Example of a practitioner project using grounded theory

This is a study of the process of setting up a therapeutic community which took the form of a day-centre. The data were interviews of the staff team, which included three managers (including: the lead, responsible for the funding negotiations, who held the clinical responsibility for the unit; the manager in charge of the service of which the community was a part; and the day to day clinical manager of the unit); one art therapist, and two nurse-therapists with training in psychodynamic models of intervention; and the service administrator. All interviews were conducted in an open style, asking the interviewee first to describe the setting up process, and then their experience of the first few months of the unit as members of the community. The aim of the research was set out as: identifying common themes and patterns emerging from the data, with the objective of providing staff with tentative findings which might assist their practice. The investigator reflects on her role as a participant in the process in each stage of the analysis.

The interviews were transcribed and analyzed, first within the broad categories which reflected the general format of the interview: the setting up process. Four initial categories were identified: route in; setting up; the unit as community; perspectives on the future. This choice of concepts introduced chronological sequence foundation to the data analysis. The amount of data quickly exceeded the use of physical cut and paste and marking up procedures, so the student turned to a qualitative data analysis package (Ethnograph Version 5.0) to work into the data more systematically. Exploration of the psychological experience of the process yielded two further core categories, which give dimension to the temporal sequence: hopes and concerns. These were used to identify additional categories, using an open coding strategy to identify sub-categories of each property, systematically building up a model of the hopes and concerns of each individual, and through comparative analysis, a model of the shared experience of the unit: both hopes (enthusiasm for the new role, and new clinical methods) and concerns (lack of opportunity to use all their skills, feeling out of place or excluded, fear of collapse of external support). The resulting substantive findings of the analytic process included: the role of the managers in the management of the impact of external factors on the boundary of the community; the impact of the clinical work on the clinical staff, and the use of peer support to sustain the pressures of the clinical work; the difficulty experienced by staff in reflecting on the process in the face of the demands on them in terms of time and the need to succeed, as part of an innovative project.

Conclusion

As can be seen from this overview of grounded theory method and its practice in psychotherapy process research, there are a variety of approaches to the research task, both in relation to the substantive areas studied, and the choice of data and context, which can be undertaken using the basic method of grounded theory. The choice of data is a primary consideration. Many existing studies use interview, or indirect evidence of the psychotherapy process itself. The direct analysis of transcripts, paying careful attention to coding for the change process would seem to be an important potential direction for analysis, as yet very little exploited. In addition, grounded theory can be used as part of a larger project, and integrated with other methods, as in Grafanaki and

McLeod (1999), and also in the illustrative project in Part IV (Lepper and Mergenthaler, 2005).

In using the method, the investigator has a series of choices to make in undertaking an analysis. The investigator must approach data selection with a set of questions: What kind of question is being asked of the data? What kind of substantive exploration would address the questions. These questions lead the investigator to another analytic choice, between the three distinct conceptual approaches, which have been identified in the above sections as 'realist', 'pragmatic' and 'hermeneutic'. The debates within the grounded theory world have centered around which version is the 'correct' or 'true' method. Does this condemn grounded theory to accusations of a lack of conceptual clarity? On the evidence of the studies reviewed above, grounded theory has been used in all of these ways, and in each case has yielded different insights into the clinical process. In some cases it has been used as a means of conceptual analysis in order to yield general categories which can identify psychotherapy process properties which can be tested, and generalized. In others, it is used to explore the clinical process in fine detail. In yet others, it has been used to explore the subjective experiences of the participants. Each of these concerns represents a discrete level of the psychotherapy process, with quite different analytic concerns. For each discrete level, grounded theory, applied in a manner appropriate to the questions asked of the data, has provided a robust method of inquiry.

SUGGESTIONS FOR FURTHER READING

Glaser, B. and Strauss, A. (1967) *The Discovery of Grounded Theory*. London: Weidenfeld & Nicolson.

Rennie, D.L. (1992) 'Qualitative analysis of the client's experience of therapy: the unfolding of reflexivity', in S. Toukmanian and D. Rennie (eds), *Psychotherapy Process Research*. Newbury Park: Sage.

Rennie, D. (2000) 'Grounded theory methodology as methodological hermeneutics: Reconciling realism with relativism', *Theory and Psychology*, 10: 481–502

Strauss, A. and Corbin, J. (1998) *Basics of Qualitative Research: Techniques and procedures for developing grounded theory*. Thousand Oaks: Sage.

CHAPTER 7

Conversation analysis

Introduction

This chapter introduces another social science research method appropriate to psychotherapy process research. Conversation analysis (Sacks *et al.*, 1974; Sacks, 1992) has been identified as a potential significant contributor to psychotherapy process research for over two decades, beginning with a study of an entire psychotherapy – *Therapeutic Discourse: Psychotherapy as conversation*, by Labov and Fanshel, in 1977. More than a decade later, another book was dedicated to the application of conversation analysis to psychotherapy discourse (Gale, 1991). In recent articles, the value of a sociological perspective on the therapeutic alliance has been proposed by Kozart (2002); and Madill *et al.* propose yet again that 'a relatively novel approach, conversation analysis, has the potential to provide useful insights into the psychotherapy process' (Madill *et al.*, 2001, p. 413). Despite this consistent interest, conversation analysis has remained a 'novel approach' and has failed to enter into the mainstream of empirical psychotherapy research.

It is only in the last decade that interest in discourse methods has permeated into the field of psychology. Conversation analysis has frequently been identified with a behaviourist, and anti-psychological stance. There are also considerable methodological problems to be resolved in applying conversation analysis to therapeutic discourse in a way that is relevant to clinical practice. The recent focus of attention in psychotherapy research on the therapeutic alliance, in particular, and on interactional features of the clinical process more generally, however, suggests that working to resolve some of the practical problems of applying conversation analysis to psychotherapeutic interaction may provide an important empirical approach for psychotherapy process research. In this chapter, some of the basic principles of conversation analysis will be introduced. There is a very wide body of findings, and therefore, no attempt will be made to cover the field. Rather, some basic applications will be demonstrated, using a limited amount of data. This will give some of the flavour of the intensive quality of the method, and how it is applied.

What is conversation analysis?

Conversation analysis (or CA) was first developed by Harvey Sacks during the 1960s. Like Noam Chomsky, he was interested in the underpinning structures of language production. However, the focus of his interest lay not in the rules by which individuals generate utterances (generative grammar), but rather, in the rules by which interactants construct meaningful talk. Influenced by Harvey Garfinkel, a sociologist who was interested in the study of everyday interaction, he developed an empirical method for the study of everyday conversations. Through this inheritance, CA is a direct descendant of the research methods developed within the interactional tradition of social science research. In common with grounded theory, the empirical project of CA rests on the assumption that meaning is an emergent production of active subjects. Unlike grounded theory, however, which focuses on systematically mapping the *content* of the emergent meaning-world generated by social actors, CA attends to the *process* by which meaning emerges in turn by turn interaction. From the perspective of CA, 'everyday reality is accomplished, and made observable/reportable, or storyable' (Sacks, 1992, vol. 1, p. 218).

CA presumes that meaning is a product of what we do as speakers and hearers. With this shift of emphasis, conversation analysis finds its place within the American philosophical tradition of pragmatics, first proposed by Charles Peirce and further developed by George Herbert Mead, an important contributor to a social theory of the self. Pragmatics focus on meaning as the 'practical consequences' of the interplay of subject and object – that is, as historically contingent. It follows that the way to understand how meaningful interaction is achieved is to study *how* speakers and hearers themselves construct hearable and understandable conversations. To do this, we have to study naturally occurring conversational data.

CA makes basic assumptions that:

- Conversation is based on orderly procedures which underpin the creation of meaning.
- These procedures are amenable to formal analysis through the study of naturally occurring turn by turn interaction.
- Interaction is 'context shaped' and 'context-renewing': that is, each turn in an interaction is locally shaped by, and provides the shape for, the next turn.

Sacks' method was to take naturally occurring talk, and to study it in intense detail, identifying by this means regularly occurring, natural phenomena which become the basis of theory building. He sought to develop a 'natural observational science of social order'. Through an iterative process of analysis, adding examples, comparing examples, and reformulating the rule as examples are studied and compared, general rules of social interaction are built. These rules are what Sacks called 'hearing rules'. It is hearing rules which enable conversational participants to design their utterances in a way which will make them understandable, and create the potential for a response which builds on each utterance. Turn taking in conversation is 'recipient designed'. Social, and inter-subjective order, are grounded in this process. The fundamental unit of discourse which CA addresses is turn taking.

CA inquiry, in seeking embedded rules of hearing, typically proceeds by asking *how* questions of the data. First questions which were asked by Sacks were:

- How does a conversation get started?
- Who gets to speak?
- How do they know when it is their turn to speak?
- How long can a person speak?
- How does the telling/exchanging of stories proceed?
- How do question and answer sequences structure the conversation?
- How do gaps, pauses, silences and overlaps help to structure the exchange?
- What happens when things go wrong?
- How does a conversation end?

Some of the earliest work in conversation analysis was done on telephone conversations recorded in an emergency psychiatric call centre. (These were the days before stringent ethics codes.) Sacks was interested in how these (often delicate and difficult) conversations were constructed. He asked the question, how do these conversations get started? One issue of importance which he noticed was that an interactional problem for the call centre operator was to elicit the name of the caller, in the event that action was needed. Often, callers did not want to identify themselves. Sacks set out to examine what happened in these conversations, and how the name of the caller might be withheld. The first exchange of the conversation yielded much useful data. Here are some examples. Compare these phone call openings:

Data samples 7.1

1.

Speaker A: Hello
Speaker B: Hello

2.

Speaker A: This is Mr Smith, can I help you?
Speaker B: Yes, this is Mr Brown

Looking at lots of examples like these, Sacks observed that the form of the first turn typically provides the form for the reply. Giving your name, in 'slot' A, was identified as an effective means of eliciting the name of the caller in 'slot' B, without asking for a name. The first speaker sets the form for the reply. All, however, does not follow this simple rule. Consider this example:

Data sample 7.2

A   This is Mr. Smith, may I help you?
B   I can't hear you.
A   This is Mr. <u>Smith</u>
B   Smith.

Here, the caller avoids the response elicited in the opening provided by Mr. Smith with 'I can't hear you'. The caller's name, as well as a reply to the question, 'may I help you', are side stepped. On the repeat of the opening 'this is Mr. Smith' , the caller provides a response, but it is not a response which provides a name, or an opening for a next turn. Sacks suggests that this caller has used a device to provide a next turn without causing the conversation to break down. He has obeyed the rule of taking turns, in an opening conversation between strangers, but has avoided giving a name.

CA is based on the observation that turn taking is a fundamental human activity. This has also been observed and documented by developmental researchers. In analyzing conversation, CA has established that speakers use rules in order to sustain conversations, and a fundamental rule is to take a turn when offered one. A question always provides for, and requires, a specific next turn: an answer. Failure to respond to a question is rude, and will normally be avoided. So questions are a good way of opening a conversation, especially between strangers. In the above case, the speaker does not provide either of the two possible responses to Mr Smith's opening offer by providing a name, or responding to the question, but does keep the conversation open with 'I can't hear you'. When things don't go according to the usual rules, other devices are employed in order to keep the conversation going. It is by looking at naturally occurring data, comparing and contrasting singular instances, and particularly by studying those that don't follow the typical pattern, that we can make generalizations about the rules which underpin successful conversations. Successful conversations are those which continue, and in which the participants collaborate to generate meaning. These basic observations form the basis of Sacks' method for the study of conversation.

Here is an example of a conversational opening, from a study of two assessment interviews conducted by the same therapist (Streeck, 2002), using standard transcription conventions which indicate non-verbal events such as the uptake of breath, or changes in tone. Detailed transcription conventions can be found in ten Have (1999) and Lepper (2000).

Data sample 7.3

(1)

Th: so what (–) brings you here to | us?

Ms R: well, I <u>was</u> again (–) at a psychiatrist (–) I don't (2.5sec silence) know now

(5 sec silence)

(2)

Ms E: With you I was able to get an appointment pretty quickly

(12.0 sec silence)

Th: So, what brings you here <u>to</u> us?

EXERCISE 7.1

Using the list of questions above, see what can be discovered about these two exchanges.

In the first extract, the therapist speaks first, and, in asking a question, gives the patient the opportunity to speak. The question also gives the hearer permission to reply with a story about her/himself, and invites the second speaker to take a long turn. Notice that the patient falters, first starting with a story ('I was again') and then falls into silence.

In the second extract, the patient speaks first, with an open ended, informal utterance to which there is no formal response. This is followed by a very long silence. The therapist then asks the question, which starts the interview in the more formal way that he customarily uses. CA studies of many medical interviews reveal that the most common opening sequence is for the 'doctor' to start the interview with a question (though there may be small talk prior to the question). 'Patients' usually wait for the question, which entitles them to talk about themselves and to take an extended turn, in order to provide an extended narrative about the problem they are bringing. This sequence is a common and well studied conversational structure. In this case, the long silence serves to set the 'small talk' of the patient apart from the formal interview, which begins when the question is asked.

Careful, observational study of thousands of examples of conversational data such as these have produced some basic rules of turn taking organization. These rules, in the first instance, are based on detailed study of turn taking, locally organized in particular conversations, in particular contexts. These early micro-studies yielded the set of observations which now form the basis of the practice of *sequential analysis*, some important aspects of which are:

- *Turn size*: rules which establish how long a speaker may speak.
- *Turn organization*: rules which underpin how each speaker knows when to speak.
- *Topic organization*: rules which underpin collaborative work to sustain a topic across turns.

Further evidence for these rules is demonstrated by what happens when things go wrong. A further important object of study is:

- *Repair organization*: how speakers restore a conversational order when something breaks down.

Here is an exchange, which occurred in a group therapy session. What turn taking phenomena can be seen in this exchange?

Data sample 7.4

1. P3: Do they know about your eating habits?
2. P7: They know ... my mum does. I told them, well I started to let them know what was happening to me – I told my mum and dad – I went especially to Tucumán to tell them (laughter) yes because I needed them to help me more than anything (noise of cars) I think my dad more than my mum – because my mum is in no condition to help me whereas my dad is.
3. T: isn't your dad an alcoholic?
4. P7: no.
(pause: 11secs)
5. T: And who would like to say anything about how they see their mother?
6. P1: I see her as very sad ... with her life – ruined (dogs barking)
7. T: ruined?
8. P1: out of tune – with everything. she is a good person, her heart is in the right place, but I don't want to be dragged down with her, that's why I don't feel right at home, I'm not comfortable, I'm not at home. Her marriage is a failure, her personal life ... I don't know, but it upsets me.
9. T: you are upset?

Some significant sequential features of question and answer sequences can be seen at work in this short extract:

- The use of a question to elicit, and provide the slot for, an extended narrative (turn 1)
- The use of a question which seems to stop the flow of the conversation (turn 3)
- The use of a question to restart the conversation (turn 5) and following questions, which 'tie' closely to the previous turn (turns 7 and 9). These constitute a repair sequence.

One question which can be asked of the data is: What is different about the question in turn 3? It elicits a response (a question requires a response), but it seems to cause a break in the interaction, on the evidence of the long pause which follows. In a recent study, Heritage (2002) studied the phenomenon of these 'negative interrogatives' – questions which take the form of 'Isn't it ...' 'Don't you ...' – as a special case of questioning. He notes that the study of news interviews provides a particularly rich source of data for the study of interrogative form, and that the forms used have general relevance to the way that interrogatives are used in ordinary conversations. He demonstrates that negative interrogatives 'project an expected answer – strong enough, when produced in association with question content that contexts an interviewee's position, to be treated as having made an assertion...' (p. 1436), and shows how this general form is used in some ordinary exchanges. He then goes on to show how this particular form of the negative interrogative serves the purposes of the news interview. The negative interrogative can often be employed, by interviewers, as a means of challenging the interviewee, and making a counter assertion. He terms them 'hostile negative interrogatives'.

In this extract from a group therapy session, the negative interrogative has a similar form: it challenges the previous utterance. The reply, 'no' is followed by a long pause, and the on-going conversation ceases. Evidence that a problem in the talk has occurred is found in the next turn: the therapist (turn 5) restarts the conversation with an open ended question, repairing the breakdown in the interaction by initiating a new sequence. More aspects of this exchange will be studied in the next sections.

The empirical study of conversational data, comparing and contrasting instances of turn taking forms, is the core methodological strategy of the discipline of conversation analysis (ten Have, 1999). The evidence for a rule is in what happens at each turn; it is what hearers do, not what researchers think, which provides that evidence. As basic science, formal CA focuses entirely on the structural features of conversation, and their generalizability across languages and cultures. By comparing, through the iterative process, large numbers of phenomena, the underlying rules are identified, and from these, a general theory of conversational interaction is being built. Early studies in CA were conducted entirely on English texts. Empirical research which can test these basic rules of conversational turn taking across different languages and cultures in order to establish to what extent these rules are genuine universals, and how they are applied locally, for specific purposes, is a more recent development. A further strand of CA research is its application in specific contexts, in order to apply its empirical methods to the study of the ways in which the rules of turn taking create and sustain everyday human institutions and practices. Heritage's study of the news interview is an example. The basic findings of CA can be used to study specific contexts, and how they are both created and sustained through languaged interaction. The application of CA to the specific context of psychotherapy will be introduced in a later section of this chapter.

Categorization analysis

The second aspect of conversational order and its underpinning structure which interested Sacks was the way in which speakers and hearers deploy categories to construct hearable utterances, which tie together to produce meaningful discourse. By using the term 'categories', he places analytic attention not on the formal meaning of words (semantics) but rather on the way words work in the context of spoken interaction as vehicles of shared meaning. This aspect of Sacks' theory has become known as Categorization Analysis (Lepper, 2000), and constitutes a somewhat separate discipline, though its concerns remain the same as sequential analysis. As with sequential analysis, the process of inquiry begins with asking questions of the data.

Sacks (1972) typically started with an observation, a scrap of data, to which he applied the kind of 'how' questioning procedure he uses with sequential analysis. In this case the data is a micro-story, told by a child of 2 years and 7 months:

Data sample 7.5

The baby cried.
The mommy picked it up.

Sacks was interested in several aspects of this fragmentary story. Most hearers will hear that this baby is the baby of the mommy, and not some other baby. This very young child still has not acquired use of personal pronouns, and yet a hearer will interpret that the story concerns a mother and her child. Sacks' question was, how does this happen? He proposed that there is an embedded 'hearer's rule': hear 'baby' and 'mother' as a unit, unless otherwise specified. They belong to the 'collection' of categories pertaining to 'family': a recognizable unit. Hearers listen for the meaningful units to which individual categories may belong, depending on the context in which they are used. Even a very young speaker has learned this basic rule of hearing, which enables a communication. Sacks proposed that in the process of learning how to use categories, the child is also learning how to put a meaningful, shared social world together.

In the next extract, the speaker is a somewhat older child, and her mother.

Data sample 7.6

A: (a little girl)   Who's that?

B: (her mother)   That's Rita. Remember when you went to the party last week and met Una? Well, that's Una's mother

---

In this fragment, we see the process by which social order is built through category management, where a skilled language user uses a rule – the 'consistency rule' – to enable a young hearer to build a relevant description. Instead of saying simply 'that's Una's mother' (a complex grammatical construction), the mother uses a micro narrative (when you went to the party and met Una) to provide the relevant description – the relationships which make up the collection 'family' – which is the answer to the question. In answering the question, she has provided the child with a complex grammatical form; she has also provided the child with valuable information about how her local social world is organized, and how to provide a description of that world. Adults answer a lot of children's questions, particularly in their first five years. From the perspective of CA, a question is an action. As noted above, questions require answers, and the young child will soon discover that a question is a good way of gaining the attention of an adult. A question is also a good way of eliciting information about how the meaning world is organized.

An older group of speakers (in a therapy group composed of adolescents, which was studied in detail by Sacks) uttered the following sentence:

Data sample 7.7

1. Joe: (Cough) We were in an automobile discussion,

2. Henry: discussing the psychological motives for

3. Mel: drag-racing in the streets.

This sentence was uttered as the next turn after the therapist introduced a new member of the group. What interested Sacks was the way in which three speakers were able to produce a perfectly grammatical sentence, seamlessly, as if it were one utterance. Here, the speakers align to a topic (automobile discussion), while at the same time (recipient design) communicating a message to both newcomer and therapist. *How* they do this is the object of study of categorization analysis. It generates question like these:

- *How* does the pronoun 'we' function to define them as a group?
- *How* do the speakers collaborate on a topic ('automobile discussion') to demonstrate their inter-subjective alliance and make it observable to a newcomer?
- *How* does the category 'drag-racing' work to provide a hearable description of their identity, not only to the newcomer, but to the therapist as well?

Sacks' primary concern was not about the subjective experience of the boys, but about how they produced a discursive unit (the co-produced sentence) which defined their identity to the newcomer.

The following are a few examples of generalized rules, derived from this empirical study of conversational data, which are of particular relevance for the study of an exchange like this.

The consistency rule

Sacks proposed that the way in which speakers and hearers collaborate to create meaning depends on the application of a consistency rule, which states that if a population of persons is being categorized, then the category used to characterize the first member of that population will be heard as relevant to the rest of the population. So, if the category 'mother' is introduced, in the absence of any other information, a subsequent 'baby' or 'child' will be heard as her own. Or take the co-produced sentence of data sample 7.7: the 'we' is hearable as the co-present group; their 'automobile discussion' defines the general topic (a 'collection' of categories) in which they are engaged; the category 'drag racing', is hearable as part of that 'collection'. If the 'we' is (observably) a group of adolescents having an 'automobile discussion' about 'drag racing in the streets', this is unlikely to include an adult. A new member can apply the consistency rule and decide which side to be on! Here is the next turn, which supports this hearing:

Data sample 7.8

1. Joe: I still say though that if you take, if you take uh a big fancy car out on the road and you're hot roddin' around you're bound to get, you're bound to get caught and you're bound to get shafted. We – look

2. Mel: Now did you do it right. That's the challenge that's the challenge you wanna try

3. Henry: that's the problem with society. Hahhh

4. Mel: and you do it right so you do not get caught

5. Henry: that's the

6. Joe: in that Bonneville of mine?

Joe follows their co-produced sentence (data sample 7.7) with the start of a story – a story about a 'big fancy car' which ties to the topic ('automobile discussion') already introduced, develops and extends the theme of 'drag-racing' ('hot roddin' around') and develops the implicit communication of the opening: the group against the adult world. Note the repeated 'we' as he gets interrupted by an overlapping contribution by Mel and Henry. It's the same structure, though this time it doesn't come off as smoothly. Here Mel and Henry compete to add to the point of the story – the conflict with 'society'. Note that Mel picks up on the category 'get caught', tying his turn to the previous utterance. Sacks calls this 'category bound activity' – i.e. 'getting caught' is heard as meaningfully related to the activity 'hot-rodding' and to the wider context of the topic, 'the problem with society'. This is how context, and shared intersubjective meaning, are shaped by the actions of speakers and hearers. All of this happened in one minute. One minute later, the boys turn their attention directly to the newcomer.

Further rules which link content to the sequence of conversations, through the management of categorization, are called tying rules.

Tying rules

Sacks demonstrated that each utterance is tied to the preceding utterance, and provides a cue (tying possibility) to the hearer to take a turn. Category ties may go back several, or many, turns in a conversation. Tying may be accomplished by a variety of devices, which include both sequential and categorization elements. The three speakers in data sample 7.8 are exceptionally closely allied both to the sequential order, and to the categorical order. Ties are often accomplished by pronouns which refer back to previous categories or collections. Ties may be accomplished by the introduction of a new category within a 'collection' (a linked set of categories, such as 'family').

One possible line of analysis is to investigate how the utterances of the speaker and hearer are tied to previous utterances in the talk. How do the categories-in-use relate to previously introduced categories or collections? What is accomplished by their use? What happens when they are not tied to the previous turn (or turns)?

These are the kinds of questions asked of the data when categorization is being studied. As with sequential analysis, what is studied are the rules of hearing which enable the speakers to take turns, to build a topic, to exchange stories, to create an inter-subjective world which includes or excludes other members.

In the first section of this chapter, the following exchange from a group psychotherapy session was examined for its specific question and answer sequences. Now, further questions can be asked about what is happening in this exchange.

EXERCISE 7.2

Examine the categories in data sample 7.4. Using the three aspects of 'tying' noted above, see what can be found out about how the topic 'mother' is managed by patients and therapist? What significance does this have for the management of the topic?

In the earlier discussion of this data, the sequential order of the questions was considered, and a comparison demonstrated that the therapist question in turn 3 was not the same as the other question and answer sequences. Some comparative research, conducted in the context of news interviews, provided a means of identifying the difference between this and the other questions. Taking categorization as well as sequential features into account can shed more light on what is happening.

In this exchange, the opening question introduces the topic 'eating habits', using the pronoun 'they', which locates the topic in the collection 'family', as we see in the text turn: P7 specifies 'mum and dad'. Within that collection, P7 further specifies that 'mum is in no condition to help me whereas my dad is'. In the subsequent turn (turn 3), the therapist ties to the category 'dad', with the negative interrogative we examined in the previous discussion of this exchange, and a break in the talk follows. Notice what the therapist does in turn 5: she returns to the talk about 'mum' offered by patient 7, with the question, 'And who would like to say anything about how they see their mother', a topic offer which is promptly taken up by P1, who collaborates in the repair.

Questions of method

Many CA studies resemble 'basic science' in that they are interested in studying the phenomenon of conversation for its own sake. These studies provide the basis for the comparative method which can then be used to apply some of the basic findings of CA in particular contexts. How do researchers studying any kind of phenomenon identify and select data? How can the researcher make generalizations on the basis of a limited number of examples? In quantitative studies, this issue is addressed through the principle of 'sampling': like samples are compared, using statistical analysis to compare them. How does CA, with its inductive strategy, solve this problem?

At first, Sacks simply selected examples of conversational exchanges which interested him. His concern was with developing what he called a 'natural observational science' of social life, comparable with the observational methods of biological science. He made a strong claim, which he termed 'order at all points': if the social world is comprehensively organized, and its organization is sustained through interactional processes such as talk, then order will be found at every point. His method of iterative comparison and building up a picture of the order which would have to exist in order for there to be meaningful interaction is similar to that of grounded theory. Early CA researchers applied the principle of 'saturation of data', using the 'constant comparison method', seeking to exhaustively search a dataset through the identification of all examples, comparison, and the building of a model, or rule, which would account for every case. This procedure is based on the principles of 'analytic induction', and its objective is to build theory. More detailed discussion of issues of reliability and validity can be found in Chapter 2.

As his corpus of findings grew, Sacks' empirical strategy addressed the issue of 'sampling' in several ways. He began to develop a more systematic strategy of data analysis, characterized by Schegloff (1992, II, p. xi) as studying:

- An order of organization, rather than a particular practice of talk;
- A class of places in an aggregate of data, rather than an extract;
- An organizationally characterized problem or form of interactional work rather than an individually designed outcome;
- Invariances of features, rather than context specific practices.

A typical project might proceed with analysis of a phenomenon which hasn't received much attention, or analysis of a particular context which is new and interesting to the researcher. Consider the example of conversational openings, which was the first focus of Sacks' analytic attention. His early research was on conversation openings in telephone conversations. This kind of comparison is called 'within type' comparison. Schegloff (1992) continued this research, examining 500 conversational openings in ordinary (social) telephone conversations, beginning a process of 'cross type' comparisons, through which universal features can be compared with context specific features. Later research on face to face conversational openings has compared instances across many kinds of settings. Openings in professional settings – medical interviews for example – reveal specific features.

In the analysis of data sample 7.4, the observation made was that the question and answer sequence in turns 3 and 4 was not the same as the other question/answer sequences. To investigate this difference, this instance was compared across types, drawing upon a study of negative interrogatives, in the particular site of the news interview (a 'within type' analysis). Heritage concludes that study by pointing out that 'research from a relatively specialized "institutional" environment will have a payoff for the study of talk in ordinary social context. Practices of talk in interaction ... have important underlying continuities across settings' (2002, p. 1444). By applying these findings to the site of the psychotherapy group, further understanding of the process of the negative interrogative was made possible. In this case, rather than a defensive response, the response was a breakdown in the talk, which then had to be repaired.

For the contemporary CA researcher, an approach to a new problem can include both the earlier method – identification of a specific practice of interest for singular analysis – and the more exhaustive methods of studying a large number of cases. For the novice, learning the method, or applying the method to a new kind of interactional setting, starting with an object of interest is still a valid entry into the CA process. The experienced researcher, working with a large dataset, however, will want to use the more developed comparative methods which emerged as Sacks refined his method.

Applying conversation analysis to psychotherapeutic interaction

For Sacks, the structural properties of conversation, some of which have been introduced in the previous sections, provide the basis for an observational science of social actions, and order. It is not the interpretation of the investigator, but the interpretations of the speakers and hearers of each others' utterances, evidenced by their turn by turn actions, which is the object of study. Though Sacks himself was interested in psychological matters, and was very interested in Freud, CA developed as a theory of social interaction (and social order), and his early collaborators took the position that 'minds' or 'intentions' were not relevant to understanding communicative interaction. They were often accused of behaviourism.

This position continues to be a widely held in the mainstream academic world of CA. The application of CA to psychology requires claims for its relevance both against the anti-psychological stance of its purist practitioners (mostly sociologists), and against the stance of the dominant cognitive/behavioural model in academic psychology, with its focus on 'shared knowledge as a matter of matching up speakers' and hearers' knowledge states' (Edwards, 1997b), rather than on the interactional dimensions of psychological functioning. Translating the basic premise of CA – that meaning is constructed, in a rule guided way, by speakers in the course of their talk – into the study of psychology has been undertaken by such theorists as Margaret Wetherell and Jonathan Potter (Potter and Wetherell, 1987), and Derek Edwards (Edwards and Potter, 1992; Edwards, 1997b). They do not deny that mental states exist, or are important, but set out to demonstrate how categories referring to mental states are employed in interaction with others, and how those communications are interpreted in the course of naturally occurring interaction. These are the processes by means of which people in interaction assess each others' intentions, feelings and thoughts. We have no other source of information about the intentions of others than the observations we make of their actions, verbal and non-verbal. Though CA is not interested in what happens 'inside' the 'mind', by implication, its focus on recipient design means that it focuses on what the interactants observably thought was meant by a previous turn, on the evidence of their response. In describing features of the world, people make available inferences about their judgements, motives and desires; and in describing features of their mind they make available inferences about events, settings and other people (Edwards and Potter, 1992). The focus of this application of conversation analysis is on inter-subjectivity, and it provides a robust empirical method for its study.

Studies in psychotherapy research based more widely on the analysis of both verbal and non-verbal aspects of psychotherapeutic interaction have been attempted at intervals during the past 30 years of psychotherapy research. Important studies include detailed investigations of psychotherapy sessions by Scheflen (1973) and Labov and Fanshel (1977), who studied the interactional features of an entire psychotherapy. More recently, Ferrara (1994) summarized a variety of different approaches to the study of psychotherapy using discourse methods. Another recent work, by Elaine Chaika (2000), an expert in schizophrenic discourse, makes the case for the direct relevance of linguistics to clinicians.

At the same time, findings from developmental psychology, and attachment theory, have focused clinical and research attention on the interpersonal processes in human development. The development of the SASB instrument (see Chapter 5), and the interpersonal model of psychotherapy proposed by Benjamin (2004) reflect this shift of focus within psychotherapy research. Further, in the last decade, review of the findings from psychotherapy outcomes research has shifted the attention of many researchers from the traditional focus on specific theoretical models to 'common factors' – variables which seem to be a common feature of all therapeutic outcomes (see Chapter 1). In particular, the 'therapeutic' or 'working alliance', or 'therapeutic relationship', is seen as the major contributing factor in good outcomes. In the context of all these developments, CA offers a powerful methodological tool for the study of therapeutic interaction, and is now being treated as a serious option for psychotherapy process research (Madill *et al.*, 2001). It presents both opportunities, and considerable methodological challenges.

The first challenge to be addressed is: what do findings from the analysis of the therapeutic interaction tell us about the clinical process? The second is: how do we identify significant clinical features in order to compare and contrast, and build a substantive case for the clinical significance of interactional features, using CA?

To illustrate these methodological challenges, consider again the sequence from the group therapy data (data sample 7.4). Using CA, some features of the question and answer sequences were identified, related to other CA research findings on Q&A sequences. The difference between the Q&A sequence at turns 3 and 4 was examined, and, with reference to research findings on 'negative interrogatives', it was noted that 'negative interrogatives' typically function as assertions, rather than invitations for information; and that, if their content is 'hostile', they elicit a defensive reply. The object of study is the form of the exchange itself, rather than its content. In this case the reply is 'no', and it is followed by a very long silence. This can now be read as a defensive reply. That it is a problem was evidenced in the next turn: the therapist re-initiates the talk by asking the kind of question which is used to invite an extended turn in the talk – an extended narrative (turn 5). Patient 1 responds, with an extended narrative, which is supported by the therapist's interjected turns, tied to the immediately preceding categories, 'ruined' and 'upset' (turns 8 and 9). There are two important things to note in the way that tying rules function in this exchange. Q&A sequences provide for ties between turns: a question requires an answer, and it also provides the topic. It's a good way to start, or continue, a coherent topic. When the on-going conversation closes down, in response to her negative interrogative, on hearing this the therapist takes steps to renew it. She reverts to the category, 'mothers', tying back to the previous turns.

What significance does this have for clinical practice? One issue which arises is the use of 'questioning'. Different forms of therapeutic practice take different approaches to the use of questions. Some systemic models use 'circular questioning' as a primary tool; psychoanalysis traditionally proscribes them. Empirical study of how question and answer sequences work in natural conversation tells us something about how they work. Comparing, contrasting and examining how Q&A sequences work in the clinical encounter, what they achieve or don't achieve as an interactional matter, may tell us quite a lot about the clinical process. In this psychodynamic group therapy, the therapist 'breaks the rules' of psychodynamic practice by asking many questions. As we can see in this extract, one question proved counter-productive; the others seem to productively start, or restart, the interactional process. It is how they are used in a specific exchange which can provide something useful to clinical understanding.

To explore this notion further, consider another observation about this extract: the therapist's use of 'reflection' (repeating another person's utterance). This is a commonly employed clinical technique intended to develop the therapeutic alliance through the demonstration of 'empathy'. Notice how the therapist turns at 7 and 9, though in 'question' format, are not actually questions at all, but are heard as what CA would call 'hearing tokens' – an invitation to continue the turn; they could also be seen as reinforcing the topic. From the clinical perspective, they can be seen as the use of reflection as a listening technique. In a study of HIV counselling, Silverman (1997, p. 86) found that the use of 'reflection' can be heard as 'I'm hearing what you say'. However, through comparative analysis of many sessions, he found that it can also be heard as 'I doubt what you said', and may elicit a defensive reply, quite different than the clinical intention.

Example of a practitioner project using conversation analysis

In a small scale student project, an exploration of the interactional process of Q&A sequences was undertaken to explore instances of refusal to answer a question in psychotherapy sessions. Having noticed its occurrence twice in a single session, the student was interested in testing the common clinical assumption that when the patient does not answer a therapist question this is evidence of resistance. The focus of attention was chosen not only for clinical interest, but also because she knew that there was a substantial body of empirical findings on question and answer sequences against which she could compare her analysis of just two exchanges.

In the analysis, she 'followed the usual convention in CA of bracketing, whenever possible, the permanent identities of the speakers and concentrated instead on the rights, obligations and expectations which are locally oriented to in the interaction.' She first analyzed turns 3–24 of the session, in which the patient begins with the following utterance:

> P: Urm, I don't know, urm, well I don't know where, I don't know where, where to begin where to begin. First of all I want to ask you just a couple of things. (pause). The tapes, er, is it only you, it's only you that listens to them, or….?

The focus of the analysis is on two sequences, both of which ask the questions which are previewed in this opening turn. A series of questions and answers follows this opening utterance, with the therapist answering the patient's questions until the following sequence occurs:

> T: But do you want me to find out for you?
> P: Well I'm just a bit anxious – well no I'm not particularly anxious that's not fair – erm, I mean, er, my name's not on there is it?
> T: No, no your name will never appear on anything.
> P. Oh, fine, oh, fine.

In this sequence, the patient avoids a direct answer to the question, the expected next turn, in favour of an explanation of her motives, followed by another question of her own. In the analysis of this pair, the student notes the 'misalignment' (questions require answers) and the therapist's resolution of the rupture in the turn taking sequence: *she* answers the patient's question – 'No, no your name will never appear on anything'.

The second unanswered question occurs in a sequence initiated with the second of the 'couple of things' the patient wanted to ask, and is explicitly tied back to the opening utterance:

> P: But that was the *other question*, how long am I in psychotherapy for?
> T: Right, was that not, that wasn't something that (*assessor*) talked about to you?

> P: I think she probably did, but I think I was probably in such a state that I didn't hear it you know
> T: We ask for a commitment of a year (*pause*) That okay?
> P: Er, so, er
> T: Er, so
> P: Oh I thought eighteen months or something
> T: Yer, yer it can be extended a bit if you want...

Here, it is the therapist who avoids answering the question, preferring instead to elicit more information relevant to the question: what was the patient told? Her reply signals that she is sensitive to the fact that the information may not have been heard: after a pause, she asks the question, 'That okay'?' To this second therapist question the patient doesn't reply. The answer does not come until 3 turns later, after some hesitation. Now the interactional problem, evident in the hesitations, is revealed: the therapist's answer ('a year') is different from the expected reply ('18 months').

Attentive to issues of sampling, the student also searched through the first five sessions, in order to explore whether there were other unanswered questions, and how they were managed by the patient–therapist couple. She found that there were two kinds of unanswered questions: those where the patient was clearly unwilling to reply – either to protect the identity of other people, or because the subject was 'too embarrassing'. There were five examples of these interactions, and they were concentrated in the first two sessions. These were reflect issues of trust and confidentiality, paramount in the early sessions. There were 16 other instances of the kind of Q&A sequences analyzed above – sequences in which a repair occurred. These instances were spread evenly throughout the five sessions. Her conclusion was that this evidence could support a working hypothesis that repair and realignment at the level of turn by turn interaction are part of the developing collaboration in the working alliance.

The turn by turn analysis of these two sequences focuses on the use of the Q&A format, and its functions and vicissitudes in the early stage of the therapy, and alliance formation. The student makes the case that the two episodes demonstrate the work being done by both patient and therapist to address issues of potential conflict in the context of trying to establish a working relationship. Not answering the questions is not, she concludes, evidence of resistance, but rather, evidence of the patient's active participation in the creation of alliance: she creates an interactional disjuncture in need of repair, alerting the therapist to the underlying problem, and providing the opportunity to both speakers to realign, and, hence, re-secure the building alliance.

In another small project, a student used categorization analysis to explore a vocalization which she noticed over and over again in sessions with her own training patient. She termed these sounds 'lipsmacks', and sought to explore Freud's proposal in *The Psychopathology of Everyday Life*:

> the interpretations of these small chance actions and the evidence for these interpretations, emerge each time with sufficient certainty from the material which accompanies them during the session, from the topic that is under discussion (Freud, 1912/1979).

Here Freud speaks of the 'evidence for interpretations'. This student sought to seek some evidence that these 'lipsmacks' could be linked to topics which aroused anxiety, and hence, to the transference. In the analysis, she identified all the occurrences of 'lipsmacks', and then identified the categories which occurred in the turns just before and after each lipsmack, using inter-rater reliability to verify her assignment of categories. She then subjected these findings to some simple quantitative analysis, demonstrating that of the 11 different categorizations found in the turns preceding and following the 38 instances of 'lipsmacks', nine were associated with just two categories: 'father' and 'husband'. Through further analysis of the categorizations (taking into account 'category bound activities', for example), she found further evidence for the same pattern. She then plotted the occurrence of lipsmacks through the whole session, by dividing it into segments of equal length, and demonstrated that after each therapist intervention addressing the issue of 'father', lipsmacks declined for a few subsequent segments. She concludes that this empirical analysis of the talk reveals evidence for the co-occurrence of anxiety and the non-verbal vocalization; and that this method might provide some empirical evidence for the interpretation of these events that Freud originally sought.

Conclusion

In his article on the analysis of counselling and psychotherapy interaction, Watson (1993b) notes that in order to analyze therapy talk, the focus of attention is on the person-in-the-talk: the object of study is the person who exists *at the moment of the talk in an inter-subjective relationship to the other speaker(s)*. In each of the examples above, we have seen how a restricted analytic frame, which attends to specific interactional events, can be linked to issues of clinical relevance (the use of questions, for example) as well as of theory (the significance of non-verbal behaviours, noted in a very early observation by Freud).

CA provides a well used method, with a large body of findings over a wide variety of interactional settings. Although it has nothing to say about clinical significance, it brings an analytic vector to the study of therapeutic interaction which is independent of clinical theory, and therefore has the power to provide evidence for clinical concepts which is not tied to clinical theory itself. Several issues of method in the application of CA to psychotherapy interaction arise from these examples.

What can be studied?

CA is uniquely suited to the study of interpersonal processes, and their unfolding in the therapeutic dialogue. As it is not bound by a psychotherapeutic model, or even by psychological theory, it provides a pan-theoretical approach to the study of therapeutic interaction. In a discussion of alliance research, Kozart (2002) proposes that the shift to a social interactional paradigm represented by CA provides an important means for the empirical investigation of the everyday interactional strategies which underpin the components of therapeutic alliance commonly identified by the psychometric measures in common use: e.g. common goals, tasks, and the therapeutic bond (Bordin, 1994). In their major study of the therapeutic alliance, Henry and Strupp (1994) conclude:

> We now believe that some type of fundamental training in the perception of moment-by-moment interpersonal process should be an initial foundation for later training in different theory-based therapies. (p. 68)

The studies cited in this chapter give some indication of the kinds of applications which can be pursued. In early studies of the therapeutic interaction, exhaustive analysis of the discourse, both verbal and non-verbal, revealed much of interest and significance (e.g., Labov and Fanshel, 1977; Scheflen, 1973). However, the practical application of their findings to clinical theory and practice have remained ungrounded, and have failed to be incorporated into clinical theory and practice. A significant problem for the researcher using CA is to identify interaction which is of clinical significance, and to link findings to clinically relevant concepts and theory. Some of the sampling methods addressed in the previous chapter on grounded theory have an important contribution to make to selecting data for CA. The examples above show several approaches to the identification of clinically significant interactions, and how they can be used to illuminate clinical theory and practice. In the first case, sampling is determined by the identification of a practical clinical problem: the management of questions. The design of the project was based on the identification of a 'class of places', which are then compared and contrasted (though due to the limited nature of the project, this was not undertaken exhaustively, as it would be in a fully developed study). In the second case, the student chose to employ 'theoretical sampling': she linked a clinical observation to a theoretical concept, and used CA to explore the hypothesis that non-verbal sounds are evidence of unconscious processes.

Reliability and validity

In these two studies, the use of the comparative method, in which the identified examples are compared both within the dataset, and with findings from adjacent studies (as in the example of questions and answers) provides for both reliability and validity in the application of CA. The principles of saturation of the data, 'constant comparative analysis', and 'deviant case analysis' must be rigorously applied to the analysis of data in order to underpin analytic findings with convincing evidence.

In order to achieve validity, classical CA seeks to identify classes of events in a dataset, and build a model of their structure through the method of saturation of the data and comparison – the 'constant comparative' method. In the small projects outlined in this chapter, validity and reliability were attended to in two ways. In the first example the principle of choice was a specific event of clinical interest. The findings were set in the context of the wider set of findings about Q&A sequences in the CA corpus. Additionally, an attempt to test the working hypothesis of the project was made by examining other instances in the dataset, to see if the hypotheses held up. In the second example the student used a simple (quantitative) time series analysis to support her finding, and establish some internal validity for her study. In a fully developed research project, saturation of the data would be the method of choice. In order to achieve this, a variety of methods might be employed, including the use of computerized search and coding methods (see Part IV) to identify and include every instance of an 'order of organization', such as Q&A sequences; or to identify and study invariant, rather than context specific, features. In the case of data sample 7.4 (from the group therapy session), the selection of this fragment of interaction for analysis was made on the principle of 'deviant case' analysis (see Chapter 2 for a discussion of deviant case analysis; and Part IV for a fuller discussion of the study from which this data comes). Using a combination of methods, this fragment was identified as clinically significant, and subjected to detailed analysis in order to extend and validate the overall analysis.

CA is a well developed empirical discourse method, which has the potential to address a wide range of clinical and research questions. It can be a useful method for the small student project, and supports clinical learning through its detailed exploration of the turn by turn interaction. The application of CA in larger studies is in its early stages. Much work needs to be done to apply the method to the specific context of therapeutic interaction.

SUGGESTIONS FOR FURTHER READING

Chaika, E. (2000) *Linguistics, Pragmatics and Psychotherapy: A guide for therapists.* London: Whurr.

Ferrara, K. (1994) *Therapeutic Ways with Words.* New York: Oxford University Press.

Labov, W. and Fanshel, D. (1977) *Therapeutic Discourse: Psychotherapy as conversation.* New York: Academic Press.

Lepper, G. (2000) *Analyzing Talk and Text: A practical introduction to categorization analysis.* London: Sage.

ten Have, P. (1999) *Doing Conversation Analysis: A practical guide.* London: Sage.

CHAPTER 8

Analyzing narratives in psychotherapy texts

Introduction

Like all of the forms of discourse analysis considered in this section, narrative analysis (NA) emerged in the post war period, as the disciplines of social science and linguistics turned their attention to the phenomenon of ordinary language and spoken interaction. NA takes as its object of inquiry the naturally occurring, first person narrative of personal experience. Used in a wide range of studies of social interaction it has become a substantial contributor to social science research across disciplines (Riessman, 1993). Within social sciences, NA is used to explore the naturally occurring phenomena of communicative action in the construction of social and personal identity. In this context, it is the natural method of 'social constructionism', which holds that reality is socially constructed through the activities of communicating subjects.

Interest in the first person, oral narrative has also been introduced into psychology. It informs a strand of contemporary developmental theory that places interaction and language at the centre of the organization of cognition (Bruner and Haste, 1987; Bruner, 1990). For these developmental psychologists, the 'constitutive role [of language] in cognition rests not only on its power to differentiate concepts, but on its power to give "ontic" status to concepts and to make them accessible for transmission as part of culture' (1987, p. 15).

Other strands of psychology which incorporate analysis of narratives are the multiple code theory (Bucci, 1997) and Main's (1991) adult attachment interview (AAI). These researchers have integrated cognitive science with theories of narrative in order to operationalize theoretically derived psychological constructs in spoken language. Using a coding frame based on discursive qualities derived from the ordinary language philosopher Grice, the AAI has demonstrated convincingly that the capacity to produce a coherent first person narrative of experience is correlated with attachment style. These findings have begun to be incorporated into some psychotherapy research. Bucci and her collaborators, working within the framework of psychoanalytic theory, have empirically investigated links between psychoanalytic theory and contemporary theories of cognitive information processing. Narratives, according to multiple code theory, provide the bridge between emotional experiencing and cognitive 'processing'. This process is termed 'referential activity', and is characterized by four discursive qualities, similar to those coded for in the AAI: *concreteness*; *imagery*; *specificity*; and *clarity*. Originally Bucci (1997) devised a coding system for referential activity. Later, a computerized measure of referential activity, originally developed in collaboration with Mergenthaler (Mergenthaler and Bucci, 1999), revealed that narrative activity waxes and wanes in the therapeutic interaction. Some further discussion of this process in psychotherapy research can be found in Chapter 9.

Both the AAI and the multiple code theory use narrative as a linguistic marker for psychological processes that lie beneath the surface phenomena of language. While they can be and are used to study psychotherapy process, their fundamental objective is the elaboration of psychological, rather than discursive, phenomena. While acknowledging the importance of both methods, they will not be treated in detail in this chapter, which will focus on methods for the systematic analysis of discursive properties of the psychotherapeutic interaction.

Narrative analysis and psychotherapy research

Narrative analysis has only recently been introduced into psychotherapy process research. In the first comprehensive review of process research methods and findings, Toukmanian and Rennie (1992) reported that 'the use of the narrative approach is relatively new and untried' (p. 235). In the subsequent decade, interest in narrative analysis has been in evidence in a wide range of studies across different 'schools' of psychotherapy.

Early interest in narrative as an important component of the therapy process was introduced into psychoanalysis by Schafer (1981, 1992). In an early multi-disciplinary conference on narrative (1981), Schafer proposed that 'the analyst has only tellings and showings to interpret, that is, to retell along psychoanalytic lines' (p. 35). His fellow psychoanalyst Donald Spence (1982), an active researcher, made the distinction between 'historical truth' and 'narrative truth', casting the psychoanalytic process in terms of the search for coherent meaning in the form of narrative, rather than historical, 'truth'. In contrast with those seeking scientific validation, Schafer and Spence made the case for a constructivist understanding of the psychoanalytic process. For Spence, the method of free association reveals the development and evolution of a life story, with its stabilizing defence mechanisms. The psychoanalytic process, in this view, provides the opportunity for the analyst to 'destabilize' this narrative (Schafer, 1992).

In a general introduction to narrative in psychotherapy, McLeod (1997) provided a useful overview of the development of a narrative approach to understanding psychotherapy process. McLeod is a 'constructionist', in the sense outlined in the introduction to the discourse methods. He holds that meaning is constructed through human interaction. He makes the case for two levels of a critical narrative approach to the study of psychotherapy. On the level of the 'meta-narrative', he points out that the interpretive framework offered by the different 'schools' of psychotherapy can be taken as organizing narratives which enable the re-telling of a coherent life story. This view accords with Schafer's suggestion (1981) that the psychoanalytic 'schools' represent meta-narratives which can be used to reframe the stories told at the level of the therapist–patient discourse. On the level of the therapeutic interaction, narrative can be understood as the way in which the individual makes sense of his or her life and its experiences. Patients, according this theory, construct their sense of self through the telling of socially grounded narratives. The therapeutic process is one of re-framing the life narrative, and McLeod makes a helpful distinction between the overall 'therapeutic narrative' and the storytelling which makes up the therapeutic talk. In a more recent paper, McLeod (1999) applies the narrative social constructionist model to the concept of 'empathy', a generic concept long recognized in psychotherapy research as one which is consistently linked with good outcomes. He argues that a narrative constructionist approach can be employed to study the process, rather than the 'quantity' of empathy captured in conventional 'measures'. The most recent contribution to narrative and psychotherapy is an edited volume (Angus and McLeod, 2004) which brings current developments in practice and theory together with research in the field.

A third contribution to the study of narrative in psychotherapy process comes from cognitive narrative psychotherapy (Goncalves and Machado, 1999). They report on research which measured the effects of writing and talking about core experiences on both psychological and health measures (Pennebaker, 1993), and find support for a method of enhancing cognitive mastery through the use of narrative as a therapeutic tool. In their own research, they used an experimental approach to elicit significant life narratives, and analyzed them, using grounded theory (see Chapter 6), in order to construct a prototype narrative for each of four diagnostic groups. These prototype narratives are assumed to provide core structures on the basis of which 'further experiences are categorized, reordered and intentionalized' (1999, p. 1187). Other empirical studies using a narrative approach which spans a variety of approaches have also identified prototypical narratives which characterize different diagnostic groups (Beutler and Malik, 2002; von Wyl, 2000). Written self-characterization narratives (derived from Kelly's Personal Construct Therapy) were treated as discourse, in order to demonstrate how family patterns can be identified as family language 'codes' and transgenerational themes (Androutsopoulou, 2001). Kuhnlein (1999) used 'social science hermeneutics' to analyze post-treatment autobiographic narratives in order to reconstruct the transformation of person schemas. A study of narrative process in schizophrenia suggested that the facilitation of narrative coherence in psychosocial interventions may make a psychotherapeutic contribution to the reformation of a coherent internal dialogue and reduce confusion or rigidity (Lysaker *et al.*, 2001). The most recent developments in NA are included in an edited volume of contributions from the main contributors to the field (Angus and McLeod, 2004). This volume integrates clinical theory and practice.

The most recent developments in narrative analysis

As can be seen from this very brief overview, interest in narrative has been applied to psychotherapy theory and research across a variety of perspectives, from cognitive science to post-modern critical theories of psychotherapy as a social discourse. In this chapter, the focus will be specifically on some basic tools for the empirical analysis of psychotherapeutic interaction, suitable for the novice researcher. The basic concepts of narrative analysis of first person stories will be introduced, and several applications studied. Finally, an important contribution to narrative analysis, specific to the study of psychotherapy, which has been developed by Lynne Angus and collaborators (1994, 1999, 2004), will be introduced in detail.

Aspects of narrative analysis

Contemporary narrative analysis has its origins in the work of William Labov, a linguistics researcher who first became interested in the naturally occurring oral narrative. He began with a study of the non-standard English of Black and Puerto Rican children in New York City (Labov, 1972). He was interested to understand how children who, although they often were unable to read and write, were nonetheless very able speakers, and lively story tellers. Part of the study was to investigate the way in which the children used language to sustain their system of values. In a seminal study, Labov and Waletsky (1967) developed an analytic method for the study of oral narratives of personal experience. Although, the authors emphasize, 'the ultimate aims of our work … are concerned with effective communication' (p. 5), in this article, they concentrate on the structures of the narratives themselves. From the large number of data samples they studied (600 interviews in which the respondents told a story about their lives, in response to a question), they derived a basic framework which they found to be common to all the narratives: a temporal sequence with a temporal juncture – in its most simple form, 'First *x*, then *y*'. The narrative typically begins with an opening phrase or clause that *orients* the story to come. This is followed by a *complication* – the action that is the point of the story. This minimum condition for a narrative was not, however, found to be a sufficient framework for a complete narrative. A complete and meaningful narrative also includes an *evaluation*: a unit of meaning by which the narrator communicates his or her attitude to the story. Stories are not simply neutral reports; they are constructions by which tellers communicate their perceptions of the world, and their moral values. They are told to make a point. In a fully complex narrative, the evaluation may be followed by a functional element that returns the story to the present, and concludes the narrative event – a *coda* – which provides an external point of view on the narrative. In the following sample narrative from one of Labov's studies, all the elements of narrative structure are present.

Date sample 8.1

1   And when we got down there her brother turned to me an whispered 'I think she's dead'

2   And when we got down there I said to myself 'My god she's dead

3   And when we got down there, I thought, She's dead

4   And when we got down there I thought she was dead

5   Later the doctors told us she was close to death.

6   I think she must have been close to death

7   You know, in cases like this it's clear that she was likely not dead

---

This story begins with a preface which gives information about the content of the story to follow (line 1). The preface is also a micro-narrative in its own right: it contains a temporal juncture, and fully sets the scene. This sequence is repeated several times, building tension around the 'action' of the story – the finding of someone who appears to be dead. It makes use of the rhetorical device of repetition to heighten the suspense, and makes it into a good (exciting) story. It conveys the feeling state of the speaker at the time. In line 5, the speaker provides the temporal link ('later') which then moves the action forward, to the resolution of the story: she is not dead. The action is evaluated: This then leads to the concluding evaluation (line 7) – 'You know...' to provide the upshot of the story (she wasn't dead), and a *coda* which brings the story back to the present, and provides the hearer with an indication of the intended point of the story: appearances can be deceiving.

Labov and Waletsky's early research provided the foundation for the study of naturally occurring story telling. Its focus was on the linguistic structure of the narrative, rather than the interactional functions of story telling. The above story gives a good example that the story is not just a vehicle of information, but a vehicle of social and affective communication. Sacks (see Chapter 7) took this concept forward in looking at the interactional characteristics of story telling. He noted the phenomenon of 'second stories' – stories that are told in response to a first story – and co-constructed stories. In response to this story, for example, the hearer can now respond, perhaps with 'second story' that acknowledges the point of the story, and takes the discussion of these kinds of experiences forward. In an extended study of naturally occurring stories *in interaction*, Jefferson (1978) demonstrated that the story structure itself is embedded in the complex activities of interaction, and that the elements of structure may be used for a variety of interactional purposes in the context of on-going conversations. She demonstrates how coherent interaction is built, and a shared and meaningful interpersonal world sustained through the sequential flow of story telling in everyday conversations.

In their first study of the structure of narrative, Labov and Waletsky (1967) noted that 'a narrative that contains only an orientation, complicating action and result is not a complete narrative. It may carry out the referential function perfectly, and yet seem difficult to understand' (p. 28). In a contemporary formulation of his original theory, Labov (1997) has revised this earlier work in the light of emerging findings and debate within the field of narrative analysis. In a special edition of the *Journal of Narrative and Life History* (1997), a collection of recent work and a critique of the original theory, the importance of the interactional characteristics of stories are brought to the fore. Contemporary findings support the original identification of the importance of evaluation as a key element in narrative story telling, and find that in naturally occurring conversation (rather than in the semi-experimental question and answer format used by Labov and Waletsky) evaluation is embedded in all components of the narrative, and forms the core of the interactional organization of talk. (Edwards, 1997a; Goodwin, 1997; Lepper, 2000).

Evaluation may be studied in relation to the structure of the narrative, the content of the narrative and the sequential order of the story within the conversational interaction. Within the structure of the story, the story teller may suspend the main narrative action in order to incorporate an evaluative sequence, which may be a sub-narrative in its own right. These embedded evaluations, or sub-narratives, orient the hearer to the direction/point of the story and often serve to increase the suspense. From the perspective of interaction, evaluation may be embedded throughout the story, and provide the hearer with cues about how the narrative is to be evaluated, to illustrate how frightening/exciting it was, for example. Evaluation may be offered from outside the narrative – the teller steps outside the narrative in order to offer a comment on its validity, relevance, or quality. Early in his work, Labov noted that 'such external evaluation is common in therapeutic interviews, where it may form the main substance of an hour's discussion. The narratives themselves may serve only as a framework for the evaluation' (Labov and Waletsky, 1967, p. 371).

The sample text comes from a large study of psychodynamic psychotherapy sessions. It contains several extended narratives, with lengthy evaluation sequences, a sequence of narratives, second stories, and a complex set of evaluative sequences built by therapist and patient. The text has already been introduced in Chapter 6, and an exercise undertaken which illustrated how grounded theory could be used to analyze the categories, and interactional processes of this exchange. Here, we return to the same text, in order to explore what analysis of the narrative structure of the event can add to the understanding of the therapist/patient interaction.

Data sample 8.2

1. A: mm. what did you think of your mother calling G immature?
2. P: um, well, she never met G, so I didn't think she was misjudging her, I mean, she was, but I just thought that um she was saying something without knowing all the facts. (mumble) I, I don't, I don't really totally discount my mother's knowledge of, of people, she's very perceptive. I was in a very uncomfortable position with a girl two years ago, when I was a sophomore. the second half of the year. and uh (sigh) I had gotten in way over my head with this girl. who was not really all there, psychologically, and uh, this girl really wanted to get married. she's a year and a half older than I am, and somehow talked me into promising to marry her at some future

time. and well basically, the whole thing was sexual, because uh, she was really sexually experienced and I was a virgin when I met her. and she, well, I mean it was, it was a fantastic thing for me, I felt so loved and everything, and so I, I, I was really young at the time, and uh, anyway, things were getting, were getting worse and worse, and uh at one point, I had brought her home for a weekend, and after the weekend, my mother said, 'oh, boy, look at this girl, she's not for you, she's not all there, she's uh, she's talking you into marrying her, and you don't really love her.' and everything, and I was furious with my mother. how could she dare say this to me? but in the end, she was right, one hundred percent right. and she really opened my eyes, and uh I had to break off with this girl.

3. A: you had to?

4. P: well, I had to because uh I was in no position to want to marry her.

5. A: and you do have a tendency to depend on people yet at the same time, while you have the tendency to depend on people, you also have a tendency to doubt whether they really know you so maybe – maybe the advice isn't so good. – it's not really ah, maybe it's you being forced to do what someone else thinks is right and not what you think is right.

6. P: yes. those were almost the exact same words I used um. – it was this summer. I, I, well, I'll tell you the story in a second but, I often do have the feeling, and I think I just realized recently, like this summer, that I let other people make up my mind for me. and the example, the thing was, I don't know if I told you. I travelled in Europe this summer, I was in L and I have relatives in E who I have never met but we had their address and I went to visit them, and they told me that I had other relatives in E and that they think that, they thought that, since I was in L already I should go up and uh, and meet the other relatives. well, I didn't really have much of a desire to go to, but I said, 'okay'. and it's a really long trip from, from L to E and I really didn't want to go, and I realized like the day afterwards, that the whole reason I had agreed to go was just because my other relatives thought that I should do it, and I was letting them make up my mind for me. And I called them up and said I can't go, and I was really proud of myself for doing that. But it was also, um, you know, it's not such a big thing but, it helped. It was like, what do you call it, a turning point when you realize something and, and I realized then that, uh, that I really do have this tendency.

In the patient's first story, we find a story with the overall structure: I had a girlfriend; I brought her home; then my mother disapproved of her; I was furious with my mother, but then I decided she was right. Embedded within the overall structure are several smaller narratives, which elaborate each part of the sequence. The evaluation – the point of the story ('my mother was 100% right') – is then taken up by the therapist in a 'second story' (interpretation) which has the basic form of a narrative: first, you depend on people, then you doubt, with its evaluation, 'maybe you [are] being forced to do what other people think is right not what you think is right'. This is followed by the patient's next story, which provides a response to, and confirmation of, the therapist's evaluation.

The hierarchical model of interpretation

Labov's approach to the analysis of narratives was generalized for all kinds of spoken narratives, or 'story telling', but has also been applied specifically to psychotherapy discourse in a collaborative single case study of the interaction in a psychodynamic psychotherapy (Labov and Fanshel, 1977). In this study of an entire psychotherapy, Labov collaborated with clinican David Fanshel in order to 'search for a definition of this situation as a whole and to discover everything we can that is relevant to this particular situation' (1977, p. 26). They sought to develop a method for the study of interaction that would address the relationship between the discourse and the actions of the therapist and the patient: 'What is the therapist trying to do in this conversational encounter? On the other hand, what is the patient doing or not doing that the therapist must be aware of?' (p. 28). Their emphasis is on communicative *action* and how it is interpreted by the interactants.

In this ambitious study, Labov and Fanshel tackled a key methodological problem for the researcher in approaching psychotherapy discourse: how to find a means of ordering the data, and identifying patterns of meaning within the text. Looking at individual turns, or at micro-sequences of the interaction, can tell us much about the ways in which the speakers are relating to each others' communicative actions. Linking text and non-verbal cues at successive moments of the interaction, they sought to link these static 'snapshots' of moments of action into larger units, including moments before and after, enriching the developing picture of the on-going therapeutic interaction. Their primary concern was 'with the mechanism of discourse as it flows from minute to minute, seeing what makes it hang together, and what makes it fall apart' (1977, p. 69).

In order to achieve their multi-level analysis of the full therapy they set out to analyze the session in terms of the 'rules of interpretation and production' that had been identified more generally through research into ordinary, everyday talk (for example, see Chapter 7). They specified several kinds of 'speech acts', which they followed systematically through the sessions: requests; challenges; coherence; narratives; and sequencing. Following these trails, they intensively examined five interactional episodes, chosen on the basis that '(1) they deal with a distinct topic drawn from everyday life or from emotional issues, and (2) the major initiative for conversation is the therapist's intervention in this area' (1977, p. 330). Then by connecting the episodes into larger units, they built a picture of the therapeutic interaction, attempting to address the question: What is the therapist trying to do?

The strategy of this study was to move beyond the micro-analysis of single exchanges, and to build an interpretive study of communicative interaction which would take into account the developing and building relationship of two speakers. Their method employs a sampling strategy, which is used by other methods of discourse analysis in order to generalize from single examples to more general findings. In this case, they sampled text from the perspective of discourse features. A question that arises, then, is to what extent these findings are clinically significant. How can they be linked to clinical theory? A weakness of this study, from the point of view of psychotherapy process research, is that it provides some interesting findings about psychotherapy discourse, but is silent on the understanding of, or application to, clinically significant issues. The contemporary researcher, whether novice or experienced, can go back to the content and method of these studies for a starting point from which to build links to clinical theory and practice.

The narrative process coding system

The narrative process coding system (NPCS) was developed by Lynne Angus (Angus and Hardtke, 1994; Angus *et al.*, 1999), in collaboration with Heidi Levitt and Karen Hardtke, with the specific aim of analyzing narrative processes in psychotherapy texts. The method evolved from Angus' original interest in the function of metaphor in the therapist's empathic attunement to the patient's emotional state (Angus, 1992). Unlike Labov's approach to narrative analysis, the NPCS is designed to identify specific characteristics of psychotherapy discourse, in terms of both content and structure, and to link them to clinical process and theory through what the authors term the 'Narrative Processes Model', which draws on dialectical-constructionist assumptions (Angus *et al.*, 2004) and Bruner's (1990) narrative developmental theory. The model holds that 'all forms of successful psychotherapy entail the articulation, elaboration and transformation of the client's self-told tale or macro-narrative' (Angus *et al.*, 1999).

The NPCS uses a coding approach. However, it is included within this chapter on discourse methods, rather than with the coding methods, because it is based on the assumption that 'all forms of successful psychotherapy entail the articulation, elaboration and transformation of the client's self-told life story or macro-narrative' (1999, p. 1256). Unlike the core conflictual relationship theme instrument (see Chapter 3), which uses conceptually driven coding elements to identify meaning units, the NPCS coding system allows meaning units to emerge from the therapeutic discourse, in a manner similar to grounded theory (see Chapter 6). It links narrative discourse theoretically with the psychotherapeutic process, and takes into account all the speakers engaged in the therapeutic interaction. It therefore accommodates all three aspects of narrative analysis: content, structure and interaction. While the NCPS is based on a theory of clinical process and outcome related to the therapeutic discourse, it is not linked to any of the specific clinical models, and can therefore be used in the empirical analysis of any psychotherapeutic modality, including both dyadic and group therapies. Its coding strategy enables it to address both the micro-processes of discourse as well as larger, comparative strategies using statistical techniques.

Analyzing narratives using the narrative process coding system

The NCPS method proceeds in two phases:

1. the identification of **topic segments** (content shifts in the talk);
2. the identification of **narrative process modes** within the topic segments.

The analytic process begins with the identification of a topic segment. Topic segments have been found to range in length from 10 to 133 transcript lines, with an average of 30 lines. A minimum of 4 sentences is needed to code accurately. Each topic segment is identified and named in terms of its:

- *relationship focus*: who the topic is addressing (self, other, self in relation to other);
- *issue focus*: what is the key issue being addressed?

The topic segments are then analyzed for:

- external narrative process sequences (description of past, present and/or future events, actual or imagined);
- internal narrative process sequences (subjective/experiential description of experience);
- reflexive narrative process sequences (analysis of current, past and/or future events)

Finally, each topic segment is examined and coded in terms of shifts between external, internal and reflexive sequences within each segment.

Identifying topic segments

Topic shifts are marked by a change in subject that occurs during the talk. A topic shift may be initiated by any speaker in the talk. In data sample 8.2, for example, a topic shift occurs when the therapist, in response to the client's story about his relationship with his mother, changes the topic to his 'tendency to depend on people' (turn 5). This topic segment can then be further categorized in terms of:

- a domain shift (a new content area, or a new relationship focus)

  or

- a facet shift (a detailed elaboration of different facets of a general content area that remains within the same relationship focus).

The therapist's topic shift in this case constitutes a facet shift: it takes the general topic (relationship to mother) and provides an elaboration of the previous narrative, in terms of the relationship of self to other. It is a more general narrative about the client's relationship of self to other. This prompts a second story from the client.

Since topic segments are interactional units, changes in either domain or facet may be initiated by any speaker. There are several discursive markers which aid the researcher in identifying topic segments:

- questions posed by the therapist;
- new topic or relationship focus introduced by the patient or therapist;
- a change in verb tense which signals the elaboration of a specific content area;
- a prolonged pause initiated by a speaker.

The end of a topic segment may be marked by:

- an affirmation of understanding by any speaker;
- a pause in the talk;
- a summary of the preceding talk.

Identify the topic segments in the sample text.
What are the topic issues?
What is the relationship focus?
What is the sequence of domain and facet shifts across the two speakers?
Do the speakers collaborate to generate an overall topic?

Identifying narrative process sequences

Once the topic segments have been identified, the researcher can then proceed with the second phase of the analysis: the identification of the narrative process sequences, which structure the talk. These, like topic segments, may be identified by characteristic markers:

Markers for external narrative sequences
- description of personal memories, probably signalled by a change in verb tense;
- concrete examples used to demonstrate issues;
- description of either a specific event or an event that is a general description or composite of many specific events;
- information giving or providing instructional guidelines.

Markers for internal narrative sequences
- therapist asks how the patient feels;
- frequent use of emotion words;
- non-verbal emotional expression;
- metaphoric descriptions of experiential states;
- long pauses in which there is a search for words to articulate an experiential state.

Markers for reflexive narrative sequences
- patient reflexively examines and/or evaluates the intentions behind and reasons for emotions and actions undertaken by self or others in personal events;
- patient plans future alternatives;
- patient discusses patterns in his or her own behaviour and/or that of others;
- self-questioning (I wonder whether, I realize, It could have been...).

Referring once again to data sample 8.2, in the first turn of talk, the client focus is specifically an external narrative focus: it provides a past tense narrative of important people and events in his life; it is a concrete and specific description of a specific event. Then there is a change.

EXERCISE 8.2

Identify the second narrative process sequence in the sample text.
What type of narrative process sequence is it?
What is the response to this sequence?
What more can now be said about the therapeutic interaction?

Close investigation of this fragment of therapeutic discourse gives some idea of how much complexity is embedded in each segment of discourse. Even without the overall context of the therapist–client interaction, some important dynamics can be identified through the examination of content and process in the therapeutic dialogue. One reading of this excerpt – at the level of sequencing – is of a client and therapist who are closely in touch with the building dialogue. The elaboration of the content (identified by topic sequences) is closely aligned from turn to turn. The talk moves between concrete (external narrative) and interpretive (reflexive narrative) and back to an external narrative (the client's second story) which confirms the therapist's intervening reflexive narrative with a concrete and vivid, external narrative. This in turn leads to an internal narrative sequence which reflects the therapist intervention.

A second reading of the interplay of content and process in the entire sequence can now be seen to reveal another level of the interaction. The client describes, through his first external narrative, a relationship episode with his mother, which the therapist then interprets with a second, reflective meta-narrative communication, suggesting that perhaps he gets 'forced to do what someone else thinks is right' in other relationship contexts as well. To this the patient replies with an affirmative ('yes, those were almost the exact same words I used'), and another external narrative, rich in content, which is offered as an illustration of the point. He completes his narrative with a reflexive narrative sequence which confirms the interactional agreement: 'I realized that, uh, that I really do have this tendency'. Is this an example of his compliance (embedded in the topic content) enacted in the interactional sequence? The answer to this clinical question would involve a sampling procedure across the course of the therapy – possibly one such as Labov and Fanshel devised for their study. The occurrence of exchanges of this kind – and any change could then be systematically studied. In this way, the micro-analysis of single examples can be built up into a generalizable analysis of a case, or set of cases.

Published applications of the NPCS method

The NPCS provides a means for the analysis of two aspects of the therapeutic process: the evolution of patterns of narrative process sequences, over time, within and between sessions; and the evolution of topics within and between sessions. The coding strategy enables the quantification of these discursive features, allowing for the systematic comparison of different therapeutic models, comparison of therapist and client contributions to the therapeutic interaction, using standard statistical tools.

In a recent study (Levitt *et al.*, 2000) the NPCS was used to explore the use of, and evolution of, the metaphor of 'burden' in a study of process-experiential psychotherapy for depression (Greenberg and Watson, 1998). Earlier single case studies have demonstrated that successful clients make use of metaphor within the therapeutic relationship, while unsuccessful clients tend to remain stuck with the metaphors they bring to the therapy, and are unable to develop or transform them (Angus, 1996). This study sought to explore differences in the use of metaphor between two patients, one of whom improved, and one who didn't. From a sample of 34 participants in a study of depression, one good outcome and one poor outcome case were selected for intensive analysis. In one case, 14 transcripts were available for analysis, in the other, 19 were available. The research process involved identifying metaphors around the theme of 'burden' (found in previous studies of depression to be an important organizing theme). The transcripts were coded for narrative process sequences using the NPCS, and for levels of experiencing, using the experiencing scale developed by Klein *et al.* (1986). The identified segments of text in which the 'burden' metaphor was identified were then compared with the NPCS coding, and it was found that there was a significant difference between the two cases. The good outcome case employed 'burden' metaphors in internal narrative sequences, marked by high levels of experiencing, while in the poor outcome case, the metaphor was associated with external narratives, where the metaphor was used to illustrate the state of mind of the client, rather than to experience it. Although the study was limited by the small sample, the authors conclude that both the process and the content analysis showed significant differences in the two cases. This enabled them to make a tentative recommendation to clinicians, that a focus on clients' feelings through attention to metaphor in the context of their lives may be a helpful strategy when working with the depressed client.

Example of a practitioner project using NPCS

A student research project sought to explore the dilemma facing a novice clinician: what should the therapist be 'doing' to help the client? What is the effect of the therapist's interventions on the therapeutic process? The student sought to explore her question, and enhance her clinical learning, by using the NPCS to analyze the process of one of her own (psychodynamic) sessions with a depressed client. She acknowledged the limitations of coding her own session (and importing her own experiences into the coding process), but felt that this limitation was more than offset by the clinical learning she gained.

She designed her analysis to address the question in three steps:

1. coding the session using the NPCS;
2. coding the topic segments for therapist interventions, using the framework developed by Stiles *et al.* (1995);
3. relating the therapist interventions to shifts in the narrative process modes.

She first identified all the topic segments, finding this somewhat less straightforward than she expected. She acknowledged that for a more extensive and formal project, working with others on the coding would be necessary. Nevertheless, she was able to create a coding table which she felt described the evolution of the topics over the session. She found, in coding the narrative process sequences against the topic segments, that some narrative sequences straddled two topic segments. She decided to count these sequences as one. Developing several graphs to represent her coding analysis, she demonstrated that the narrative process sequences changed from predominantly external in the early phase of the session to predominantly reflexive towards the end of the session. The analysis revealed that the client was more active at the beginning of the session, and the therapist more active at the end, while therapist and client were equally active in initiating narrative sequences in the middle phase of the session.

In the second step of the analysis, analyzing the therapist interventions, she adapted the Stiles rating scale to develop a coding instrument based on six scales, with sub-categories. She found that there was no opportunity in the Stiles rating scale for identifying 'mistakes' – i.e., mishearings or misunderstandings. She added this category to her coding frame, and discovered such a therapist intervention in one turn. Building a graph to represent the shifts in intervention type across the session, she found a clear increase in interpretive interventions. Finally, in step 3, by relating the therapist intervention code to the narrative sequences coded in step 1, she was able to demonstrate a clear relationship between the therapist's supportive interventions and the developing external narrative sequences, interspersed with emotion-directed supportive interventions which increase following a 'mistake' in the middle of the session. She comments about this interactional event that this client is inclined to feel misunderstood. This event is followed by a higher incidence of interpretive intervention, and a higher level of reflective narrative sequences, towards the end of the session. The relationship of intervention to narrative process is represented in a table which assembles all the information from steps 1, 2 and 3. The student noted that her findings were consistent with other findings derived from the use of the NPCS, regarding the characteristic pattern of psychodynamic psychotherapy, which tends to be characterized by high levels of external and reflective narrative process sequences. These represent the psychodynamic strategy of engendering new perspectives on interpersonal conflict and relationships through interpretation of life events and memories.

A statistical analysis was not used in this single session, single case study. Nevertheless, use of tables and graphs was adequate to demonstrate the changing relationship between topic, narrative sequence and therapist intervention. The student concluded:

> It has been an interesting project and has helped me a lot to understand the dynamics of a therapy session, and the complex interaction of the client and the therapist. I think what I have really learnt is that therapy is a co-construct, a working together within limits of tolerance, understanding and shared experience. There are aims and choices of activity, but they can only be employed within a shared space that is created by two people interacting. I think, as a training therapist, I was unconsciously looking for certainties to hang on to, I was looking for 'laws representing predictable relationships between antecedents and consequences' (Toukmanian and Rennie, 1992, p. 246). I have found the world of therapy a far richer place.

Conclusion

Narrative analysis is a not a single method, but an approach to the analysis of everyday and therapeutic discourses which encompasses a variety of perspectives. The focus of an analysis may be on content, on narrative structures, or on the interactional processes which evolve in the course of a dialogue. While some of the methods throw one or other of these perspectives into sharper focus, all of those working with narrative agree that the integration of these three domains of narrative is required for a fully developed analysis of narrative processes. All the methods proceed inductively from identification of units of discourse to the development of generalizations about the nature of the text or texts under scrutiny, although the different methods embed different strategies for the selection of text for analysis. Elements of quantification can be built into the methods, enabling generalization on the basis of systematically selected data from a larger dataset. Narrative analysis provides a flexible research approach, which can be used for a wide variety of purposes at different levels of discourse, from small units of interaction to larger, comparative research designs.

SUGGESTIONS FOR FURTHER READING

Angus, L. and McLeod, J. (2004) *The Handbook of Narrative and Psychotherapy: Practice, theory, research.* London: Sage.

Angus, L.E., Hardtke, K. and Levitt, H. (1999) 'The narrative processes coding system manual: research applications and implications for psychotherapy practice', *Journal of Clinical Psychology*, 55: 1255–70.

Journal of Narrative and Life History, 7 (1997). Special Edition on narrative analysis.

McLeod, J. (1997) *Narrative and Psychotherapy.* London: Sage.

Toukmanian, S.G. and Rennie, D.L. (eds) (1992) *Psychotherapy Process Research: Paradigmatic and narrative approaches.* Newbury Park: Sage.

CHAPTER 9

The therapeutic cycles model (TCM)

Introduction

This chapter introduces the therapeutic cycles model (TCM), which was developed by Erhard Mergenthaler, a researcher with a background in linguistics and computer science who collaborates with psychotherapy colleagues at the University of Ulm. The model evolved out of a series of experimental content analyses, using a statistical modelling method to explore the frequencies of target words (Mergenthaler and Kachele, 1996). The discourse methods examined in the previous chapters would be characterized as 'qualitative' methods. Their analytic strategies rely on direct analysis of the text, and their focus of attention is on meaning, or meaning-making. The TCM method, by contrast, is the most quantitative process research method studied in this book. Its primary strategy is to produce a statistically derived map of the text of a psychotherapy session, in the form of a graph which can then be examined in much the same way as any map would be used. It enables the researcher to locate a place of clinical interest. The TCM is included with the group of 'discourse methods' because its object of analysis meets the fundamental definition of discourse: 'a connected series of utterances, forming a unit for analysis'.

The TCM differs in another way both from the other discourse methods introduced in this part of the book, and from the computerized analysis packages which are discussed in Part IV. Though based on computerized data analysis, unlike other computerized methods, it is not a theory-neutral tool used for the purpose of manipulating data. At the same time, it is unlike the other discourse methods introduced in the previous chapters, which have nothing to say about events specifically of clinical interest. The TCM is grounded in clinical theory. It is intended to provide a tool for mapping clinical process and change by means of identifying linguistic patterns expressed in the therapeutic discourse. The basic TCM unit of analysis is the text of a single session. The resulting graph can be used to identify within-session clinical features. In addition, TCM analysis can set the individual session into a larger unit of analysis –

for example, an entire therapy. It could be compared to a geological map: it reveals the surface features of underlying, and not immediately visible, phenomena of interest. It provides the researcher with a powerful tool for surveying large datasets, and identifying clinical features of interest for in-depth, or comparative, analysis in conjunction with other methods.

The development of the therapeutic cycles model

The TCM was originally created 'to develop a computer-aided system that is able to identify key moments in transcripts from psychoanalytic sessions and to provide an adequate theory of change' (Mergenthaler and Kachele, 1996, p. 1306). It was anticipated from the beginning that the method would be applicable to other forms of psychotherapy, as long as the focus was primarily on verbal interaction. It is built on computerized 'dictionaries' of words which were chosen as markers for 'abstract' talk, and for 'emotion' talk occurring in the therapeutic dialogue. The choice of these two kinds of words was based in clinical theory and practice. The experience of emotion is recognized as central to most psychotherapeutic methods. In the TCM, experience of emotion is assumed to be represented by the presence of marker words for emotion in the transcript. In addition, it is assumed that the process of reflection on experience is another of the primary constituents of therapeutic process and change. The identification of 'abstraction' words is intended to provide markers for those parts of the clinical process in which reflection is taking place. It is assumed by the TCM model that it is the conjunction of emotion and abstraction (reflection on experienced emotion) that marks key moments in the psychotherapy process.

The dictionaries were built, and then applied to a variety of different kinds of texts by multiple raters in order to test their reliability. The marker words are not necessarily based on overt content, but on their likely occurrence in discursive units which are characterized as 'emotion' talk or 'abstract' talk. The first dictionary created by this process was in German. Later, the same method was applied to other languages, and dictionaries for English, Spanish and Italian, as well as German, are now in use.

The TCM method is supported by the 'CM' software, which calculates the occurrence of marker words in texts. The transcribed session is imported into the program, and a few alternatives are offered. The user may choose the length of the 'word block' – the basic unit of calculation. Word blocks may be of any length, but in practice it has been established

Figure 9.1 Therapeutic cycle model

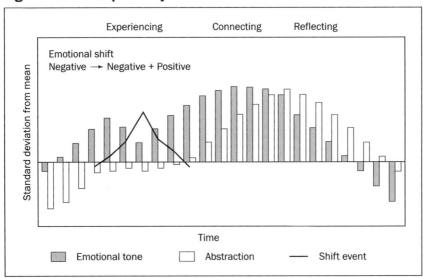

that word blocks of 150 words length give the clearest results. The user may also choose to calculate the speech patterns for each speaker, and for all speech taken together. The proportion of words for each speaker can also be calculated. A further calculation performed by the CM software represents the fluctuation of positive and negative emotion tone. For this measure, the 'emotion' dictionary is divided into those words which denote positive or negative tone. The output of this calculation appears on the graph as a black line. Once all the parameters are selected, the calculation proceeds automatically. The software generates a graph, an 'ideal' version of which looks like Figure 9.1.

The vertical axis of the table represents standard deviations from the mean expected incidence of the TCM dictionary marker words. The horizontal axis represents word blocks – the division of the text into pre-defined blocks of words, the length of which can be changed for the purposes of the research. Visible in each cell are two bars which represent the different kinds of marker words in the dictionaries: abstraction (white), and emotion tone (grey). The mean is represented by 0 on the vertical axis with $+(1-3)$ above and $-(1-3)$ below, representing standard deviations above and below the mean.

In the idealized version of the cycles above, the rising and falling of the two kinds of marker words, representing changes in the discourse of the text, is clearly visible. There are four possible combinations, and these have been given names according to their possible interpretations:

- both abstract and emotion words are below the mean (low activity, or 'relaxing')
- abstraction above and emotion below the mean ('reflecting')
- abstraction below and emotion above the mean ('experiencing')
- both abstraction and emotion above the mean, ('connecting')

The TCM assumes that the emergence of emotion/abstraction patterns of discourse which result in cycles are not random events, but are a periodic process which is a marker for underlying mental and biological processes, such as affect regulation.

Interpreting the CM graph

Interpretation of the CM graph begins with the identification of 'cycles'. The patterns of emotion and abstraction can be considered for each speaker, and for all speakers together. Each of these possibilities is expressed in a different graph on the print out. Cycles may appear in the discourse of any of the speakers, or in the graph of the combined talk of speakers. If transcripts for an entire therapy are available, a further possibility is to aggregate all the sessions in a therapy, and to calculate the emotion/abstraction patterns across the entire therapy. Typically, it has been found, one cycle will be completed in the full course of short-term therapies. In the TCM analysis of the aggregated sessions of 4 year psychoanalytic psychotherapy, several cycles were found to occur.

A 'cycle' is defined as the sequence preceding and following a 'connecting' word block in which at least one of the bars exceeds +1 standard deviation. The beginning of the cycle is marked by the first block after a 'relaxing' block, and the end by the last block before the next 'relaxing' block.

Through the application of the CM to many transcripts, it has been observed that cycles do not necessarily appear in every session. Application of the CM to multi-party talk reveals that although the cycles may not exist for individual speakers, they may occur for the combined discourse of all the speakers.

The TCM software can be used to analyze psychotherapy texts quickly and easily. As a result, large numbers of sessions can be analyzed and compared for these features of the therapeutic discourse. The first research task becomes: What do the cycles say about the therapeutic process? How can they be interpreted?

In practice, analyzing real psychotherapy texts produces a far less perfect result, which looks more like Figure 9.2.

Figure 9.2   CM graph, session 4

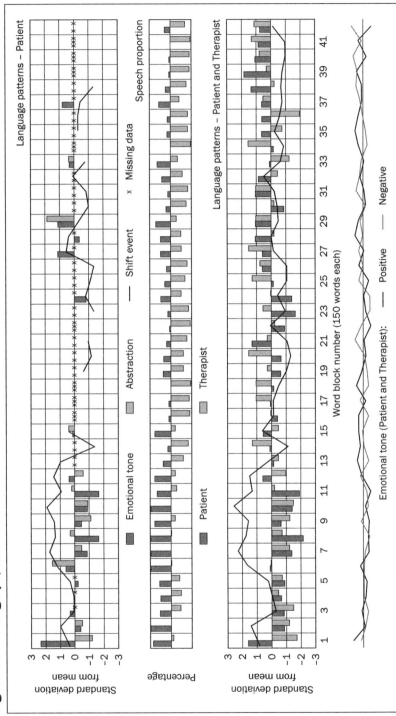

The print out in Figure 9.2 shows four kinds of information available to the researcher. The first graph represents the ebb and flow of marker words for abstract and emotion in the 4th session of a brief psychodynamic psychotherapy, for the patient's speech only. This table is based on 150 word blocks (WB). Clearly visible are two peaks of high incidence of both abstract and emotion words. These are 'connecting' word blocks. There are many word blocks which are marked by an X, indicating missing data. There aren't enough words spoken by the patient in these word blocks to be reliably compared. The second graph, which represents the proportion of words used by patient and therapist in the course of the session, by word block, explains why. The proportion of words spoken by the patient is on the top row, and those of the therapist on the bottom row. Notice how active the therapist is in this session. The lower graph gives the graph of emotion and abstraction words for both therapist and patient speech combined. Notice that the pattern for the two speakers differs considerably from that for the patient only. Three cycles are identifiable: the first is identified by finding, in WB 21, a 'connecting' word block (both emotion and abstraction are positive, with one measure above $+1$), and identifying the first 'relaxing' block before and after it: the cycle begins in WB 14, and continues until WB 21. A second cycle begins in WB 25, and continues until WB 29, followed by the 'relaxing' block at WB 30. Then a third cycle immediately begins again, continuing until the final WB 42. This could also be interpreted as one long cycle with a brief pause.

The black line which crosses the graph represents the level of narrative (or referential) activity. The session is characterized by a high level of narrative in the first 13 word blocks, which then falls away for the rest of the session, where the cycles are at their highest. This is a common feature of the TCM pattern for psychodynamic sessions: a cycle is typically preceded by a high level of narrative activity, which falls away as a cycle begins. The linear chart shows the relative relationship of positive to negative emotion tone, also calculated by word block. It has to be read in conjunction with the graphs. Emotion tone is a measure of the density of positive and negative emotion words within a word block. Mergenthaler provisionally defines good therapeutic moments, leading to insight, as those in which a connecting moment is accompanied by a shift from negative to positive emotion tone. This hypothesis remains to be tested.

The graph for all 8 sessions of this therapy was also calculated (Figure 9.3). Notice that it has one long cycle, which occurs at sessions 3 and 4.

Figure 9.3   CM graph, all sessions

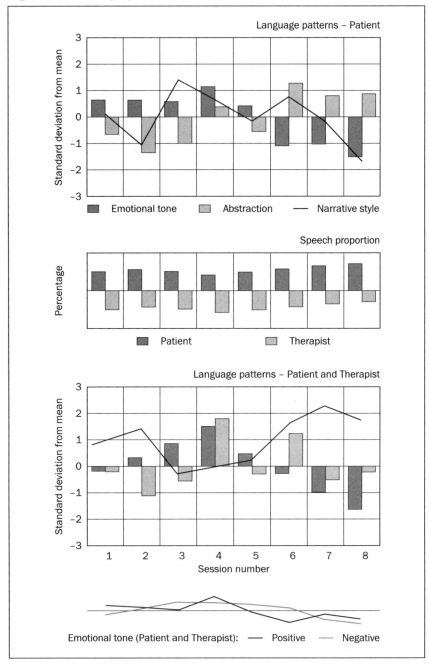

Findings from studies using the TCM

The usefulness of the TCM rests in its ability to enable the investigator reliably to identify clinical phenomena of interest. The first studies testing the TCM were designed to assess its reliability. Mergenthaler analyzed a large dataset from the Penn Psychotherapy Study (Luborsky and Crits-Christoph, 1990), which consisted of 73 psychodynamic treatments. The study was designed to test his hypothesis that the incidence of the phenomenon of 'connecting' would be higher for improved patients than for those who weren't; and that 'connecting' would be more likely to appear towards the later stages of the treatment. This hypothesis was borne out by the analysis. In a single case study of one of the sessions, TCM analysis revealed that while the emotion and abstraction patterns for therapist and patient taken together achieved a high degree of convergence, when analyzed separately they were significantly different from the mean in the rest of the dataset, with a significantly higher emotion score for the patient, and higher abstraction score for the therapist. This finding suggests that the therapist adapted to the specific discursive presentation of the patient, and supports a linguistic assumption that the patient and therapist form a linguistic unit with its own set of characteristics. Two later studies further explore this assumption (see the example in the next section).

In other studies, the TCM has been used to identify discourse features of the clinical interaction, and compare them with findings from a variety of other methods. TCM patterns were compared with analysis of video recorded data (including the above 28 session therapy) which were analyzed using Horowitz's behavioural rating method, the States of Mind Model (Horowitz, 1987). Significant correlations were found (Mergenthaler and Horowitz, 1994). More recently, TCM was used in a study of the Adult Attachment Interviews (Main, 1991) in order to explore the relationship between discourse characteristics of the interviews, using the Computerized Referential Activity function of the TCM, and emotion/abstraction patterns. The interviews studied were of a non-clinical sample of 40 subjects, matched to eliminate any socio/demographic differences. Twenty subjects from this set were identified as representing the 'secure' attachment style, 10 as 'dismissing', and 10 as 'preoccupied'. The study demonstrated that the computerized text analysis was able reliably to distinguish between the different attachment styles.

The assumption that the TCM can be applied to a range of models of psychotherapy has been tested in two studies, one of which applied the TCM to transcripts of a series of cognitive behavioural therapy (CBT) sessions. The results of this study demonstrated that the cycles appear as consistently in CBT as in psychodynamic therapeutic discourse. However, it was discovered that the cycles in CBT assumed a different shape than those of the psychodynamic transcripts. Rather than starting with a 'relaxing' pattern (low abstraction and low emotion), they typically started with a high 'reflection' (high abstraction, low emotion) pattern. Semerari *et al.* (2003a and b) concluded that this difference represents the different discursive pattern of the method itself: where in psychodynamic psychotherapy, the process of 'free association' provides the basis for the emergence of clinically significant actions, in CBT, it is the therapist who structures the interaction with active questioning, and initiates the clinical process.

Application of the TCM to group therapy transcripts (Fontao and Mergenthaler, 2002) confirmed that the TCM may also be used to analyze multi-party talk. This study discovered that although the cycles did not emerge in the talk of individual participants, the analysis of the talk of all participants taken together revealed the presence of cycles over the whole therapy. This finding supports the theoretical proposition that the overall pattern of combined speech of the participants represents collaborative work on the part of the speakers. In a further study of this data, using a single session, Lepper and Mergenthaler (2005) tested the hypothesis that the presence of a cycle for the group as a whole might be a marker for the clinical construct of 'group cohesion'. For a discussion of this study, see the example at the end of Part IV.

The TCM is intended to provide a means for the process researcher to identify significant clinical moments reliably, and to deal with large amounts of clinical data which can be easily identified through the analysis of transcribed sessions. The regularly occurring features of the cycles have been identified as common to all the methods of psychotherapy studied, and enable the researcher to ask questions of data, and to identify relevant text with a view to developing a systematic understanding of psychotherapeutic process. The method is suitable for projects of all sizes: a single session case study can be a valuable way of testing an hypothesis (Lepper and Mergenthaler, 2005) or a full scale case study of an entire therapy. Alternatively, the method can be used to compare an identified clinical feature across different therapies, using the TCM to identify and locate specific clinical events across a large number of transcripts.

Application of the TCM: an exercise

Here is an example of a project a novice researcher might undertake. Examine the graph of patient and therapist speech for session 4 in

Figure 9.2. At word block 30, there is a 'relaxing' block, which immediately follows, and is followed by, a 'connecting' word block. A question of interpretation is raised: Was this really two cycles, or one cycle which paused, or broke down? Now the researcher can go to the text in order to examine it more closely, and develop a hypothesis about what this feature in the table might signify. The text for word block 30 is given in data sample 9.1 (notice the numbers in parentheses: the CM program inserts the number of the word block after each 150 words, or whatever number of words the investigator has requested). What hypothesis might be considered about the therapeutic interaction at this point in the session? How could this hypothesis then be tested?

Data sample 9.1

A: I suppose there's lots of threatening and, frightening feelings around, that er. and these threatening (29) and frightening feelings are brought out. particularly when we try, to understand what's going on between us. because it's here and now, and it's it's always easier to talk about things that happened a long time ago or, happening outside the room, than it is to, look together at what's happening and what what we're making each other feel here. (pause 14 sec)

P: I am, I am a vulnerable person.

A: mm-hm

P: very. (pause 17 sec) I suppose I don't want to lose the safeness.

A: mm-hm

P: (pause 6 sec) that the person I really am you won't like. (pause 6 sec)

A: because that felt like it was the the lesson of your childhood. because the person that you really are, no-one would like.

P: sorry, I?

A: it just seemed to me that the fear that the person you really are no-one will like, is, something very important that goes back a long way it's very (30), it's, you've always had the kind of be a nice person, and not show something inside that people wouldn't like.

One obvious feature of the discourse in this segment of the text is the introduction of the notion of the 'feelings in the room'. This is followed by a 14 second pause – a very long pause in a dialogue – and soon after by two more pauses. It appears that there is considerable disturbance of the interaction following this therapist intervention. The great strength of the TCM method is that it enables easy identification and comparison of similar features in a large number of texts. An investigator could decide to search out and compare all comparable pauses in cycles across a single therapy (there were quite a few in the 8 sessions of this therapy, for example). Two questions to be asked of the data might be: What characteristics do these events share? How often are such events related to therapist interventions? Should a pattern emerge, a hypothesis might be developed, and then tested using other texts from other therapies to compare events.

Strengths and weaknesses of TCM

The TCM is an automated program, which can be downloaded for use at no charge, upon registration with the *Sektion Informatik der Psychotherapie* of the University of Ulm (http://sip.medizin.uni-ulm.de/informatik/software. html). It is easy to use – simple entry of data into the package is all that is needed to generate the graphs, with all their information components. As the only data analysis package designed specifically for the content analysis of psychotherapy texts, it can provide information that no other analytic tool can. For the clinician researcher who wants to study the underpinning communicative processes of psychotherapy, the TCM provides a powerful analytic tool for mapping the data, and the basis for a structured comparative analysis of process events within and between sessions and therapies.

Another aspect of the TCM is its basis in clinical theory, which becomes part of the way in which the component analytic parts are analyzed. Unlike other IT applications, it is not theory-neutral. TCM is a tool which is designed to locate clinically significant events in textual data. This provides the process researcher with a powerful means of identifying clinically relevant text for further analysis. However, at this stage in its development, interpretation of the graphs is not straightforward, and it is still being tested and refined. Therefore, for any substantial piece of work, consultation with expert users is essential.

SUGGESTIONS FOR FURTHER READING

Lepper, G. and Mergenthaler, E. (2005) 'Exploring group process', *Psychotherapy Research*, 15(4): 433–44.
Mergenthaler, E. (1996) 'Emotion-abstraction patterns in verbatim protocols: A new way of describing psychotherapeutic processes', *Journal of Consulting and Clinical Psychology*, 64: 1306–15.

PART IV

Data analysis and documentation

Introduction

It should be clear by now that, while the elements of the research process have a sequential form, starting with the question, the design of the study, followed by the data collection and analysis, these processes are not separate and discrete, nor are they necessarily strictly sequential. At each stage, the researcher will be looking forward to the other elements of the inquiry, in order to ensure that the project is viable. For example, the most interesting question is not going to be practicable if the data is unavailable, or ethical permission would not be forthcoming. Equally, not every stage of the process is necessarily complete before the next is begun. In particular, the process of data collection may overlap with the analysis of the emerging data, as the researcher begins to analyze early data while waiting for the final data collection to be completed. For example, in a process/outcome study, analysis of transcripts might begin as they are being transcribed, and much of the process analysis might have been completed before the final outcome data is gathered. In more exploratory research designs, such as a grounded theory project, it will be part of the analytic process itself to formulate exploratory hypotheses, and select further data for analysis on the basis of emerging findings. However, the general principle that a research question is addressed through the systematic process of inquiry outlined in the previous chapters remains the underpinning basis for the reliability and validity of any form of inquiry.

An additional issue for process researchers at the stage of the analysis of data is the complex process of reliability and validity of the analysis of transcripts. Questionnaire-based research using established instruments can be conducted by a single researcher on the basis that the validity and reliability of the instruments have been established elsewhere. However, in order to analyze data reliably, process researchers invariably need to have access to collaborators. The reason for this is that in process research we are not relying on answers to questions by clients or therapists: responses that, it could be argued, have their own validity. Instead we have to rely upon judgements made by the researchers who are studying the transcribed material. The quality of those judgments depends on the training and experience of the researcher.

In order to gain good reliability of coding there normally needs to be a training process. The extent of training required depends upon the amount of inference required by raters. Hill (1991) points out that highly operationalized variables (such as, for instance, the length of pauses or volume of response) can be rated by inexperienced judges whereas very abstract concepts (such are transference) require experienced clinicians. In the case of some coding methods, such as SASB (see Chapter 5), this can take many hours of practice: itself a limiting factor in using particular methods within small scale research. For large and complex projects, Hill advises screening raters with a sample task and hiring more than you think will be required. Florsheim and Benjamin (2001) advise on the elimination of judges who do not readily adjust to the process of coding for SASB.

Reliability of coding is established through comparing the ratings of different coders to ensure a reasonable degree of consistency. This is usually done using the 'Cohen's kappa' inter-rater reliability measure within a PC-based statistical program. Where there is a clear sequence of categories – as in adjacent interpersonal circle segments (see Chapter 5) – a weighted kappa can be used which measures not only the actual agreement but also the closeness of disagreements to provide a more accurate measure. Hill (1991) points out that while most researchers see a kappa of 0.7 as adequate, this leaves a lot of room for error. For this reason she advises that more than one rater is used for all ratings unless a very high level of agreement (about 0.95 or above) has been demonstrated in trial runs. Attention also needs to be paid to the distribution of codings between judges to ensure that there is not a problem of bias with a particular judge which is skewing the overall findings. In order to eliminate social pressures and preconceptions on the coding process it is conventional for raters to code separately and to rate material blind (to the research hypothesis, temporal sequence of therapy extracts, outcome etc.).

In contrast, some coding methods (e.g. the Assimilation Model), and most discourse analytic methods, emphasize the importance of immersion and consensus in the process of assigning codes or categories to the material. For these methods, teamwork is essential. Our research supervision programme includes on-going, open ended research groups which provide the collaborative basis for the process of analyzing data. Each member of the research group becomes familiar with a project as it develops, and the group as a whole contains the expertise of those who have already undertaken similar analyses.

Assuming that by now the researcher is able to demonstrate the validity and reliability of the design and the methods being used, and has collected sufficient data, the data analysis proceeds in earnest. Its aim is to link the findings to the original research question. This process will vary, depending on the kind of analysis undertaken, but the same basic principles which underpin the reliability and validity of the entire process are equally essential to this stage of the inquiry. In the case of statistically driven, theory testing strategies, the process of data collection may constitute the largest expenditure of time and effort, and the data analysis will be relatively straightforward analysis of numerical data, using agreed instruments, and automated statistical data analysis. Obviously, a basic honesty is required in the use of statistical tests and the interpretation of results. While a negative result – for instance, the failure to find an effect which can confidently be claimed as resulting from the experimental condition rather than chance – can be disappointing, it needs to be remembered that this can be as interesting and important as a positive result. As researchers, we should not be in the business of pushing a particular doctrine but rather in inquiring openly about the processes that take place in psychotherapy.

For exploratory, theory building designs, on the other hand, the process of data analysis may be the most time and energy demanding part of the process – particularly where existing data in the form of transcripts are being used. Equally the challenges of analysis and the relationship of findings to the original question will be different. The original question is likely to have been more exploratory, and the findings may reveal elements which were not previewed in the original question. In this kind of research design, the danger of using findings to support a preconceived assumption, disguised as a question, is greater than that of the interpretation of findings expressed statistically.

Much of the emphasis in discussions about research design is concerned with trying to ensure that there is good generalizability of research findings. While employing methods within each study which can contribute to the generalizability of its findings, no one study can stand on its own, and documentation is an integral part of the gradual accumulation of evidence, which can be compared against other findings, through replication, as in group designs, or, in the single case design, perhaps through a constant comparative analysis on a case by case basis. The purpose of documentation is to provide a structure for the presentation of findings which will enable the wider dialogue of ideas and evidence between individual studies and findings across a field of inquiry.

While it is the main aim of formal research, generalizability may not be the main concern of small scale practitioner-based research. The quite legitimate aim may instead be a fuller contextual understanding of the work with a particular client, perhaps as part of the training process. This could have as a goal the improvement of clinical practice through the process of systematic analysis of the work from a different perspective. It is part of the intention of this book, however, to provide the small scale, clinically focused researcher, equally as well as the researcher aiming for more formal research, with the basic tools of the process of inquiry so that this kind of research can take its place within the wider context of psychotherapy process research. It is through the transparency of the research process, and its representation in the documentation process, that these findings can be interpreted and incorporated into practice, as *part* of the much larger process of inquiry, to which a limited study, despite limitations in its scope, can make its contribution.

In all research, the management of data is a major task. Ensuring that all transcripts have been systematically sampled, that the process of the analysis is recorded so that it can be rendered transparent, and managing textual and/or statistical analysis as it emerges through the application of the chosen methods, are the crucial tasks for the investigator at the stage of data analysis and presentation of the findings. For all but the smallest scale studies, today's researcher will want to turn to the power of information technology to help in this task. In the following chapter, we introduce some of the data analysis software packages which are suitable for the analysis of transcript data. This leads us to the final stage in the process of inquiry: the interpretation and presentation of results. In Chapter 11, we outline the process of documentation, and illustrate the whole process with a research report submitted by one of our students.

CHAPTER 10

Computerized data analysis

Introduction

In the past two decades, there has been an enormous development in the potential for computer aided research. The capacity to manipulate huge datasets, the speed of making statistical calculations, and the ability to link actual text, recorded and videoed speech to coding systems have moved from the domain of the large scale, professional research study to the desk of every researcher who has access to a PC. This section will discuss some of the systems available to the small project researcher. We have chosen one package from each of three main types: a text coding system (C-I-SAID); a textual analysis programme (NVivo); and the well established social sciences statistical analysis package (SPSS). We are not attempting a full tutorial on each of the systems, but rather a taster. Researchers who wish to use them will need to learn the systems from manuals and help files (or in the case of SPSS from published books). These packages are designed to be used in a variety of settings and with different theoretical or coding models. Those tied to particular coding systems, such as the therapeutic cycles model and SASB, are mentioned respectively in the sections on discourse approaches and coding approaches.

Process research places two competing demands on the researcher. On the one hand, the researcher wants to be close to the data, attending to specific characteristics of the psychotherapy process, rather than to the more general population patterns which outcome research seeks to measure. On the other hand, especially in larger datasets, dealing directly with texts generates vast amounts of potential data. The researcher can be overwhelmed with the quantity of data available for analysis, and faces the problem of finding, selecting and analyzing relevant text from the available corpus. IT can aid this process considerably. It can also impose its logic on the analysis, and distance the researcher from his or her engagement with the text.

In the following sections, several very different applications available to psychotherapy process researchers will be illustrated in order to give some idea of the ways in which IT can aid the process of data analysis, some suggestions about what they can do, and some examples. The strengths and weaknesses of the methods in relation to psychotherapy process research will be reviewed, and the final section will demonstrate an IT approach with an exemplar data analysis which makes use of several methods.

Example 1 – C-I-SAID: The Code-A-Text System

The first software package to be introduced is 'Code-A-Text Integrated system for the Analysis of Interview and Dialogues' (C-I-SAID), developed by Alan Cartwright at the University of Kent. Like the TCM, this package was originally developed specifically to analyze psychotherapy texts. Later, the original program (Code-a-Text) was adapted so that it can be applied to a wide variety of text, audio and video data for more general social science research purposes, and renamed C-I-SAID. It is a complex program with many features, which can be adapted to all kinds of textual research. To use the full analytic power of C-I-SAID requires considerable practice and experience. However, it is possible to learn and use parts of the programme for more limited analytic purposes, and its design makes it suitable for a variety of projects, ranging from small, single case study designs to large and complex studies.

C-I-SAID is built to provide the researcher with a flexible framework for coding and analyzing text using text windows, through which codes can be applied directly to the text visible in the window. The researcher may choose to use existing coding systems, such as CCRT (see Chapter 3) or the Assimilation Model (see Chapter 4) or narrative process coding system (see Chapter 8). Alternatively, the researcher may want to use C-I-SAID to develop and use his or her own coding frame. This may be a particularly helpful exercise for student clinician/researchers who may want to explore their own clinical questions in small projects which systematically analyze session texts, without being constrained by an existing coding system. These small projects may form first steps towards larger and more developed formal research designs. Using C-I-SAID enables the student to explore clinical phenomena very close to the actual process. A tutorial introduces the new user to the program, and provides a first set of skills with which to get started on a simple project.

Using C-I-SAID

C-I-SAID is divided into two parts – the Document Manager and the Report Manager. Each of these features is described below.

Document Manager

Document Manager is the entry point for data, which can be imported into C-I-SAID as text, audio or video files. Transcriptions of therapeutic dialogue (some transcription conventions must be observed) can then be parsed by the software into numbered 'segments' which represent the speech units, or turns, of each speaker. Document Manager can accept and represent multiple speakers, so that C-I-SAID can be used for analysis of both dyadic and multi-party talk. Before beginning analysis, a 'project' must be set, and filled with data. A coding frame for the project can then be set. The coding frame can accommodate nominal (true/false), categorical (multiple value) and numerical scales which can represent, for example, the number of words in each segment. For any particular project, the researcher can employ pre-existing codes, which are imported into the 'coding grid' before the analysis begins, or alternatively, develop a coding frame for the purposes of a project. This can begin within Document Manager, and a coding frame can be developed in the process of analyzing the texts. Codes may also be derived from a lexical analysis of the text in the Report Manager (see the next section).

The process of coding a text takes place within the Document Manager function. Windows can be accessed through the button bar, and sized and moved to suit the researcher, and enable movement back and forth between the 'coding grid' and the text window. There are several methods by which coding can be undertaken. When undertaking the first coding of the text, the most direct and easy method to use is probably the coding window, with the text immediately available. Later coding can be done directly into data tables, derived from the original coding, or from other functions within the program, such as lexical analysis for example.

Report Manager

The Report Manager is the second part of the C-I-SAID software. It has two functions: it enables the statistical analysis of the coding which has been undertaken in the Document Manager (Rating Scale Analysis); and it provides opportunities for analysis of the lexical properties of the texts in a variety of forms (Lexical Analysis). This dual function gives the researcher great flexibility in design and analytic strategies.

The Lexical Analysis function

C-I-SAID automatically creates an index of every word in a project. These provide for several possible content analyses. Using the Lexical

Analysis function, the researcher can order a count of all the words in use and organize words in use into 'word groups' for whatever analytic purpose he or she may have. The word groups created (or imported) by the researcher can then be used as coding scales in Document Manager; or alternatively, the 'word groups' can be analyzed statistically as lexical features. Selecting 'Lexical Analysis' from the drop down menu in 'Lexicon' provides a variety of automatic lexical analysis functions, including 'document word counts'; 'compare speakers word use'. 'document work group counts'; 'compare word groups by speaker across documents' – and others. These functions provide an immediate statistical analysis of the lexical properties of the text, some expressed in table form which includes chi-square and probability analyses, and others in graph form (format can be selected for the purpose at hand). Information from any of these can also be represented in 'tab delimited files', which can be further edited, and exported into a statistical data analysis package such as SPSS for further analysis.

Further functions which are enabled by the lexical analysis function are the facility of linking words or word groups directly to their occurrence in the text. In this way the researcher can move back and forth from data analysis to content very directly, checking, for example, on context: does the word accurately represent the coding in the context of its use? The lexical function combines content analysis, which can be closely linked to the actual text, with statistical analysis which can give a broad picture of the same data.

The Rating Analysis function

The Rating Analysis function is located in the 'Rating' drop down menu. Like a lexical search, a scales search provides for the analysis of data within the C-I-SAID program. First, using the 'searches' function, a data grid which displays the selected scales is produced (this data grid can be edited and printed in a word processor). From this data grid, a statistical analysis of the scales coded in a project in the Document Manager can then be undertaken, using the 'analysis' function, which outputs the analysis in the form of rich text format (RTF) tables. As with the Lexical Analysis, a menu of possible analytic tests appears, which generate statistical tests and output in the form of a table or graph. Within the C-I-SAID program, the investigator can, for example, 'plot sequential scales sequentially', 'compare means in categories', or 'cross tabulate two categorical scales'. Data in a grid can also be exported to SPSS.

Strengths and weaknesses of C-I-SAID

C-I-SAID is a comprehensive and complex software package, which can serve a wide range of possible analytic needs. It can be used for quite simple projects, as well as for complex ones. In the project outlined in the last section of this chapter, there is an illustration of a use of the 'Lexicon' function in a project which aimed to identify 'topic' in a set of psychotherapy transcripts. In this project, all the IT methods outlined in this chapter were used to undertake an analysis of an 8 session brief psychodynamic psychotherapy. This was a medium sized project, and it was essential to have the lexical analysis functions available in C-I-SAID. The lexical analysis function is also very useful for the first stage of a grounded theory (see Chapter 6) project, and can be used even in quite small projects, once the use of the package is mastered, to provide an accurate calculation of the main categories in use in the text – something which can be time consuming and inaccurate when done by hand.

For many researchers, student or advanced, the main strength of C-I-SAID will lie in its coding facility, and the ease with which imported coding systems such as CCRT and the Assimilation Model can be scored and analyzed. More adventurous researchers, and some students, may also find that the generation of coding categories derived from close contact with the data and designed for a particular analytic purpose will provide new and deeper insights into psychotherapy process, enhance research creativity and eventually yield new clinical insights. It was for this that C-I-SAID was originally designed, and even in its highly evolved form, it can still serve that function. Of all the packages introduced in this chapter, C-I-SAID offers the process researcher the widest range of potential for data analysis. The analysis of text, audio and video data can be handled within one project, enabling coding and analysis of both verbal and non-verbal components of interaction. This feature potentially enables the user of this package to undertake the most complex and demanding analysis of therapeutic interaction, at present only addressed in parts. The possibility of using existing coding frames, or of developing new coding frames out of the data analysis itself, means that C-I-SAID is suitable for both theory testing and theory building research strategies for the investigation of the therapeutic process.

The strengths of C-I-SAID also constitute some of its weaknesses. It is an immensely complex program, which requires a lot of learning. For simple projects, involving imported coding frames, it may be accessible for the novice researcher. However, to make the most of its facilities, considerable learning and a large research project would be more rewarding for the researcher considering using it as a tool.

Example 2 – NVivo (QSR)

The NVivo package, like C-I-SAID, is the latest version of a program which has developed over time from earlier versions (i.e., several versions of NUD*IST). It is a general all purpose package developed for 'qualitative' social science research, but has many features which make it well suited to psychotherapy process research. Its underlying structure is built to support the logic of the grounded theory approach to data analysis. It is based on a strategy which enables the free coding of text fragments, and subsequent retrieval of all instances of comparable fragments for further analysis. However, unlike the coding frameworks of C-I-SAID, which are translated into units for quantitative analysis, the coding done within N-Vivo yields systems of relations, designated as 'nodes', 'trees' and 'sets', which can be represented in graphical form. Tables and other aspects of project data can be exported for statistical analysis, but this is a secondary rather than primary strategy of the program. NVivo requires the researcher to develop an analysis which is grounded in the data itself, rather than one which chunks the data into coding units based on an external theoretical or analytical framework, and leads to quantitative analysis. It is best suited to the process of analytic induction and theory building. In keeping with the principle of grounded theory analysis, higher order categories are the final output, not the starting point, of data analysis. As such, it is particularly suitable for an inductive, hermeneutic approach to analysis of psychotherapy texts (Rennie, 2000a).

Using NVivo

To begin using NVivo, the researcher must create a Project, which is then managed through the Project Pad, which appears on the screen when the program is opened. All documents relevant to a project can be organized within the frame of this project, and can include a wide variety of different kinds of texts, which can be linked in the process of exploration of the data through hyperlinks. The primary logic of the package aims to enable the researcher to sustain a flexible framework for data analysis, so that categories can be built and refined, given higher order values in the form of attributes, which can be retested and reframed as the data analysis proceeds.

First, the researcher begins to code the data, with the text in the open window of the 'Document Browser', and a panel at the side (the 'Coding Stripes'), which displays the coding as it proceeds. As the researcher browses the text, building codes through the identification of words or chunks of text, NVivo records the codes in the form of 'nodes', which can store codes, and ideas, notes, and links to other documents within the project. Nodes are built into the project as the researcher browses the text and makes connections between elements in the text, and ideas, or other elements in the project. Nodes may be 'free', or they may be structured into 'trees', by creating a group marked by a slash mark. For example, to create a tree of 'emotion' words, the code might begin with '/feeling/' after which a string of 'emotion' words could be added: /feeling/afraid/safe/ angry/. All nodes, whether 'free' or 'trees', can then be retrieved using the 'Node explorer', and examined, added to, and compared in depth, consistent with the grounded theory 'constant comparative' method.

The next phase of the analytic process involves the creation of links between the two systems of data that have been created by the coding process: the document system and the node system. The elements of each of these systems can be linked internally, and to each other, in the form of sets, which can be represented graphically. In this way, the content can be represented visually in a way which enables connections and links to be made which are not superficially visible in the text.

A unique, and powerful, aspect of the NVivo environment is that it also allows for an audit trail of the analytic process. This makes it ideally suited to a team project, so that the analytic decision-making process of the research can be tracked and accounted for. This feature addresses issues of validity and reliability in inductive, theory building methods, enabling saturation of the data, and constant comparative analysis of the data to be tracked, re-visited, and re-analyzed successively, while a record of each level of the process is stored. This is a particularly important feature for a hermeneutic analysis, where the consistency and transparency of the process is vital for its claims to validity and reliability (see Chapter 6).

The analytic strategy built into NVivo provides for maximum flexibility in the analysis of content, documenting a branching, organic process through which pattern and form in the content of the data emerges through the analytic process. As such, it is ideally suited to inductive, theory building projects, small or large. The method is well suited to the novice clinician/researcher who wants to explore the clinical process with a view to understanding and enhancing his or clinical learning and practice. It is relatively easy to learn the basic techniques, and in this respect may be better suited to the novice IT data analysis user than C-I-SAID. It gives the researcher the widest possible freedom in the design of a project, and is particularly suited to exploratory research. It is less suitable for a research design which needs to incorporate quantification at a later stage, or for projects whose strategy is theory testing. For projects where a combination of qualitative and quantitative analysis is envisioned, C-I-SAID might be a better choice.

Example 3 – The Statistical Package for the Social Sciences (SPSS)

There is often a need for some basic statistical calculations in psychotherapy process research. Even the most qualitative project may need some counting of categories and matching of two variables. Some of these functions are built into the programs discussed above. It is possible also to use a basic spreadsheet, such as Microsoft Excel, to provide key statistical information: frequencies, means, basic statistical tests etc. However, in order to go beyond fairly basic statistics a custom built package is advised. This will normally allow data entry, reporting on the characteristics of the data such as frequencies, and more sophisticated mathematical techniques ranging from chi-square analysis, tests of statistical significance and regression to factor analysis and logistic regression.

SPSS is the 'big daddy' of statistical packages within psychology and the social sciences generally. It is a very sophisticated program which goes well beyond the requirements of most small scale psychotherapy researchers, and we will not attempt to outline its capabilities except in very broad terms. SPSS was developed at the University of Chicago in the late 1960s, when computers were becoming a potential tool in quantitative social sciences research. SPSS for Windows has since been developed with many specialist packages and is at the time of writing in version 12.0 (http://www.spss.com). SPSS quickly spread through university social sciences departments in the 1970s and has been established as the leading social science statistical package since that time. When SPSS was first used, requests for statistical analysis had to be typed onto punch-cards, then left for the operators to feed into the computer for analysis. The results were printed out and the resulting volumes of paper left in the researcher's tray, usually on the following day. Any minor mistake in syntax was rewarded with an error print out. The calculations which took a day to arrive at are now are done on a PC or laptop in a few seconds.

The development of SPSS and other statistical packages for the PC has the advantage that fast mining of the data in very sophisticated ways is now possible. This has the disadvantage that often very complicated statistical calculations are made without the researcher having any idea of the underlying mathematics or the real significance of the result. It is important for the researcher wishing to use SPSS to decide in advance which statistical tests to apply based upon a good understanding of what is appropriate, and only use methods that are understood. In other words, keep it simple unless you are very confident about the meaning of your results.

The layout of SPSS is like a spreadsheet, with the columns assigned to variables and the rows to cases. Variables can be defined into various categories, of which the important ones for the process researcher are 'numeric' and 'string'. Numeric variables are those which are entered in numbers, on which it is possible to perform statistical calculations. However, the numeric variable is also used for ordinal variables, which have an ordering if not an absolute numerical meaning. These are important in most psychological questionnaire-based material. For instance on psychotherapy outcome instruments the patient is often asked to give a 1–5 score against a problem area to indicate severity of the problem. While this does not produce a true interval variable (i.e. where the score '5' is truly five times the score '1' as it would be in age or weight data), this kind of variable is usually treated as such for statistical calculation. String variables can be used for basic categorization, such as gender, or in the case of textual data, for the coding category of a part of text.

Once data has been taken into SPSS – either entered directly or imported from a spreadsheet or other package – the basic facilities are given in the menu bar at the top of the screen in standard Windows fashion. These include *Data* and *Transform* which enable you to locate material, to sort according to a particular variable or to split and merge files, transform variables, recode, assign missing values etc. It is often necessary to spend considerable time cleaning up the data, checking that it has all been entered correctly, that gaps are filled or coded as missing, and transforming variables so that basic calculations can be made. For instance, in order to look at the association between particular codes for patient communication and the preceding therapist intervention it may be necessary to simplify the codings into a new variable that divides into (in SASB terms) affiliative or disaffiliative communications. It may be desirable to rationalize a variable into a dichotomous variable (e.g. high/low empathy) rather than, say, a five point Likert-type scale commonly used in instruments in order to show an effect more clearly. SPSS allows the variables to be transformed into ways that effects can be demonstrated, but it is important for the researcher to be clear on the rationale or validity of this process. There is a risk with such powerful tools at our command that data is transformed until an effect is found. This increases the chance of a Type 1 error – supporting the hypothesis when the effect is random.

The main statistical power of SPSS lies in the *Analyze* sub-menu. This provide options for providing basic reports and descriptive data: for instance how many cases are within which category or means in the case of numerical data. Each time an analysis is initiated a new Output window opens presenting the data in tabular form which can be printed or exported. This section of the package also allows the calculation of significance – for instance, whether an observable difference from one time to another is likely to be random or significant (probability of chance less that 5% or 1%, ie $p < 0.05$ or < 0.01). It provides the possibility of doing this calculation on non-numerical data through the chi-square calculation (*Analyze/Descriptive Statistics/Crosstabs*). It is also possible to calculate correlations of numerical data using two or more variables.

More complex statistical calculations are probably beyond most small scale or practitioner psychotherapy research. However, some of these are frequently used when developing a new instrument and may need to be called upon. For instance *Analyze/Scale/Reliability Analysis* is used to produce an alpha test of the extent to which different scale (say, questionnaire) items produce consistent results that can be seen as forming a construct. Another method which is popular for establishing the validity of an instrument is factor analysis (*Analyze/Data Reduction/Factor*), which is a technique for defining factors within numerical (or ordinal) data with a large number of variables, as in the case of a large questionnaire where you wish to test which items can be factored in with others to form sub-scales.

Many of these statistical techniques will not be needed by process researchers who are dealing with single case data or predominantly non-numerical data. However, some of the methods do produce numerical data – for instance word counts, or frequency of occurrences of particular phenomena – which can be analyzed using a statistical program like SPSS.

Which package?

Each of the IT methods outlined above has its own special characteristics, strengths and weaknesses. Like the research methods outlined in the preceding chapters, IT tools enable and constrain the analytic process by the very nature of their organization and logic. A further consideration in the decision to use IT is the degree to which a data analysis package fits with the chosen research method. The choice of a data analysis package, must be thought through carefully. On the one hand, the deepening of complexity of research into the interplay of social, psychological and possibly even biological factors which underpin the complex process of psychotherapy, will require the analytic power which only IT methods can offer. For the novice researcher, or for any small project, on the other hand, it should be noted that a word processor may be sufficient to aid some simple analytic procedures: the 'search and find' function of a word processor, for example, can be used to find and count key words; the 'table' function in a word processor can be used to organize and structure counts from a small dataset for presentation or further analysis; and simple calculations, and graphs, can be accomplished on Excel, by exporting tables or by setting data into Excel form as a first procedure. In the following example, a project moved from a small, hand-analyzed project using minimum IT resources, to a larger project, with a much bigger dataset, which used several of the IT methods mentioned in this book.

A project using several IT methods

In the first of a series of studies, using group therapy data, Fontao and Mergenthaler (2002) demonstrated that cycles identified by the therapeutic cycles model software (see Chapter 9) can be identified in the talk of all the participants of the group, although cycles cannot be identified in each speaker's talk. The purpose of the research was twofold: to provide empirical evidence at the level of discourse for the characteristics of the therapeutic interaction of which the cycles are markers; and to enable the use of the cycles to identify specific characteristics of the psychotherapeutic discourse for detailed empirical analysis of the clinical process. The findings suggested that the cycles model might be capturing a phenomenon of group process, known as 'group cohesion' in the literature. Some subjective measures of 'group cohesion' have been developed and tested, but no systematic method has been developed which will connect 'group cohesion' to specific features of the therapeutic discourse. The observation that cycles occur regularly in the multi-party talk of the group suggested a further level of investigation: what phenomena at the level of clinical interaction the cycles might be capturing. A pilot study (Lepper and Mergenthaler, 2005) explored the hypothesis that the TCM cycles could be linked to high levels of 'topic coherence' – a concept derived from conversation analysis (see Chapter 7). To analyze the transcript of just one session, the 'search and find' option in the Edit menu of Word was used to identify the categories in use, using a 'grounded theory' approach. This step was followed by the aggregation of categories in use into topics, which were then identified in the text and represented in a table, constructed in the Word 'Table' function. This table was then exported into SPSS and analyzed. The findings of this pilot study provided strong statistical evidence for a link between the cycles and three dimensions of topic coherence identified by empirical study of multi-party talk: content; sequential order and participation structure (Linell and Korolija, 1997). A linguistic feature of the discourse at the level of interaction was thus connected with a statistically derived linguistic feature at the level of content. Is it possible that this finding could contribute to a description of the 'group cohesion' construct at the level of empirical observation, rather than subjective report?

This positive finding prompted a further stage of analysis, in which an 8 session brief psychodynamic psychotherapy, from the Sheffield Psychotherapy Project (Shapiro and Firth, 1987), for which outcome data were available, was analyzed using a similar method. The case was chosen because the transcripts demonstrated strong TCM cycle features, and the outcome was very good. The questions asked of the data were:

- Would the finding of the link between topic coherence and cycles hold up in a larger dataset?
- Could the link between cycles and topic coherence be indicative of the presence of therapeutic alliance?

The study proceeded in four stages, using three data analysis packages in the process of the analysis. First, all the transcripts were analyzed using the therapeutic cycles model software, in order to identify all of the cycles which occurred within the 8 sessions, as a basis for the comparative analysis of elements of topic coherence between interaction within the cycles, and interaction outside of the cycles. An additional objective of the study was to use the results of this detailed analysis of the text to provide additional evidence for the formal rules for defining a cycle.

In the second phase of the study, C-I-SAID was used to identify the topics, and locate them in the text. First, the transcripts were imported into a project, and parsed so that each speech turn was represented as a 'segment'. Using the Lexical Analysis function, all the words in the 8 documents were counted. Working from this list, categories in use in the sessions (nouns, verbs and descriptive words) were identified, and grouped, using the 'word group' function. This strategy was used in order to identify the content of topics in the sessions. In the next step in the process, the identification of word groups within the discourse was recorded by counting the word groups by segment; this analysis was then automatically represented as a table, using the Lexical Analysis option 'Word group counts by segment'. The table was then converted into a tab-delimited file, which showed each word group as a column, and each segment (speech turn) as a row. With this table, further coding could then be undertaken. First, each segment was compared with the text, and coding of the word group examined in relation to the context. In some cases, frequently used categories proved not to signify a consistent topic. For example, the word group 'death' proved not to be connected to a topic, but rather to unrelated aspects of several different narratives. It was dropped from the table. Other word groups proved, on inspection in context, to be allied to others in context, and were more accurately represented as one topic. Where this occurred, the word groups were therefore collapsed into one. Segment by segment analysis also enabled the exclusion or inclusion of some categories represented in a cell, when aspects of context were taken into account. Finally, further coding was added to the tables. First, a column was added to indicate which segments of talk fell within a TCM cycle, and which outside a TCM cycle. Then, in order to represent the sequence of topics – where both speakers oriented to the same topic – a column was added to identify those segments in which a topic (word group) was carried over from one segment (speaker turn) to the next.

In the next phase, the tables were exported to SPSS, to test the frequency, and significance, of topic features in relation to the cycles. Again, the findings showed highly significant correlations between the frequency of topic coherence elements and the cycles (Figure 10.1).

Figure 10.1   TCM cycles and topic coherence

Content (measured as the chain length of topics, mean number of topics by word block, $n = 19$ different topics)

Cycle	$M = 6.46$	$SD = 0.483$
Non Cycle	$M = 4.91$	$SD = 0.704$

t-test: $t(14) = 5.132$
$p < 0.001$ (two-sided)

Topic sequences (measured as the frequency of topic words occurring across speaker turns, mean by session, $N = 8$) were higher within the cycles to the level $p < 0.005$ for all the topics taken together.

Participation structure. All the topic sequences were analyzed to determine which speaker initiated the sequence. The analysis revealed no significant differences. This suggests that patient and therapist were equal partners in the creation and maintenance of topics.

Finally, we returned to the text, using the cycles identified by the TCM to locate the segments of text at the end of each cycle. These segments of text were analyzed in detail, using conversation analysis, to explore what is happening at the level of the talk at the moment when a cycle ends. The interaction between therapist and patient at the end of each cycle was examined on a turn by turn basis. We found that one of three kinds of discourse events occurred in every case:

1. a rupture in topic sequences across speaker turns which was repaired;
2. a rupture in topic sequences which was not repaired; or
3. a 'withdrawal' – talk marked by pauses, which resulted in a withdrawal from a previous topic.

In those cases where a rupture in the topic sequencing was repaired, the cycle was renewed; where a rupture was not repaired, or where the talk showed evidence of a 'withdrawal', the cycle came to an end, and a period of 'relaxing' followed. This finding was noted, and linked to some of the contemporary findings on alliance ruptures (Safran and Muran, 1996). To take this finding forward, it is planned to undertake an intensive micro-analysis of these events, using conversation analysis, in order to investigate these significant moments in the therapist/patient interaction. This analysis, it is hoped, will yield specific findings about therapist interventions, relevant to clinical practice.

Conclusion

This example was presented to show how the use of IT methods greatly enhances the scope of both statistical and textual analysis, and enables the researcher to combine methods in a variety of ways to support both theory testing and theory building strategies. The objectives of this single case study included both a *confirmatory* (Hilliard, 1993) element (to replicate a previous finding, and to test a hypothesis concerning the relationship between the computerized content analysis of the TCM, and discursive features at the level of the therapeutic interaction); and an *exploratory* element (the hypothesis that the construct of 'therapeutic alliance' may be linked to discursive phenomena in the therapeutic interaction, and rendered 'observable' by the TCM). Each of these studies involved selection of single cases from a larger dataset, for which outcome and other empirical data were available. Selection of cases, and combining methods, enables the researcher to link clinical findings from single case studies empirically to more general findings from other studies, and other disciplines. In this way, a combination of strategies, both quantitative and qualitative, enhanced by computerized techniques, gives heightened validity to the single case study, and provides the scaffolding for theory building.

SUGGESTIONS FOR FURTHER READING

Dancey, C.P. and Reidy, J. (2002) *Statistics Without Maths for Psychology. Using SPSS for Windows*[TM]. Harlow: Prentice Hall.
Fielding, N.G. and Lee, R.M. (1998) *Computer Analysis and Qualitative Research*. London: Sage.

CHAPTER 11

Documentation of the research

Introduction

The final aim of any research project, large or small, theory testing or theory building, is to take its place as part of a growing body of knowledge. Research is a 'dialogue of ideas and evidence' (Ragin, 1987). The project should begin with a question which grows out of the current state of knowledge; and it should aim to add to that knowledge base, by confirming or disconfirming the original proposition, through the systematic exploration of evidence. To achieve this aim, and to become part of the overall evolution of generalized findings, the individual research process must be documented, and linked to the other research. The process of documentation, therefore, is an integral part of the inquiry, and must be attended to throughout the process of the research. This involves several principles.

In documenting the research, each stage of the process must be described and the decision-making process made clear. In the case of group designs, for example, demographic data, decisions to include or exclude some subjects, and the analytic tools used in the interpretation of the data must be made clear. In the case of exploratory single case designs, the decision-making process at each stage of the analysis must be made clear (it should have been documented as the analysis proceeded), including the method of ensuring the reliability of coding or interpretation. In some of the discourse analytic methods, transparency is at the centre of the claim to validity: the data itself should be included in the research report, and available for critical examination by the reader (Perakyla, 1997).

There is no absolute rule about how a research report should be written, but if the researcher wants to present findings in a way that is recognizable and acceptable to other members of the research community, and perhaps get them published, then observation of the conventional form of the research report is a good way to start. The conventional report has a standard form:

- It begins with an introduction, which articulates the question to be addressed, and locates it in the context of previous research.

- This will normally include, or be followed by, a review of the relevant literature.
- The data to be studied and the method to be used are then described in some detail. In some studies, this part of the report will be the largest.
- The analysis of the data then follows. A description of the process, which will typically be longer in the case of discourse-based studies, will be included in this section.
- Finally, the conclusions to be drawn from the data analysis, and their implications for the question asked, will be set out.
- A critical evaluation of the research, its limitations, and its implications for future study are often discussed to conclude the report.

As can be seen, the standard form of the research report is structured within the general principles of the process of inquiry.

In order to illustrate the way a research report will look, and to demonstrate what can be addressed in a small scale student project, this chapter reproduces in its entirety a research project which was submitted as partial requirement for the clinical doctorate in psychotherapy at the University of Kent, May 2003. The project is based on transcripts from two of the student/clinician's own sessions. The transcripts were included with the original submission, with the consent of the patient, but are omitted here for reasons of confidentiality. The references which were included with the original project have been included within the references given at the end of the book.

Example of a practitioner project – Stories and metaphors: exploration of the narrative and figurative language in one patient–therapist dyad: a pilot study

Philippa Shadrach Long

Introduction

Psychotherapy research has now established certain facts (if facts are defined as consistently replicated findings) (Bergin and Garfield, 1994). These include the following: the general effects of psychotherapy exceed spontaneous remission; therapy effects are generally positive and exceed placebo controls; there is relative equivalency in outcome for a large number of therapies, therapeutic modalities and temporal arrangements; outcomes vary due to therapist factors rather than technique factors; the therapist–patient relationship has central importance in predicting and possibly causing positive personality change (Lambert and Bergin, 1992).

That good outcome in therapy is related to the strength of the working alliance has been demonstrated by Orlinsky and Howard (1986) and Orlinsky *et al.* (1994), amongst others. The fit between therapist and patient is also a factor and conceptual levels and values seem more important in this respect than simpler correlations such as age or sex (Posthuma and Carr, 1975; Welkowitz *et al.*, 1967). Additionally Kelly and Strupp (1992) showed that both participants in therapy dyads influenced one another in terms of the assimilation of values.

Therapist factors that influence good outcome include responsiveness (Stiles *et al.*, 1995), experience (Westerman and Foote, 1995) and the ability to form a warm and supportive relationship (Luborsky *et al.*, 1985). For patient characteristics, there is strong evidence in process research studies that their influence on outcome is central (Rennie, 1992b) and that their capacity for self-healing is more important than differences in technique (Tallman and Bohart, 1999). Joyce *et al.* (1995) showed that the client's preparedness to respond to an interpretation was the key issue in predicting its effectiveness, rather than the way the therapist framed it. Other studies have shown that the client's original level of object relating can predict therapeutic alliance and outcome (Joyce and Piper, 1998; Piper *et al.*, 1995). On the basis of these findings, process research has had to provide a variety of more flexible techniques, more complex conceptual models (Stiles *et al.*, 1990) and more complex methods of analysis to study the multivariate and complex phenomena of therapy and the change process.

One approach, influenced by both hermeneutic or social constructionist perspectives, is narrative. Some researchers have elaborated the analogy of psychotherapy to hermeneutics (Frank and Frank, 1993) and have explored 'the assumption that all forms of successful psychotherapy entail the articulation, elaboration, and transformation of the client's self-told life story' (Angus *et al.*, 1999). It may be that a change in the patient's 'assumptive world' (hypothesized by Frank and Frank (1993) to underpin successful psychotherapy) is significantly influenced by a change in narrative. Further, in facilitating a change in narrative, effective psychotherapists co-create a plausible 'myth' that the patient can accept (Frank and Frank, 1993). Some researchers have, therefore, studied the narrative, either through within-session descriptions of relationship events or micro-narratives, or through models that can examine the macro-narrative. This offers a middle ground for analyzing process that lies 'between atomistic, line by line discourse analyses and global theories as offered in stage models' (Bob, 1999). Luborsky and Crits-Cristoph's (1990) core conflictual relationship theme (CCRT) and the narrative process coding system (NPCS) developed by Angus *et al.* (1999) exemplify this middle ground from the micro-narrative and from the macro-narrative perspective respectively.

Luborsky and his co-researchers (Luborsky and Crits-Christoph, 1990) initiated the first major research programme to take the 'top-down' approach of operationalizing their models of narrative process through the construction of a coding manual which is then applied by trained raters to produce quantitative measures of the frequency of occurrence of relevant variables' (McLeod and Balamoutsou, 1996). They have shown how their categorization method can analyze the structure and content of stories to reveal 'the core conflictual relationship themes' and demonstrate how these change over the course of therapy. They differentiate between client and therapist narratives.

Angus *et al.* (1999), using their narrative process coding scheme (NPCS), focus on the strategies and processes by which a client and therapist transform the events of everyday life into a meaningful story that both organizes and represents the client's sense of self and others in the world. They found a correlation between particular narrative patterns and different theoretical orientations and, in a study of poor and good outcome therapies (Angus and Hardtke, 1994), found that positive outcomes were associated with higher numbers of topic segments in each session, substantially higher frequencies of reflexive processing, and lower frequencies of internal processing sequences.

Apart from studying the narrative, Angus, in collaboration with Rennie (1988, 1989) and Korman (2002) has also studied the use of metaphor in psychotherapy for 'the selective analysis of recurring metaphor themes may be a particularly productive and meaningful method for tracing both the development of productive working alliances in therapy relationships as well as for tracing the specific conceptual and experiential stages entailed in the successful resolution of longstanding interpersonal problems' (Angus, 1996, p. 82).

The relationship between metaphor and affect, and between metaphor, affect and insight deserves further investigation. Frank and Frank (1993) note that 'the success of all forms of psychotherapy depends on the patient's experiencing emotional arousal' (p. 69). 'Figurative language springs from strong affect that cannot be conveyed in any other way' (Siegelman, 1990, p. 16). In this regard the use of metaphor is a critical but under-researched area of psychotherapy (Angus and Rennie, 1988). Empirical studies of metaphoric expression in therapy are relatively few and lack sufficient emphasis on the subjective meaning of metaphors to the patient–therapist dyad, not least because of the methodological challenge this poses (McMullen, 1996). Angus and Rennie (1988) found that the link between metaphor and creative insight and problem solving was evident only in those dyads where the therapist operated from a collaborative style.

Glaser (1990) made explicit some of the parallels between the methods of rhetoric and psychotherapy which include vivid metaphors. Angus and Rennie's (1989) analysis of the role of metaphor in therapy showed that a critical function of metaphor is to help the client access a contextual network of associated meaning and memories, and also provide a shared entry into aspects of the client's self-identity and modes of relating. Metaphor then is inextricably linked to the narratives we construct about ourselves: 'we seek out personal metaphors to highlight and make coherent our own pasts, our present activities, and our dreams, hopes and goals as well' (Lakoff and Johnson, 1980, p. 232).

The pilot study which follows examines how a client and therapist co-construct a macro-narrative 'such that the life story, in essence, the sense of self, may be transformed at the conclusion of the therapeutic relationship' (Angus *et al.*, 1999). A therapy in progress which seemed particularly rich in metaphor was used for analysis which addressed the beginning stages of the narrative. The aims were:

- To assess, with an early and limited portion of a therapy, the usefulness of an instrument designed to explore the process of co-construction of the macro-narrative, i.e. the NPCS.
- To compare findings from the use of this method with that of CCRT.
- To compare key themes that emerged from an analysis of the metaphors used in this study to those of CCRT and NPCS.

Methodology

In choosing one empirical method over another, it was felt that the NPCS was relevant to the issues this study sought to explore for the following reasons:

Firstly the NPCS argues that three narrative-process sequence types serve an important function in '*the co-construction of the client's macro- or self narrative*' which directly addresses the question of <u>how</u> the story or myth becomes co-constructed.

Secondly the NPCS is a theory-neutral model that provides a standard unit of analysis (i.e. the topic segment) for psychotherapy session transcripts and can be used to track the processes of narrative construction in therapy across differing therapeutic approaches. It would, therefore, not limit a study to one theoretical orientation. This was relevant to the view that theoretical orientation is, within certain constraints, of little relevance to outcome (Imber *et al.*, 1990; Shapiro *et al.*, 1990; Sloane *et al.*, 1975).

Thirdly the NPCS was chosen because of its link to analysis of metaphoric expression (Angus and Rennie, 1988, 1989; Rasmussen and Angus, 1996) which paralleled the current study's interest in the place of metaphor in the transformation of the patient's interpretation of their narrative. Indeed, narratives have been described as an extended metaphor. Angus *et al.* (1999) 'found the use of individual metaphor phrases' (Angus, 1996) to be particularly productive within the context of 'internal narrative sequences' (p. 1258).

Explanation of the NPCS

The NPCS was developed by Lynne Angus in collaboration with others (1994, 1999) with the specific aim of analyzing narrative processes in psychotherapy texts in order to study how the micro-narratives of the therapy content come to be linked together into a macro-narrative that organizes, represents, and ultimately, may transform the client's sense of self. It is primarily a coding technique, as follows:

- The analytic process begins with the identification of a topic segment.
- Each topic segment is identified and named in terms of its:
  - relationship focus: (self, other, self in relation to other);
  - issue focus: (the content).
- The topic segments are then analyzed for:
  - external narrative process sequences (description of events, real, imagined, past, present or future);
  - internal narrative process sequences (subjective/experiential description of experience);
  - reflexive narrative process sequences (analysis of current/past/future events).
- Each topic segment is examined and coded in terms of the pattern of shifts between internal and reflexive sequences within each segment.

Angus *et al.* (1999) argue that it is the *pattern* of the shifts from one to another of the three narrative process sequences that is important to practitioners and researchers since they may:

a. capture differential therapeutic processing strategies representing differing therapeutic approaches;
b. be predictive of good or poor outcome.

For comparative purposes sessions were also analyzed using Luborsky's core conflictual relationship method, a transference-related method that guides clinical judgement of the content of the central relationship patterns in psychotherapy sessions (Luborsky *et al.*, 1994b). This was chosen as one method that had been extensively used in Europe and the United States and has been used to develop a new method of brief psychotherapy (Book, 1997). The primary data to be scored for CCRT are a minimum of 10 narrative episodes about relationships. The judge identifies for each episode the types of each of three components:

- the patient's main wishes, needs or intentions toward the other person in the narrative;
- the responses of the other person;
- the responses of the self.

Within each component the types with the highest frequency across all relationship episodes are identified and their combination constitutes the CCRT.

Previous empirical work on analyzing metaphor in psychotherapy has largely used qualitative analyses of participants' tape-aided recollected accounts of metaphoric events, recorded within 24 hours of the session (Angus and Rennie, 1988, 1989). This methodology was beyond the scope of this study.

The method developed for this study was as follows. Each metaphor or metaphoric allusion was identified. It was decided to include dream symbols as metaphors, given their central importance to the generation of metaphors within the sessions. Each metaphor was then marked as originating from therapist or patient. Even if a metaphor were from a dream that was not the patient's, the reporting of it by the patient was deemed to be a patient generation. Each metaphoric instance was then transcribed into one of two columns, either patient generated or therapist generated, and listed in temporal sequence. This method allowed the cross-fertilisation, or co-construction, of metaphors to be seen more clearly, as can be seen in Table 11.7 (p. 219).

Procedure

The NPCS (Angus *et al.*, 1999) was used to analyze two sequential taped sessions from the early part of a forty session, brief focal psychodynamic psychotherapy individual treatment with a fifty-six-year-old woman suffering from depression. The therapist was a psychoanalytic psychotherapist with 25 years of clinical experience. The patient's written consent was acquired prior to taping Session 17 in its entirety and 70% of Session 18. Sessions were then analyzed and coded according to the NPCS by two judges: the researcher (an experienced psychoanalytic psychotherapist) and an experienced cognitive-behavioural psychotherapist.

Results

Inter-rater agreement

It was found that, for identification of topic-segment units and the labelling of central issues and relational focus, the raters in this study achieved 82% agreement (Cohen's kappa = 0.74) (Cohen, 1968).

For the identification and categorization of narrative-sequence units the raters for this study reached inter-rater agreement levels of 81%. (Cohen's kappa = 0.74)

Topic segment length

The average length of topic segments was 25 lines (range 4–69 lines).

Analysis of narrative process sequences

Table 11.1 shows the patterning of Reflexive narrative-process sequences (Ref); External narrative-process sequences (Ext) and Internal narrative-process sequences (Int).

Table 11.1   Patterning of narrative-process sequences

Session 17   Ext /Ref /Ext /Ref /Int /Ref /Ext /Int /Ref /Int   *Session 18*   Ext /Int /Ref /Int /Ref /Ext /Ref /Int /Ext

The percentage use of different narrative-process sequences, rather than their chaining, was: Reflexive sequences were 45% of the total, Internal 27% and External 26% (see Table 11.2 overleaf).

Core themes

Although analysis of two sequential therapy sessions cannot track core themes across a treatment, it can collate and sort individual topic segments into recurring relational and/or issue-based themes. Table 11.2 is a sequential table of the abbreviated issues initially allocated to each topic shift in the rating of the transcripts.

Although it would have been possible to extrapolate some core themes even from this scant information, it was felt that to do justice to this aspect of the NPCS, the raters should amplify their topic segment issues somewhat. A further rating of the transcripts produced the topic lists shown in Table 11.3.

Table 11.2 Issues allocated to topic shifts

Session 17	Session 18
Issues	*Issues*
Visit to daughter	Dream
Relationship with daughter	Relationship with son
Daughter's dream and associations	Defence/detachment
Daughter	Relationship with friends
Relationship with son and daughter	Detachment
Relationship with son	Goal of therapy
Self and guilt	Relationship with son and daughter
Self esteem and relationship with others	Detachment
Job	
Analysis of self/detachment	

Table 11.3 Amplified topic issues

Session 17	Session 18
Issues	*Issues*
Visit to daughter	Pushing away child/feeling
Controlling, critical relationship with daughter	Clearer perception of son
Child/feelings shut out	Defences of detachment with others
Daughter's repressed feelings	Giving-up in the face of demands
Cutting off from partner	Detachment with others
Mother–daughter reversal of roles	Dilemma to reconnect or not
Fear of son's judgement of her	Perception of children
Guilt about her mothering	Cut-off in the face of disappointment
Fear of son's attitude to her	
Need to be liked	
Disappointment re job	
Lack of sense of self	
Feelings in therapy	

Table 11.4 Generalized topic issues

Painful affects
Defence of detachment
Guilt re damage done to loved others
Fear of return of affects
Intolerance of demands or disappointments that threaten detachment
Difficulty re awakening of affects in therapy

Table 11.4 presents the results of collating and sorting topics into more generalized and abstract themes.

Not only did this offer a coherent focus and formulation but it also reflected the sense of coherence in the sessions. 'Findings from a qualitative, comparative analysis of metaphoric expression in psychodynamic therapy with borderline and non borderline clients indicate the non borderline clients and their therapists identify experiencing a sense of narrative coherence in their therapy sessions in which topic-facet shifts occur predominantly in the context of core client issues' (Angus *et al.*, 1999, p. 1266).

Patient or therapist initiated shifts

The narrative processes coding system also offers an empirical method of assessing the ratio of therapist initiated to client initiated topic shifts or narrative-sequence shifts. In this study topic shifts were initiated by the patient in 33% of cases and by the therapist in 66%. Narrative process sequences were initiated by the patient in 44% of cases and by the therapist in 55% of cases.

Session analysis using CCRT

Using the CCRT method (Luborsky *et al.*, 1994b), relationship episodes in the two sessions were scored into tailor-made categories and then translated into the standard categories (see Table 11.5 overleaf).

Core themes compared using NPCS and CCRT methods

Table 11.6 gives a comparison between the categories analyzed by CCRT method and those analyzed by NPCS method.

Table 11.5   18 relationship episodes categorized into CCRT standard category clusters

Wishes	
To be distant and avoid conflicts	88%
To be loved and understood	11%
Responses from Other	
Rejecting and Opposing	62%
Upset	37%
Responses of Self	
Unreceptive	62%
Disappointed and Depressed	18%
Anxious and Ashamed	18%

Table 11.6   Comparison of core themes as analyzed by CCRT and NPCS methods

CCRT	**NPCS**
To be distant and avoid conflicts	Detachment and intolerance of demands or
Unreceptive	disappointments that threaten detachment
Disappointed and Depressed	Fear of return of painful affects/ difficulty re
Anxious and Ashamed	awakening of affects in therapy

Metaphor

Table 11.7 shows the metaphors used by patient and therapist in temporal order, illustrating where and how metaphors were co-elaborated. Table 11.8 shows these metaphors collated into categories.

Discussion

These findings accord with Angus *et al.* (1999) in terms of inter-rater agreement levels and topic segment lengths. Angus *et al.* (1999) state that 'in terms of inter-rater agreement levels for the identification of topic segment units in the transcript, it was found that after 20–25 hours of training, raters were able to establish a 90% hit rate … for both the

Table 11.7   Therapist and patient metaphors in sequence

Time	THERAPIST	Co-elaborated metaphors (Summary)	PATIENT
	*step toward/step back /***balance***/* **dance**/ *wired-up/heart-***broken**/*locked-out/* *Afraid to let in/***break** *something* /**push away**	**balance** **broken** **dance**	*Bunged-up/fragile mountain easy to collapse//* *delicately* **balanced**/ **Do the dance**/*warm glow/bit stuck/* Go through hoops/no core/half
	Torture/**Repair** *Final straw/* **pushing away/part of yourself** */ black bag/put it in the rubbish/ *Little boy making demands/* part of you **put in the rubbish, kill off** *a loving you/* **Life** *and* **Death**/ *Observer of a* **car crash**/*Person outside Shinto temple/* **pushed her away**/ pushed away, drown/ *under the water/* **drowned, disconnected**	**death** **push away** black/rubbish **kill off** car crash **drown** **dis**/ **connection** repairs life	**Dead/push away with black plastic bin liner/drowned**/ *Hadn't saved him/***killed him off**/ Getting rid **of**/*didn't give a toss* *Seeing him clearly/fogged things /figment in my mind/* *demon/hiding seething can/* *mass of everything/on my knees/looking at a* **car** /**crash** Chaos, not **killing** that/ *Blank/blankness/***detachment**/ *shut people out/* *Bleeding hearts/***detached** *person/bleeds*
	duck out/ get to you, get hold of you ***Throws the switch*/** Drowned/kill *them off/* **Kill** *a part of you/*		**Reconnected**/*tying to* **live, do repairs**/*trying* **to connect** Repairs/*trying* **to connect**/ *seeking/backs off seeking;* *moving sideways/slam door/* *mess/nightmare/***cut off**/ Purging/don't fill my head/ **Chop, Chop**/

Table 11.8 Categorization of therapist and patient metaphors

Therapist	Patient	Therapist	Patient
Metaphor: Barrier		**Metaphor: Disposal/rubbish**	
Not let in	Locked out	Push away	Push away with bin liner
	Out/shut put	Push away	Getting rid of
	Slams door	Black bag/in the rubbish	
			Seething can/ mass
		Put it in the rubbish	
		Push away/ pushed away	Mess/chaos
Metaphor: Disconnection		**Metaphor: Death/Murder**	
Break	Blank/blankness Detachment/	Torture	Collapse
Disconnected	detached		No core/half dead
Duck out			Drowned/not saved
	Back off / Cut off		Killed/demon/car crash
Throw the switch			
	Chop / Chop		
		Kill off	Killing
		Life and Death	Bleeding/bleeds
		Car crash/drowns Under the water	Nightmare
		Drowned/kill	
Metaphor: Movement		**Metaphor: Reconnection**	
Dance/step toward	Balanced	Repair	Wired-up/warm glow
Step back	Do the dance		
	Bit stuck/go		Reconnected
Get hold of/get to	through hoops		Trying to connect
	Moved sideways/ seeking		
Metaphor: Vision		**Metaphor: Body/Feeling**	
Observer	Seeing clearly/ fogged		Heart-broken/ bleeds
			Bleeding/on my knees
	Looking/seeking		Fill my head

Table 11.9 Metaphors as related to core themes identified by CCRT and NPCS

Core themes	Metaphors
Distant	Barriers
Avoid conflicts	Disposal
Detachment	Disconnection
Fear of return of affects	Death and Murder
Wish for love and understanding	Reconnection
	Movement
	Feeling

identification of Topic-Segment units and the labelling of central issues and relational focus' (p. 1261). That raters with fewer hours of training achieved similar levels of inter-rater agreement may reflect the fact that sample sessions were unusually clear in terms of their categories.

With the same level of training Angus *et al.* (1999) found that raters were able to identify reliably and categorize Narrative-Sequence units in therapy session transcripts to an 'acceptable level' (inter-rater agreement levels of 83% to 88%). Current levels of inter-rater reliability obtained with minimally trained judges are therefore broadly in accord with previous ratings deemed 'acceptable.'

Angus *et al.* (1999) found that the length of topic segments varied from dyad to dyad. The average length of a topic segment in the current study of 25 transcript lines accords with findings by Hardtke (1996) using 5 therapy dyads across 75 sessions (average 30; range 10–133 lines).

Differences between the findings of Angus *et al.* (1999) and the current study emerge in terms of how therapists with different theoretical orientations demonstrate different patterns of combinations of narrative process sequences.

The narrative processes coding system was designed to identify and track patterns of narrative sequences and to test the hypothesis that different theoretical orientations would utilize different combinations of narrative-process sequences, in line with their theory driven goals and methods of treatment. In a study by Angus *et al.* (1999) for example, the psychodynamic therapy sessions showed a pattern of Reflexive (40%) and External (54%) predominating in which both therapist and patient engaged in a process of meaning construction (Reflexive) linked to the patient's descriptions of past and current memories These results bear more similarity to Angus *et al.*'s (1999) findings for process-experiential therapy modes, than for a psychodynamic orientation: i.e. 'a pattern of Internal (29%) and Reflexive (46%) narrative sequences in which the client and therapist engaged in a process of identifying and differentiating emotional experiences (Internal) and then generating new understanding of those experiences (Reflexive) during the therapy hour' (p. 1265). The current study's results were also more in line with the chaining pattern of narrative sequences for perceptual processing rather than for psychodynamic modes.

Angus *et al.* (1999) argue that these different patterns are consistent with the stated goals and aims of different therapy approaches and compare the aim of the Psychodynamic model (to link memories (External) with new understanding and insight (Reflexive) into intra and inter personal issues) with that of the Process Experiential model (to develop more functional emotional schemes (Internal) and integrate new feelings, beliefs and attitudes (Reflexive); and that of Perceptual Processing Therapy (to facilitate an extended client inquiry into core self-related issues in which automatic processing patterns were identified and challenged). Factors related to methodology, and therapist and client characteristics may explain the variance between the chaining pattern of this study of psychodynamic therapy and previous research.

Firstly a sample of 1.7 sessions of one client–therapist dyad may be atypical of therapy sessions overall. Secondly, it may also be that an experienced therapist (as was the therapist in this study) is more flexible and eclectic in aims and techniques than therapists following a manualized approach. Goldfried *et al.*'s (1998) findings support this: comparison of cognitive-behavioural and psychodynamic 'master therapists' found that 'the portions of the sessions judged by therapists to be clinically significant appeared to reflect a blending of both orientations' and concluded that the interventions of 'master-therapists' were less pure theoretically than manual-based treatment. Thirdly, it may be that the nature of this particular client's difficulties and interpersonal style are such that therapist responsiveness (Stiles *et al.*, 1998) dictated a more emotion generating approach as indicated by the analysis of core themes within sessions.

Angus *et al.* (1999) argue that the NPCS can offer a way to name and trace the emergence and fate of core themes across the therapy process. The results of this study demonstrate that the use of NPCS can show the emergence of core themes from the analysis of just less than two sessions.

The higher proportion of Reflexive over Internal and External narrative process sequences in the current study reflect Angus *et al.*'s (1999) findings, which was also correlated with good outcome in therapy. Goldfried *et al.*'s (1998) study of 'master-therapists' supports this:

'Regardless of theoretical orientation, the session portions judged to be clinically significant involved a greater focus on clients' ability to observe themselves in an objective way, their evaluation of their self-worth, their expectations about their future, their thoughts in general, their emotions, and aspects of their functioning' (p. 809).

The comparison of the NPCS with the CCRT methods of analysis led to similar formulations of the main themes in therapy. As the CCRT is designed to analyze micro-narratives and the NPCS to analyze macro-narratives, the similarity of the findings from both methods raises some interesting questions about the relationship of micro-narratives to the macro-narrative.

As the NPCS does not allow for more specificity than a relational focus of self/other/self and other it does not allow for comparison with the CCRT's Response of Other. In this study, the Response of Other, according to CCRT analysis, was 'Rejecting and Opposing and Upset'. The CCRT analysis also revealed a wish to be loved and understood that did not emerge from the NPCS topic issues analysis. It may suggest that an implicit wish can only be discerned through the analysis of the Response of Other or that the NPCS method of topic segmentation is generally not subtle enough to discern an implicit wish.

Angus *et al.* (1999) argue that 'the therapist's facilitation of topic-facet shifts helps both clients and therapists to develop a more differentiated, contextual understanding of clients' key concerns and aids in the germination of core themes that integrate disparate client experiences across sessions' (p. 1267). The greater proportion of therapist facilitated topic-shifts to client initiated topic-shifts in this study would appear to reflect this argument. Given that therapists and clients are viewed as co-constructing meaning during the therapy hour, it is expected that both clients and therapists will initiate narrative-sequence shifts during the therapy hour. The NPCS offers an empirical index of therapist and client agency, in the therapeutic relationship, by generating a precise accounting of the number of narrative-mode shifts initiated by client and therapist. The relatively equal initiation of narrative-sequence shifts by client and therapist in this study confirms this expectation and also accords with various findings by Angus and her co-researchers.

The results of the analysis of the metaphors within this study did confirm the hypothesis that the metaphors used would relate to core themes, as arrived at by the NPCS and the CCRT. The co-construction and joint elaboration of the metaphors within these two sample sessions was also demonstrated in Table 11.7. Ferrara (1994) points out that joint construction of extended metaphor and the ratification of each other's metaphors build rapport in the therapy dyad, facilitate further client self-expression, and foster insight. 'Some metaphors are accepted and some are rejected. The point is that they are all negotiated. Their meaning is not static but 'interactive'. (McMullen, 1985) concluded that in successful cases 'there might be a greater degree of "sharing" of figures between client and therapist' (p. 618). Angus and Rennie (1988) found that the collaborative elaboration of a metaphor by a client and therapist was associated with 'the development of a mutually shared understanding of the meaning of a metaphor' (p. 552) and seemed to be a marker of the collaborative nature of the therapeutic relationship itself.

Figurative language is a frequent and important aspect of therapy discourse: Lenrow (1966) found that there was an average of three metaphors per 100 words in a single hour of therapy. This study yielded double that figure. Angus (1996) found that good-outcome dyads had an average of 53 metaphors per session, while poor outcome dyads averaged 73, evidencing as explanation for this counter-intuitive finding that 'intensive sequential analysis of therapy sessions revealed that therapist and clients in good-outcome dyads tended to co-create and reuse a core set of metaphoric phrases or themes in their therapeutic conversations.' (Angus, 1996, p. 75). This study demonstrated an average of 50 metaphors per session, further supporting the evidence above that metaphors in this study related to core themes and demonstrated a cohesiveness that argues for a strong working alliance.

Overall the results of this study confirm the usefulness of the NPCS as a tool for studying narrative, especially at the macro-narrative level, but even at the micro-narrative level. NPCS has obvious value in generating hypotheses about ongoing treatment and prediction of outcome. Topics suggested for further study on the basis of the current pilot include the role of metaphor in the co-construction and transformation of the micro- and macro-narratives in therapy and the link between the generation of emotion within the session and the use of metaphor.

Conclusion

In this introduction to process research methods, we have aimed to guide the student practitioner through the stages of the systematic investigation of the psychotherapy process, using some of the methods in current use. The starting point for most research is a question. The researcher then needs to consider ways of finding answers to this question, either from established research methods or by devising a new research strategy. We have sought to demonstrate that the research process, like the clinical process, can be conducted in a spirit of open minded inquiry, using methods appropriate to the task. The research project needs to be designed to address the clinical questions that the researcher wants to ask in a way that ensures transparency, consistency and reasonable validity and reliability. However, no project, whether big or small, should follow slavishly a particular research methodology, but rather should approach the question in an open and enquiring way and devise research strategies which are realistic and appropriate to investigate the question. The value of the small scale, individual practitioner or student research project may not necessarily be in the actual findings, or in the potential generalizability of these findings into other settings. It is, rather, the discipline of the process of inquiry, and the immersion in the process itself, which can deepen understanding of both the clinical and the research process.

In many research traditions the emphasis is upon the practitioner being separate from the researcher, and this is the case in much large scale psychotherapy research. This is consistent with an approach which emphasizes the need for objectivity, blind coding etc. However, within the clinical field of psychotherapy the importance of not trying to separate the clinician from the clinical process, as in the original 'blank screen' emphasis of Freud, has been recognized for many years. It is now recognized that the psychotherapist is an active participant in the therapeutic relationship with feelings and reactions, typically referred to as counter-transference responses. The impossibility of separating the observer from the observed has been recognized in other scientific fields. We have attempted in this book to highlight the benefit of research being practitioner-based. This not only ensures that research questions and methodologies are clinically meaningful, but also has a sometimes unexpected pay off in clinical terms. It has been our experience in teaching research to trainee and qualified psychotherapists that while they frequently show resistance to engaging in the research process, they commonly experience this as of immense value to their work as clinicians.

For this reason it seems appropriate to conclude this exploration of process research with the reflections of the student/practitioner whose project has been reproduced above, on her experience of undertaking research for the first time:

In conclusion, I should like to make some personal observations about the process of this study that I feel have relevance for clinicians and for the issue of practitioner research. For this researcher, the experience of undertaking and completing this study has been an immensely instructive and salutary experience in the following ways:

Firstly, much of the literature on empirical process research of psychotherapy was unknown to me. This might seem merely a regrettable but unsurprising fact, except that I am a well qualified and experienced clinician with twenty-five years practice. I have undertaken a professional training with one of the leading psychoanalytic psychotherapy bodies in the U.K.; I have a Diploma in Supervision of Counsellors; I have developed and run a Psychodynamic Counselling Diploma Course that achieved British Association of Counsellors and Psychotherapists (BACP) accreditation; I am a BACP accredited Senior Practitioner, Supervisor and Trainer. That I was so ignorant of the evidence-based body of knowledge about the psychotherapy process, some of which was counter-intuitive or challenging of partisan beliefs within any particular orientation, suggests that other clinicians may be in a similar position. This has a direct impact on clinical practice: at the crudest level, for instance, if a clinician is unaware that meta-analyses have shown that good outcome is correlated with, in descending order of importance, factors within the patient and their external situation (40%); working alliance, (30%); placebo effects (15%) and therapist technique, (15%) (Bergin and Garfield, 1994) then there are obvious implications to the handling of, and response to, the process. I and other clinicians are denied, through their ignorance, important and efficacious knowledge to guide their practice, regardless of their expertise in the theoretical and technical aspects of their particular model.

This also raises questions about training and the apparent deficiency in many professional trainings of research-based knowledge and the fostering of a critical and research-orientated weltanschauung. The relationship between theory and practice is a complex and creatively dialectical one and we need constantly to cross fertilise the two. 'Concepts may broaden and expand as clinical experience is gained and observations are sharpened and refined' (Sandler, 1983) but equally we need to inform our experience with new knowledge, new theories, tested and refined.

Secondly, an awareness of the process research is helpful in raising awareness of the change factors in the psychotherapeutic process and the commonalities across orientations. This fosters mutual respect and communication between practitioners and is instrumental in building a cohesive, co-operative identity in a profession that has been riven with schisms and splits, which must, in the final analysis, benefit the consumer, our clients. I have worked closely with clinicians of different theoretical persuasions but it was gratifying to find evidence for our mutual respect. It has also allowed me to be more informed and effective in deciding with prospective patients/ clients whether my model is more appropriate for their needs or whether, and where, I might refer them.

Thirdly, the mere fact of engaging in a reflective and exploratory process about one's work has a refreshing and developmental effect on one's practice. The process of transcribing my sessions has allowed me to become more aware of myself, my interventions and their impact on my clients than even a process record, carefully supervised, could have done. In addition, the analysis of these transcripts has clarified and sharpened my thinking about my clients, the formulations I had made and the process of the therapy. This has extended into my thinking about clients/ patients not included in the study. Since doing the research project I feel that my listening has been enriched: that I am able to hear my patients on a number of additional levels that include the narrative sequence they are engaged upon, their use of metaphor and references to core conflictual issues; that I am more attuned to cues about the state of the working alliance and more sensitised to their responses to my interventions.

Overall, my experience would suggest that the benefits of engaging in practitioner research to further one's own development and one's clinical practice outweigh any resistances or effort involved.

Philippa Shadrach Long

References

Albani, C., Villmann, T., Korner, A., Reulecke, M., Blaser, G., Pokorny, D., Geyer, M. and Kachele, H. (2001) 'Zentrale Beziehungsmuster im Vergleich verschiedener Objekte [Central relationship patterns in comparison with different objects]', *Psychotherapie, Psychosomatik und Medizinische Psychologie*, 7: 298–300.

Alden, L.E., Wiggins, J.S. and Pincus, A.L. (1990) 'Construction of circumplex scales for the Inventory of Interpersonal Problems', *Journal of Personality Assessment*, 55: 521–36.

American Psychiatric Association (1994) *Diagnostic and Statistical Manual of Mental Disorders*, 4th edn. Washington DC: APA.

Androutsopoulou, A. (2001) 'The self-characterization as narrative tool: Applications in therapy with individuals and families', *Family Process*, 40(1): 79–94.

Angus, L.E. (1992) 'Metaphor and the communication interaction in psychotherapy: a multi-methodological approach', in S.G. Toukmanian and D.L. Rennie (eds), *Psychotherapy Process Research: Paradigmatic and narrative approaches*. Newbury Park: Sage.

Angus, L.E. (1996) 'An intensive analysis of metaphor themes in psychotherapy', in J. Mio and A. Katz, (eds), *Metaphor: Implications and applications*. Mahwah, NJ: Lawrence Erlbaum Associates.

Angus, L. and Hardtke, K. (1994) 'Narrative processes in psychotherapy', *Canadian Psychology*, 35: 190–203.

Angus, L.E. and Korman, Y. (2002) 'A metaphor theme analysis: Conflicts, coherence and change in brief psychotherapy', in S.R. Fussel (ed.), *The Verbal Communication of Emotions: Interdisciplinary perspectives*. Mahwah, NJ: Lawrence Erlbaum Associates.

Angus, L. and McLeod, J. (2004) *The Handbook of Narrative and Psychotherapy: Practice, theory, research*. London: Sage.

Angus, L.E. and Rennie, D.L. (1988) 'Therapist participation in metaphor generation: Collaborative and non-collaborative styles', *Psychotherapy*, 25: 552–60.

Angus, L.E. and Rennie, D.L. (1989) 'Envisioning the representational world: The client's experience of metaphoric expressiveness in psychotherapy', *Psychotherapy*, 26: 373–9.

Angus, L., Levitt, H. and Hardtke, K. (1999) 'The Narrative Process Coding System: Research applications and implications for psychotherapy practice', *Journal of Clinical Psychology*, 55: 1255–70.

Angus, L., Lewin, J., Bouffard, B. and Rotondi-Trevisan, D. (2004) 'What's the story? Working with narrative in experiential psychotherapy', in L. Angus and J. McLeod (2004), *The Handbook of Narrative and Psychotherapy: Practice, theory, research*. London: Sage.

Annells, M. (1996) 'Grounded theory method: Philosophical perspectives, paradigm of inquiry, and postmodernism', *Qualitative Health Research*, 6(3): 379–94.

Asay, T.P. and Lambert, M.J. (2000) 'The empirical case for the common factors in therapy: quantitative findings', in M. Hubble, B. Duncan and S. Miller (eds), *The Heart and Soul of Change*. Washington DC: American Psychological Association.

Athern, J. and Madill, A. (1999) 'How do transitional objects work? The therapist's view', *British Journal of Medical Psychology*, 72: 83–96.

Athern, J. and Madill, A. (2002) 'How do transitional objects work? The client's view', *Psychotherapy Research*, 12(3): 369–88.

Barber, J.P. and Crits-Cristoph, P (1993) 'Advances in measures of psychodynamic formulations', *Journal of Consulting and Clinical Psychology*, 61(4): 574–85.

Barber, J.P., Foltz, C., DeRubeis, R.J. and Landis, J.R. (2002) 'Consistency of interpersonal themes in narratives about relationships', *Psychotherapy Research*, 12(2): 139–58.

Barber, J.P., Luborsky, L., Crits-Christoph, P. and Diguer, L. (1995) 'A comparison of Core Conflictual Relationship Themes before psychotherapy and during early sessions', *Journal of Consulting and Clinical Psychology*, 63: 145–8.

Barkham, M. (1996) 'Individual therapy: Process and outcome findings across successive research generations', in W. Dryden (ed.), *Handbook of Individual Therapy*. London: Sage.

Barkham, M., Margison, F., Leach, C., Lucock, M., Mellor-Clark, J., Evans, C., Benson, L., Connell, J., Audin, K. and McGrath, G. (2001) 'Service profiling and outcomes benchmarking using the CORE-OM: Toward practice-based evidence in the psychological therapies', *Journal of Consulting and Clinical Psychology*, 69(2): 184–96.

Barkham, M., Stiles, W.B., Hardy, G.E. and Field, S.D. (1996) 'The assimilation model: Theory, research and practical guidelines', in W. Dryden (ed.), *Research in Counselling and Psychotherapy: Practical Applications*. London: Routledge.

Barlow, J.M., Pollio, H.R. and Fine, H.S. (1977) 'Insight and figurative language in psychotherapy', *Psychotherapy: Theory, Research and Practice*, 14: 212–22.

Barnes, D. (1996) 'An analysis of the grounded theory method and the concept of culture', *Qualitative Health Research*, 6(3): 429–42.

Benjamin, L.S. (1974) 'Structural analysis of social behaviour', *Psychological Review*, 81: 392–425.

Benjamin, L.S. (1988) *The Short Form INTREX User's Manual, Part I*, Salt Lake City: University of Utah.

Benjamin, L.S. (1994) 'SASB: A bridge between personality theory and clinical psychology', *Psychological Inquiry*, 5(4): 273–316.

Benjamin, L.S. (1996a) *Interpersonal Diagnosis and Treatment of Personality Disorders.* New York: Guilford.

Benjamin, L.S. (1996b) 'A clinician-friendly version of the interpersonal circumplex: Structural analysis of social behaviour', *Journal of Personality Assessment,* 66(2): 248–66.

Benjamin, L.S. (2004) 'Interpersonal theory of personality disorders: The structural analysis of social behavior and interpersonal reconstructive therapy', in M. Lenzenweger and J. Clarkin (eds), *Major Theories of Personality,* 2nd edn. New York: Guilford Press.

Benjamin, L.S. and Cushing, G. (2000) 'Reference manual for coding social interactions in terms of Structural Analysis of Social Behaviour', unpublished update for Benjamin, L.S., Giat, L. and Estroff, S.E. (1981) 'Manual for coding social interactions in terms of Structural Analysis of Social Behaviour'.

Bergin, A.E. and Garfield, S.L. (eds) (1994) *Handbook of Psychotherapy and Behaviour Change,* 4th edn. New York: Wiley.

Bergin, A.E. and Lambert, M.J. (1978) 'The evaluation of therapeutic outcome', in S.L. Garfield and A.E. Bergin (eds), *Handbook of Psychotherapy and Behaviour Change,* 2nd edn. New York: Wiley.

Bhaskar, R. (1979/1989) *The Possibility of Naturalism.* New York: Harvester Wheatsheaf.

Birtchnell, J. (1993) *How Humans Relate. A new interpersonal theory.* Westport, CT: Praeger.

Birtchnell, J. (1994) 'The interpersonal octagon: An alternative to the interpersonal circle', *Human Relations,* 47: 511–29.

Birtchnell, J. (1999) *Relating in Psychotherapy.* London: Praeger.

Bob, S.R. (1999) 'Narrative approaches to supervision and case formulation', *Psychotherapy,* 36(2): 146 –53.

Bolger, E. (1999) 'Analysis of emotional pain', *Psychotherapy Research,* 9(3): 342–62.

Book, H.E. (1997) *How to Practice Brief Psychodynamic Psychotherapy: The Core Conflictual Relationship Theme Method.* Washington DC: American Psychological Association.

Bordin, E.S. (1976) 'The generalisability of the psychoanalytic concept of the working alliance', *Psychotherapy: Theory, research and practice,* 16: 252–60.

Bordin, E. (1994) 'Theory and research on the therapeutic working alliance: New directions', in A.O. Horvath and L.S. Greenberg (eds), *The Working Alliance: Theory, research, practice.* New York: John Wiley.

Bressi, C., Amadei, G., Caparrelli, S., Cattaneo, C., Cova, F., Crespi, F., Crespi, S., dell'Arringa, M., Ponti, F., Zirulia, V. and Invernizz, G. (2000) 'A clinical and psychodynamic follow-up study of crisis intervention and brief psychotherapy in psychiatric emergency', *New Trends in Experimental and Clinical Psychiatry,* 16(1–4): 31–7.

Bruner, J. (1990) *Acts of Meaning.* Cambridge, MA: Harvard University Press.

Bruner, J. and Haste, H. (eds) (1987) *Making Sense: The child's construction of the world.* London: Routledge.

Bucci, W. (1997) *Psychoanalysis and Cognitive Science: A multiple code theory*. New York: Guilford.

Bucheim, A. and Mergenthaler, E. (2003) 'The relationship among attachment representation, emotion – abstraction patterns and narrative style: A computer-based text analysis of the adult attachment interview, *Psychotherapy Research*, 10(4): 390–407.

Carson, R.C. (1969) *Interaction Concepts of Personality*. Chicago: Aldine

Cartwright, A., Hyams, G. and Spratley, T. (1996) 'Is the interviewer's therapeutic commitment an important factor in determining whether alcoholic clients engage in treatment?', *Addiction Research*, 4(3): 215–30.

Cassidy, J. and Shaver, P.R. (eds) (2002) *Handbook of Attachment: Theory, research and clinical applications*. New York: Guilford.

Chaika, E. (2000) *Linguistics, Pragmatics and Psychotherapy: A guide for therapists*. London: Whurr.

Chance, S.E., Bakeman, R., Kaslow, N.J., Farber, E. and Burge-Callaway, K. (2000) 'Core conflictual relationship themes in patients diagnosed with borderline personality disorder who attempted, or who did not attempt, suicide', *Psychotherapy Research*, 10(3): 337–55.

Chassan, J.B. (1979) *Research Design in Clinical Psychology and Psychiatry*. New York: Wiley.

Cierpka, M., Strack, M., Benninghoven, D., Staats, H., Dahlbender, R., Pokorny, D., Frevert, G., Blaser, G., Kachele, H., Geyer, M., Korner, A. and Albani, C. (1998) 'Stereotypical relationship patterns and psychopathology', *Psychotherapy and Psychosomatics*, 67: 241–8.

Cohen, J. (1968) 'Weighted kappa: Nominal scale agreement with provision for scaled disagreement or partial credit', *Psychological Bulletin*, 70: 213–20.

Covington, C. (1995) 'No story, no analysis: The role of narrative in interpretation', *Journal of Analytical Psychology*, 40: 405–17.

Crits-Christoph, P. and Luborsky, L. (1990) 'Changes in CCRT pervasiveness during psychotherapy', in L. Luborsky and P. Crits-Christoph, *Understanding Transference*. New York: Basic Books.

Crits-Christoph, P., Barber, J.P. and Kurcias, J.S. (1993) 'The accuracy of therapists' interpretation and the development of the therapeutic alliance', *Psychotherapy Research*, 3, 25–35.

Crits-Christoph, P., Cooper, A. and Luborsky, L. (1988a) 'The accuracy of therapist interpretation and the outcome of dynamic psychotherapy', *Journal of Consulting and Clinical Psychology*, 56, 490–5.

Crits-Christoph, P., Demorts, A., Muenz, L.R. and Baranackie, K. (1994) 'Consistency of interpersonal themes', *Journal of Personality*, 62: 499–526.

Crits-Christoph, P., Luborsky, L., Dahl, L., Popp, C., Mellon, J. and Mark, D. (1988b) 'Clinicians can agree in assessing relationship patterns in psychotherapy: The Core Conflictual Relationship Theme method', *Archives of General Psychiatry*, 45: 1001–4.

Culler, J. (1959) 'Introduction', in F. de Saussure, *Course in General Linguistics*. New York: Fontana/Collins.

Curtis, J.T., Silberschatz, G., Sampson, H. and Weiss, J. (1994) 'The Plan Formulation Method', *Psychotherapy Research*, 4: 197–207.

Cutcliffe, J.R. (2000) 'Methodological issue in grounded theory', *Journal of Advanced Nursing*, 31(6): 1476–84.

Dahl, H. and Teller, V. (1994) 'The characteristics, identification, and application of FRAMES', *Psychotherapy Research*, 44: 253–76.

DeWitt, K.N., Kaltreider, N.B., Weiss, D.S. and Horowtiz, M.J. (1983) 'Judging change in psychotherapy', *Archives of General Psychiatry*, 40, 1121–8.

Dolan, B., Evans, C. and Norton, K. (1995) 'Multiple Axis-II diagnoses of personality disorder', *British Journal of Psychiatry*, 166: 107–12.

Duranti, A. and Goodwin, C. (1992) *Rethinking Context*. Cambridge: Cambridge University Press.

Eames, V. and Roth, A. (2000) 'Patient attachment orientation and the early working alliance – A study of patient and therapy report of alliance quality and ruptures', *Psychotherapy Research*, 10(4): 421–34.

Edwards, D. (1997a) 'Structure and function in the analysis of everyday narratives', *Journal of Narrative and Life History*, 7(1–4): 139–46.

Edwards, D. (1997b) *Discourse and Cognition*. London: Sage.

Edwards, D. and Potter, J. (1992) *Discursive Psychology*. London: Sage.

Elkin, I. (1994) 'The NIMH treatment of depression collaborative research study', in A.E. Bergin and S.L. Garfield (eds), *Handbook of Psychotherapy and Behaviour Change*, 4th edn. New York: Wiley.

Elliott, R. (1985) 'Helpful and nonhelpful events in brief counseling interviews: An empirical taxonomy', *Journal of Counseling Psychology*, 32: 307–22.

Elliott, R. (1986) 'Interpersonal Process Recall (IPR) as a psychotherapy process research method', in L.S. Greenberg and W.M. Pinsof (eds), *The Psychotherapeutic Process: A research handbook*. New York: Guilford.

Elliott, R., Greenberg, L.S. and Lietaer, G. (2003) 'Research on experiential psychotherapies', in M.J. Lambert (ed.), *Bergin and Garfield's Handbook of Psychotherapy and Behaviour Change*, 5th edn. New York: Wiley.

Elliott, R., Slatick, E. and Urman, M. (2001) 'Qualitative change process research on psychotherapy: Alternative strategies', in J. Frommer and D.L. Rennie (eds), *Qualitative Psychotherapy Research – Methods and Methodology*. Lengerich, Germany: Pabst Science Publishers.

Ervin-Tripp, S. and Kuntay, A. (1996) 'The occasioning and structure of conversational stories', in T. Givon (ed.), *Conversation: Cognitive, communicative and social perspectives*. Amsterdam: John Benjamins.

Evans, C., Connell, J., Barkham, M., Mellor-Clark, J., McGrath, G. and Audin, K. (2002) 'Towards a standardised brief outcome measure: psychometric properties and utility of the CORE-OM', *British Journal of Psychiatry*, 180: 51–60

Eysenck, H.F. (1952) 'The effects of psychotherapy: An evaluation', *Journal of Consulting Psychology*, 16: 319–24.

Ferrara, K.W. (1994) *Therapeutic Ways With Words*. Oxford: Oxford University Press.

Florsheim, P. and Benjamin, L.S. (2001) 'The structural analysis of social behavior observational coding scheme', in P.K. Kerig and L.M. Lindahl (eds), *Family Observational Coding Systems: Resources for systemic research.* Hillsdale, NJ: Lawrence Erlbaum Associates.

Florsheim, P., Tolan, P.H. and Gorman-Smith, D. (1996) 'Family processes and risk for externalizing behavior problems among African American and Hispanic boys', *Journal of Consulting and Clinical Psychology*, 64(6): 1222–30.

Fonagy, P., Gergely, G., Jurist, E.L., Target, M. (2004) *Affect Regulation, Mentalization, and the Development of the Self.* London: Karnac.

Fonagy, P., Leigh, T., Steele, M., Steele, H., Kennedy, R., Mattoon, G., Target, M. and Gerber, T. (1996) 'The relation of attachment status, psychiatric classification, and response to psychotherapy', *Journal of Consulting and Clinical Psychology*, 64: 22–31.

Fontao, M.I. and Mergenthaler, E. (2002) 'Das Therapeutische Zyklusmodell: Eine Evaluation im pruppenpsychotherapeutischen Setting'. *Gruppenpsychotherapie und Gruppendynamik*, 38(4): 349–71.

Foucault, M. (1973) *The Birth of the Clinic.* London: Tavistock Publications.

Foucault, M. (1990) *The History of Sexuality: An introduction.* New York: Vintage Books.

Frank, J.D. and Frank, J.B. (1993) *Persuasion and Healing*, 3rd edn. Baltimore, MD: Johns Hopkins University Press.

Freedman, M.B., Leary, T., Ossorio, A.G. and Coffey, H.S. (1951) 'The interpersonal dimension of personality', *Journal of Personality*, 20: 143–61.

Freud, A. (1938) *The Ego and the Mechanisms of Defence.* London: Hogarth Press.

Freud, S. (1912/1979) *The Dynamics of Transference.* London: The Pelican Freud Library.

Fried, D., Crits-Christoph, P. and Luborsky, L. (1992) 'The first empirical demonstration of transference in psychotherapy', *Journal of Nervous and Mental Disease*, 180: 326–31.

Gale, J.E. (1991) *Conversation Analysis of Therapeutic Discourse: The pursuit of a therapeutic agenda.* Norwood, NJ: Ablex.

Gill, M., Newman, R. and Redlich, F.C. (1954) *The Initial Interview in Psychiatric Practice.* New York: International Universities Press.

Glaser, B. (1978) *Theoretical Sensitivity: Advances in the methodology of grounded theory.* Mill Valley, CA: The Sociology Press.

Glaser, B. (1992) *Emergence vs Forcing: Basics of grounded theory analysis.* Mill Valley, CA: The Sociology Press.

Glaser, B. and Strauss, A (1967) *The Discovery of Grounded Theory.* London: Weidenfeld & Nicolson.

Glaser, S. (1990) 'Rhetoric and therapy', in M.J. Mahoney (ed.), *Psychotherapy Process: Current issues and future directions.* New York: Plenum Press.

Goldfried, M.R., Raue, P.J. and Castonguay, L.G. (1998) 'The therapeutic focus in significant sessions of master therapists: A comparison of cognitive-behavioural and psychodynamic-interpersonal interventions', *Journal of Consulting and Clinical Psychology*, 66: 803–10.

Goncalves, O.F. and Machado, P.P. (1999) 'Cognitive narrative psychotherapy: research foundations', *Journal of Clinical Psychology*, 55(10): 1179–91.

Goncalves, O., Machado, P., Korman, Y. and Angus, L. (2002) 'Assessing psychopathology: A narrative approach', in L. Beutler and M. Malik (eds) *Rethinking the DSM: A psychological perspective*. Washington DC: American Psychological Association.

Goodwin, M.J. (1997) 'Toward families of stories in context', *Journal of Narrative and Life History*, 7(1–4): 107–12.

Gore, N. (1977) *Psychological Functions of Metaphor*. Dissertation Abstracts International, 38 6B 286.

Grafanaki, S. and McLeod, J. (1999) 'Narrative processes in the construction of helpful and hindering events in experiential psychotherapy', *Psychotherapy Research*, 9(3): 289–303.

Greenberg, J.R. and Mitchell, S.A. (1984) *Object Relations in Psychoanalytic Theory*. Cambridge, MA: Harvard University Press.

Greenberg, L.S. (1986) 'Change process research', *Journal of Consulting and Clinical Psychology*, 54: 4–9.

Greenberg, L.S. and Pinsof, W.M. (ed.) (1986) *The Psychotherapeutic Process: A research handbook*. New York: Guilford.

Greenberg, L.S. and Watson, J. (1998) 'Experiential therapy of depression: Differential effects of client centred conditions and active experiential interventions', *Psychotherapy Research*, 8: 210–25.

Grunbaum, A. (1984) *The Foundations of Psychoanalysis*. Los Angeles: University of California Press.

Hall, W. and Callery, P. (2001) 'Enhancing the rigor of grounded theory: Incorporating reflexivity and relationality', *Qualitative Health Research*, 11(2): 257–73.

Hardtke, K. (1996) 'Characterising therapy focus and exploring client process: Investigating therapeutic modalities from a narrative approach', unpublished Master's thesis. Dept. of Psychology, York University, Toronto, Ontario, Canada.

Hardy, G, Aldridge, J, Davidson, C, Rowe, C, Reilly, S and Shapiro, D.D. (1999) 'Therapist responsiveness to client attachment styles and issues observed in client-identified significant events in psychodynamic-interpersonal psychotherapy', *Psychotherapy Research*, 9: 36–53.

Henry, W.P. (1996) 'Structural analysis of social behavior as a common metric for programmatic psychopathology and psychotherapy research', *Journal of Consulting and Clinical Psychology*, 64: 1263–75.

Henry, W.P. and Strupp, H.H. (1994) 'The therapeutic alliance as interpersonal process', in A.O. Horvath and L.S. Greenberg (eds), *The Working Alliance: Theory, research, practice*. New York: John Wiley.

Henry, W.P., Schacht, T.E. and Strupp, H.H. (1986) 'Structural analysis of social behavior: Application to a study of interpersonal process in differential psychotherapeutic outcome', *Journal of Consulting and Clinical Psychology*, 54(1): 27–31.

Henry, W.P., Schacht, T.E. and Strupp, H.H. (1990) 'Patient and therapist introject, interpersonal process and differential psychotherapy outcome', *Journal of Consulting and Clinical Psychology*, 58: 768–74.

Henry, W.P., Strupp, H.H., Schacht, T.E. and Gaston, L. (1994) 'Psychodynamic approaches', in A.E. Bergin and S.L Garfield (eds), *Handbook of Psychotherapy and Behavior Change*. New York: Wiley.

Heritage, J. (2002) 'The limits of questioning: negative interrogatives and hostile question content', *Journal of Pragmatics*, 34(10–11): 1427–46.

Hill, C.E. (1991) 'Almost everything you ever wanted to know about how to do process research on counseling and psychotherapy but didn't know who to ask', in C.E. Watkins and L.J. Schneider (eds), *Research in Counseling*. London: Sage.

Hill, C.E. and Lambert, M.J. (2003) 'Methodological issues in studying psychotherapy processes and outcomes', in M.J. Lambert (ed.), *Bergin and Garfield's Handbook of Psychotherapy and Behaviour Change*, 5th edn. New York: Wiley.

Hilliard, R.B. (1993) 'Single-case methodology in psychotherapy process and outcome research', *Journal of Consulting and Clinical Psychology*, 61: 373–80.

Hilliard, R.B., Henry, W.P. and Strupp, H.H. (2000) 'An interpersonal model of psychotherapy: linking patient and therapist developmental history, therapeutic process and types of outcome', *Journal of Consulting and Clinical Psychology*, 68: 125–33.

Hobson, R.F. (1985) *Forms of Feeling*. London: Tavistock.

Honos-Webb, L. and Stiles, W.B. (1998) 'Reformulation of assimilation analysis in terms of voices', *Psychotherapy*, 35: 23–33.

Honos-Webb, L., Stiles, W.B., Greenberg, L.S. and Goldman, R. (1998a) 'Assimilation analysis of process-experiential psychotherapy: a comparison of two cases', *Psychotherapy Research*, 8: 264–86.

Honos-Webb, L., Surko, M. and Stiles, W.B. (1998b) 'Manual for rating assimilation in psychotherapy', Unpublished manuscript. Oxford Ohio: Miami University.

Honos-Webb, L., Surko, M., Stiles, W.B. and Greenberg, L.S. (1999) 'Assimilation of voices in psychotherapy: The case of Jan', *Journal of Counseling Psychology*, 46: 448–60.

Horowitz, L.M. and Rosenberg, S.E. (1994) 'The consensual response psychodynamic formulation: Part 1. Method and research results', *Psychotherapy Research*, 4: 222–33.

Horowitz, L.M., Rosenberg, S.E., Baer, B.A., Ureno, G. and Villasenor, V.S. (1988) 'Inventory of interpersonal problems: Psychometric properties and clinical applications', *Journal of Consulting and Clinical Psychology*, 56: 885–92.

Horowitz, L.M., Rosenberg, S.E. and Bartholemew, K.. (1993) 'Interpersonal problems, attachment styles, and outcome in brief dynamic psychoterapy', *Journal of Consulting and Clinical Psychology*, 61: 549–60.

Horowitz, L.M., Rosenberg, S.E., Ureno, G., Kalehzan, B.M., O'Halloran, P. (1989) 'Psychodynamic formulation, consensual response method, and interpersonal problems', *Journal of Consulting and Clinical Psychology*, 57: 599–606.

Horowitz, M.J. (1987) *States of Mind: Configurational analysis of individual psychology*. New York: Plenum.

Horvarth, A.O. and Bedi, R.P. (2002) 'The alliance', in J.C. Norcross, *Psychotherapy Relationships that Work. Therapist contributions and responsiveness to patients*. New York: Oxford University Press.

Horvarth, A.O and Greenberg, L.S. (eds) (1994) *The Working Alliance: Theory, research and practice*. New York: Wiley.

Howard, K.I., Kopta, S.M., Krause, M.S. and Orlinsky, D.E. (1986) 'The dose-effect relationship in psychotherapy', *American Psychologist*, 41: 159–64.

Howard, K.I., Orlinsky, D.E. and Lueger, R.J. (1995) 'The design of clinically relevant outcome research: Some consideration and an example', in M. Aveline and D.A. Shapiro (eds), *Research Foundations for Psychotherapy Practice*. New York: Wiley.

Humphrey, L.L. (1989) 'Observed family interactions among subtypes of eating disorders using structural analysis of social behavior', *Journal of Consulting and Clinical Psychology*, 57(2): 206–14.

Hyams, G., Cartwright, A. and Spratley, T. (1996) 'Engagement in alcohol treatment: the client's experience of, and satisfaction with, the assessment interview', *Addiction Research*, 4(2): 105–23.

Imber, S.D., Pilkonis, P.A., Sotsky, S.M., Elkin, I., Watkins, J.T., Collins, J.F., Shea, M.T., Leber, W.R. and Glass, D.R. (1990) 'More specific effects among treatments for depression', *Journal of Consulting and Clinical Psychology*, 58: 352–9.

Jacobson, N.S. and Truax, P. (1991) 'Clinical significance: A statistical approach to defining meaningful change in psychotherapy research', *Journal of Consulting and Clinical Psychology*, 59(1): 12–19.

Jefferson, G. (1978) 'Sequential aspects of storytelling in conversation', in J. Schenkein (ed.), *Studies in the Organization of Conversational Interaction*. New York: Academic Press.

Jorgensen, C.R., Hougaard, E., Rosenbaum, B., Valbak, K. and Rehfeld, E. (2000) 'The dynamic assessment interview (DAI), interpersonal process measured by structural analysis of social behavior (SASB) and therapeutic outcome', *Psychotherapy Research*, 10(2): 181–95.

Joyce, A.S. and Piper, W.E. (1998) 'Expectancy, the therapeutic alliance and treatment outcome in short-term individual psychotherapy', *Journal of Psychotherapy Practice and Research*, 7(3): 236–48.

Joyce, A.S., Duncan, S.C. and Piper, W.E. (1995) 'Task analysis of "working through" responses to dynamic interpretation in short-term individual psychotherapy', *Psychotherapy Research*, 5: 49–62.

Kelly, T.A. and Strupp, H.H. (1992) 'Patient and therapist values in psychotherapy: Perceived changes, assimilation, similarity and outcome', *Journal of Consulting and Clinical Psychology*, 60: 34–40.

Kendall, J. (1999) 'Axial coding and grounded theory controversy', *Western Journal of Nursing Research*, 21(6): 743–58.

Kiesler, D. (1971) *Psychology of Commitment: Experiments linking behaviour to belief*. New York: Academic Press.

Kiesler, D. (1981) 'Empirical clinical psychology: Myth or reality?', *Journal of Consulting and Clinical Psychology*, 49: 212–15.

Kiesler, D. (1983a) 'The 1982 interpersonal circle: A taxonomy for complementarity in human transactions', *Psychological Review*, 91: 185–214.

Kiesler, D. (1983b) 'The paradigm shift in psychotherapy process research'. Summary discussant paper presented at the National Institute of Mental Health Workshop of Psychotherapy Process Research, Bethesda, MD.

Kiesler, D. (1992) 'Interpersonal circle inventories: Pantheoretical applications to psychotherapy research and practice', *Journal of Psychotherapy Integration*, 2: 77–99.

Kiesler, D. (1996) 'From communications to interpersonal theory: A personal odyssey', *Journal of Personality Assessment*, 66(2): 267–82.

Kirk, J. and Miller, M.L. (1986) *Reliability and Validity in Qualitative Research*. Beverly Hills: Sage.

Klein, M., Mathieu-Couglan, P. and Kiesler, D. (1986) 'The experiencing scales', in L.S. Greenberg and W.M. Pinsoff (eds), *The Psychotherapeutic Process: A research handbook*. New York: Guilford.

Kogan, S.M. (1998) 'The politics of meaning making: Discourse analysis of a "postmodern" interview', *Journal of Family Therapy*, 20: 229–51.

Kozart, M.F. (2002) 'Understanding efficacy in psychotherapy: An ethnomethodological perspective on the therapeutic alliance. *American Journal of Orthopsychiatry*, 72(2): 217–31.

Kuhnlein, I. (1999) 'Psychotherapy as a process of transformation: Analysis of post-therapeutic autobiographic narrations', *Psychotherapy Research*, 9(3): 274–88.

Labov, W. (1972) *Language in the Inner City: Studies in black English vernacular*. Philadelphia: University of Pennsylvania Press.

Labov, W. (1997) 'Some further steps in narrative analysis', *Journal of Narrative and Life History*, 7(1–4): 395–415.

Labov, W. and Fanshel, D. (1977) *Therapeutic Discourse: Psychotherapy as conversation*. New York: Academic Press.

Labov, W. and Waletsky, J. (1967) 'Narrative analysis: oral versions of personal experience', *Journal of Narrative and Life History*, 7(1–4): 4–38.

Laitila, A. and Aaltonen, J. (1998) 'Application of the assimilation model in the context of family therapy: A case study', *Contemporary Family Therapy*, 20(3): 277–90.

Laitila, A., Aaltonen, J., Wahlstroem, J. and Angus, L. (2001) 'Narrative process coding system in marital and family therapy: An intensive case analysis of the formation of a therapeutic system', *Contemporary Family Therapy: An international journal*, 23(3): 309–22.

Lakoff, G. and Johnson, M. (1980) *Metaphors We Live By*. Chicago: University of Chicago Press.

Lambert, M.J. (ed.) (2003) *Bergin and Garfield's Handbook of Psychotherapy and Behaviour Change*, 5th edn. New York: Wiley.

Lambert, M.J. and Barley, D.E. (2002) 'Research summary on the therapeutic relationship and psychotherapy outcome', in J.C. Norcross (ed.), *Psychotherapy*

Relationships that Work. Therapist contributions and responsiveness to patients. New York: Oxford University Press.

Lambert, M.J. and Bergin, A.E. (1992) 'Achievements and limitations of psychotherapy research', in D.K. Friedham (ed.), *History of Psychotherapy: A century of change.* Washington DC: American Psychological Association.

Lambert, M.J. and Ogles B.M (2003) 'The efficacy and effectiveness of psychotherapy', in M.J. Lambert (ed.), *Bergin and Garfield's Handbook of Psychotherapy and Behaviour Change,* 5th edition. New York: Wiley.

Lambert, M.J., Garfield, S.L. and Bergin, A.E. (2003) 'Overview, trends, and future issues', in M.J. Lambert (ed.), *Bergin and Garfield's Handbook of Psychotherapy and Behaviour Change,* 5th edition. New York: Wiley.

Leary, T. (1957) *Interpersonal Diagnosis of Personality.* New York: Ronald.

Leiman, M. and Stiles, W.B. (2001) 'Dialogical sequence analysis and the zone of proximal development as conceptual enhancements to the assimilation model: the case of Jan revisited', *Psychotherapy Research,* 11(3): 311–30.

Lenrow, P.B. (1966) 'The use of metaphor in facilitating constructive behaviour change', *Psychotherapy,* 3 (4), 145–8.

Lepper, G. (2000) *Categories in Text and Talk: A practical guide to categorization analysis.* London: Sage.

Lepper, G. (2001) 'Values and ethics in researching psychotherapy', in F. Palmer-Barnes and L. Murdin (eds), *Values and Ethics in the Practice of Psychotherapy and Counselling.* Milton Keynes: Open University Press.

Lepper, G. and Mergenthaler, E. (2004) 'Therapeutic alliance as an interactional accomplishment: a multi-method investigation of the patient/ therapist interaction in a brief psychodynamic therapy', panel presentation, International conference, Society for Psychotherapy Research, Rome.

Lepper, G. and Mergenthaler, E. (2005) 'Exploring group process', *Psychotherapy Research,* 15(4): 433–44.

Levitt, H. (2001) 'Sounds of silence in psychotherapy: the categorization of clients' pauses', *Psychotherapy Research,* 11(3): 295–309.

Levitt, H., Korman, Y. and Angus, L. (2000) 'A metaphor analysis in treatments of depression: Metaphor as a marker of change', *Counselling Psychology Quarterly,* 13(1): 23–35.

Linell, O. and Korolija, N. (1997) 'Coherence in multi-party conversation: Episodes and contexts in interaction', in T. Givon (ed.), *Conversation: Cognitive, communicative and social perspectives.* Amsterdam/Philadelphia: John Benjamins.

Luborsky, L. (1986) 'Evidence to lessen Professor Grunbaum's concern about Freud's clinical inference methods', *Behavioral and Brain Sciences,* 9: 247–9.

Luborsky, L. and Barber, J.P. (1994) 'Perspectives on seven transference-related measures applied to the interview with Ms Smithfield', *Psychotherapy Research,* 4: 152–4.

Luborsky, L. and Crits-Christoph, P. (1990) *Understanding Transference: The CCRT method.* New York: Basic Books.

Luborsky, L. and Crits-Christoph, P. (1998) *Understanding Transference,* 2nd edn. New York: Basic Books.

Luborsky, L. and Singer, B. (1975) 'Comparative studies of psychotherapies: Is it true that "everyone has won and all must have prizes"?', *Archives of General Psychiatry*, 32: 995–1008.

Luborsky, L., Diguer, L., Seligman, D.A., Rosenthal, R., Krause, E.D., Johnson, S., Halperin, G., Bishop, M., Berman, J. and Schweizer, E. (1999) 'The researcher's own therapy allegiances: A 'wild card', in comparisons of treatment efficacy', *Clinical Psychology Science and Practice*, 6: 95–106.

Luborsky, L., McLellan, A.T, Woody, G.E., O'Brien and Auerbach, A. (1985) 'Therapist success and its determinants', *Archive of General Psychiatry*, 42: 53–63.

Luborsky, L., Popp, C. and Barber, J.P. (1994a) 'Common and Special Factors in Different Transference-related Measures', *Psychotherapy Research*, 4: 277–86.

Luborsky, L., Popp, C., Luborsky, E. and Marx, D. (1994b) 'The core conflictual relationship theme' *Psychotherapy Research*, 4: 172–83.

Lysaker, P.H., Lysaker, J.T. and Lysaker, L. (2001) 'Schizophrenia and the collapse of the dialogical self', *Psychotherapy: Theory, research, practice, training*, 38(3): 252–61.

Macdonald, J. (2001) 'An analysis of data relating to client-therapist interaction and engagement in treatment in an alcohol service', unpublished manuscript, Christ Church University College, Canterbury.

Madill, A., Widdicombe, S. and Barkham, M. (2001) 'The potential of conversation analysis for psychotherapy research', *The Counselling Psychologist*, 29(3): 413–34.

Mahler, M. (1968) *On Human Symbiosis and the Vicissitudes of Individuation*. New York: International Universities Press.

Main, M. (1991) 'Meta-cognitive knowledge, meta-cognitive monitoring and singular (coherent) vs. multiple (incoherent) models of attachment: findings and directions for future research', in P. Marris, J. Stevenson-Hinde and C. Parkes (eds), *Attachment Across the Life Cycle*. New York: Routledge.

Malan, D.H. (1976) *Toward the Validation of Dynamic Psychotherapy*. New York: Plenum Press.

Margison, F.R., Barkham, M., Evans, C., McGrath, G., Mellor Clark, J., Audin, K. and Connell, J. (2000) 'Measurement and psychotherapy. Evidence-based practice and practice-based evidence', *British Journal of Psychiatry*, 177: 123–30.

Marmar, C.R., Horowitz, M.J., Weiss, D.S. and Marziali, E. (1986) 'The development of the therapeutic alliance rating system', in L.S. Greenberg and W.S. Ponsoff (eds), *The Psychotherapy Process: A research handbook*. New York: Guilford.

Mason, O. and Hargreaves, I. (2001) 'A qualitative study of mindfulness-based cognitive therapy for depression', *British Journal of Medical Psychology*, 74: 197–212.

McConnaughy, E.A., DiClemente, C.C., Prochaska, J.O. and Velicer, W.F. (1989) 'Stage of change in psychotherapy: A follow-up report', *Psychotherapy*, 26: 494–503.

McConnaughy, E.A., Prochaska, J.O. and Velicer, W.F. (1983) 'Stage of change in psychotherapy: Measurement and sample profiles', *Psychotherapy: Therapy, research and practice*, 20: 368–75.

McLeod, J. (1994) *Doing Counselling Research*. London: Sage.

McLeod, J. (1997) *Narrative and Psychotherapy*. London: Sage.

McLeod, J. (1999) 'A narrative social constructionist approach to therapeutic empathy', *Counselling Psychology Quarterly*, 12(4): 377–94.

McLeod, J. and Balamoutsou, S. (1996) 'Representing narrative process in therapy: A qualitative analysis of a single case', *Counselling Psychology Quarterly*, 9(1): 61–76.

McMullen, L.M. (1985) 'Methods for studying the use of novel figurative language in psychotherapy', *Psychotherapy*, 22: 610–19.

McMullen, L.M. (1996) 'Studying the use of figurative language in psychotherapy: The search for researchable questions', *Metaphor and Symbolic Activity*, 11(4): 241–55.

McNamee, S. and Gergen, K. (eds) (1992) *Therapy as Social Construction*. London: Sage.

Melia, K.M. (1996) 'Rediscovering Glaser', *Qualitative Health Research*, 6(3): 368–79.

Mergenthaler, E. (1996) 'Emotion-abstraction patterns in verbatim protocols: A new way of describing psychotherapeutic processes', *Journal of Consulting and Clinical Psychology*, 64: 1306–15.

Mergenthaler, E. and Bucci, W. (1999) 'Linking verbal and nonverbal representations: computerized analysis of referential activity', *British Journal of Medical Psychology*, 72(3): 339–54.

Mergenthaler, E. and Horowitz, M.J. (1994) 'Linking computer aided text analysis with variables scored from video tape', in F. Faulbaum (ed.), *SoftStat'93: Advances in statistical software*. New York: Fischer.

Mergenthaler, E. and Kachele, H. (1996) 'Applying multiple computerized text analytic measures to single psychotherapy cases', *Journal of Psychotherapy Practice and Research*, 5(4): 302–17.

Meyer, B. and Pilkonis, P.A. (2002) 'Attachment style', in J.C. Norcross, *Psychotherapy Relationships that Work. Therapist contributions and responsiveness to patients*. New York: Oxford.

Miller, S.I. and Fredericks, M. (1999) 'How does grounded theory explain?', *Qualitative Health Research*, 9(4): 538–52.

Najavits, L.M. and Strupp, H. (1994) 'Differences in the effectiveness of psychodynamic therapists: A process-outcome study', *Psychotherapy*, 31: 114–23.

Newman, D.W. and Beail, N. (2002) 'Monitory change in psychotherapy with people with intellectual disabilities: The application of the assimilation of problematic experiences scale', *Journal of Applied Research in Intellectual Disabilities*, 15: 48–60.

Norcross, J.C. (2002) *Psychotherapy Relationships that Work: Therapist contributions and responsiveness to patients*. New York: Oxford.

Orford, J. (1986) 'The rules of interpersonal complementarity: Does hostility beget hostility and dominance, submission?', *Psychological Review*, 93: 365–77.

Orlinsky, D.E and Howard, K.I. (1986) 'The psychological interior of psychotherapy: Explorations with the therapy sessions reports', in L.S. Greenberg and W.M. Pinsof (eds), *The Psychotherapeutic Process: A research handbook*. New York: Guilford.

Orlinsky, D.E., Grawe, K. and Parks, B.K. (1994) 'Process and outcome in psychotherapy – Noch Einmal', in A.E. Bergin and S.L. Garfield (eds), *Handbook of Psychotherapy and Behaviour Change*, 4th edn. New York: Wiley.

Orlinsky, D.E., Ronnestad, M.H. and Willutzki, U. (2003) 'Fifty years of psychotherapy process-outcome research: Continuity and change', in M.J. Lambert (ed.), *Bergin and Garfield's Handbook of Psychotherapy and Behaviour Change*, 5th edn. New York: Wiley.

Paddock, J.R., Terranova, S. and Giles, L. (2001) 'SASB goes to Hollywood: Teaching personality theories through movies', *Teaching of Psychology*, 28: 117–20.

Parker, I. (1992) *Discourse Dynamics: Critical analysis for social and individual psychology*. London: Routledge.

Pennebaker, J.W. (1993) 'Putting stress into words: Health, linguistic and therapeutic implications', *Behaviour Research and Therapy*, 31: 539–48.

Perakyla, A. (1997) 'Reliability in research based on tapes and transcripts', in D. Silverman, (ed.), *Qualitative Research: Theory, method and practice*. London: Sage.

Pincus, A.L., Gurtman, M.B. and Ruiz, M.A. (1998) 'Structural analysis of social behavior (SASB): Circumplex analyses and structural relations with the interpersonal circle and the five-factor model of personality', *Journal of Personality and Social Psychology*, 74(6): 1629–45.

Piper, W.E., Joyce, A.S., McCallum, M. and Azim, H.F.A. (1993) 'Concentration and correspondence of transference interpretations in short-term psychotherapy', *Journal of Consulting and Clinical Psychology*, 61: 586–95.

Piper, W.E, Boroto, D.R, Joyce, A.S., McCallum, M. and Azim, H. (1995) 'Patterns of alliance and outcome in short-term individual psychotherapy', *Psychotherapy*, 32: 639–47.

Pittenger, R.E., Hockett, C.F. and Donehy, J.J. (1960) *The First Five Minutes: A sample of microscopic interview analysis*. Ithaca, NY: Martineau.

Posthuma, A.B. and Carr, J.E. (1975) 'Differentiation matching in psychotherapy', *Canada Psychological Review*, 16: 35–43.

Potter, J. and Wetherell, M. (1987) *Discourse and Social Psychology: Beyond attitudes and behaviour*. London: Sage.

Ragin, C.C. (1987) *The Comparative Method: Moving beyond qualitative and quantitative strategies*. Berkeley: University of California Press.

Ragin, C.C. (1994) *Constructing Social Research: Unity and diversity of method*. Thousand Island, CA and London: Pine Forge Press.

Rasmussen, B. and Angus, L.(1996) 'Metaphor in psychodynamic psychotherapy with borderline and non-borderline clients: A qualitative analysis', *Journal of Analytic Social Work*, 4(4): 53–7.

Rennie, D.L. (1992a) 'Explanation on psychotherapy process research', in S. Toukmanian and D.L. Rennie (eds), *Psychotherapy Process Research: Paradigmatic and narrative approaches*. Newbury Park: Sage.

Rennie, D.L. (1992b) 'Qualitative analysis of the client's experience of therapy: the unfolding of reflexivity', in S. Toukmanian and D. Rennie (eds), *Psychotherapy Process Research*. Newbury Park: Sage.

Rennie, D.L. (1994a) 'Clients' accounts of resistance', *Canadian Journal of Counselling*, 28: 28–43.

Rennie, D.L. (1994b) 'Clients' deference in psychotherapy: A qualitative analysis', *Journal of Counselling Psychology*, 41: 427–37.

Rennie, D.L. (1994c) 'Storytelling in psychotherapy: The client's subjective experience. psychotherapy', 31: 234–43.

Rennie, D.L. (1998) 'Grounded theory methodology: The pressing need for a coherent logic of justification', *Theory and Psychology*, 8(1): 108–11.

Rennie, D. (2000a) 'Grounded theory methodology as methodological hermeneutics: Reconciling realism with relativism', *Theory and Psychology*, 10: 481–502.

Rennie, D. (2000b) 'Aspects of the client's control of the therapeutic process', *Journal of Psychotherapy Integration*, 10: 151–67.

Rice, L.N. and Greenberg, L.S. (eds) (1984) *Patterns of Change: Intensive analysis of psychotherapy process*. New York: Guilford.

Riding, N.C. and Cartwright, A. (1999) 'Interpreting the inventory of interpersonal problems: Subscales based on an interpersonal theory model', *British Journal of Medical Psychology*, 72: 407–20.

Riessman, C.K. (1993) *Narrative Analysis*. Newbury Park: Sage.

Rogers, C.R. (1957) 'The necessary and sufficient conditions of therapeutic personality change', *Journal of Consulting Psychology*, 22: 95–103.

Rohovit, D. (1960) 'Metaphor and mind: A re-evaluation of metaphor theory', *American Imago*, 17: 289–309.

Roth, A. and Fonagy, P. (2005) *What Works for Whom: A critical review of psychotherapy research*, 2nd edn. London: Guilford.

Rubino, G., Barker, C., Roth, T. and Fearon, P. (2000) 'Therapist empathy and depth of interpretation in response to potential alliance ruptures: The role of therapist and patient attachment styles', *Psychotherapy Research*, 10(4): 408–20.

Russell, R.L., Van Den Broek, P., Adams, S., Rosenberger, K. and Essig, T. (1993) 'Analysing narratives in psychotherapy: a formal framework and empirical analyses', *Journal of Narrative and Life History*, 3: 337–60.

Sacks, H. (1972) 'On the analyzability of stories by children', in J.J. Gumperz and D. Hymes (eds), *Directions in Sociolinguistics: The ethnography of communication*. New York: Reinhardt & Winston.

Sacks, H. (1992) *Lectures in Conversation, Vols I and II*. Oxford: Blackwell

Sacks, H., Schegloff, E.A. and Jefferson, G. (1974) 'A simplest systematics for the organization of turn-taking in conversation', in J.N. Schenkein (ed.), *Studies in the Organization of Conversational Interaction*. New York: Academic Press.

Safran, J.D. (1992) 'Extending the pan-theoretical applications of interpersonal inventories', *Journal of Psychotherapy Integration*, 2: 101–6.

Safran, J.D. and Muran, J.C. (1996) 'The resolution of ruptures in the therapeutic alliance', *Journal of Consulting and Clinical Psychology*, 64(3): 447–58.

Safran, J.D. and Muran, J.C. (2000) *Negotiating the Therapeutic Alliance: A relational treatment guide*. New York: Guilford.

Safran, J.D., Muran, J.C., Samstag, L.W. and Stevens, C. (2002) 'Repairing alliance ruptures', in J.C. Norcross (ed.), *Psychotherapy Relationships That Work*. New York: Oxford University Press.

Sandler, J.J. (1983) 'Reflections on some relations between psychoanalytic concepts and psychoanalytic practice', *International Journal of Psychoanalysis*, 64: 35–45.

Schaefer, E.S. (1971) 'From circular to spherical models for parent behavior and child behavior', in J.P. Hill (ed.), *Minnesota Symposium of Child Psychology, Vol. 4*. Minneapolis: University of Minnesota Press.

Schafer, R. (1981) 'Narration in the psychoanalytic dialogue', in J.W.T. Mitchell (ed.), *On Narrative*. Chicago: University of Chicago Press.

Schafer, R. (1992) *Retelling a Life: Narration and dialogue in psychoanalysis*. New York: Basic Books.

Scheflen, A.E. (1973) *Communicational Structure: Analysis of a psychotherapy transaction*. Bloomington: Indiana University Press.

Schegloff, E.A. (1992) 'Introduction', in H. Sacks, *Lectures in Conversation Vol II*. Oxford: Blackwell.

Schmidt, J.A., Wagner, C.C. and Kiesler, D.J. (1999) 'Psychometric and circumplex properties of the octant scale impact message inventory (IMI-C): A structural evaluation', *Journal of Counseling Psychology*, 46(3): 325–34.

Seitz, P.F.D. (1966) 'The consensus problem in psychotherapy research', in L. Gottschalk and A. Auerbach (eds), *Methods of Research in Psychotherapy*. New York: Appleton-Century-Crofts.

Semerari A., Carcione A., Dimaggio G., Falcone M., Nicolò G., Procacci M. (2003a) 'Assessing Problematic States in patients' narratives: the grid of problematic states.', *Psychotherapy Research*, 13: 337–53

Semerari A., Carcione A., Dimaggio G., Falcone M., Nicolò G., Procacci M., Alleva G. (2003b) 'How to evaluate metacognitive functioning in psychotherapy? The metacognition assessment scale and its applications', *Clinical Psychology and Psychotherapy*, 10: 238–61.

Shapiro, D.A. and Firth, J. (1987) 'Prescriptive v. exploratory psychotherapy: Outcomes of the Sheffield Psychotherapy Project', *British Journal of Psychiatry*, 151: 790–9.

Shapiro, D.A., Barkham, M., Hardy, G.E., Morrison, L.A., Reynolds, S., Startup, M. and Harper, H. (1990) 'University of Sheffield Psychotherapy Research Programme: Medical Research Council/Economic and Social Research Council Social and Applied Psychology Unit', in L.E. Beutler and M. Crago (eds), *Psychotherapy Research Programmes*. Washington DC: American Psychological Association.

Shapiro, D.A., Barkham, M., Rees, A., Hardy, G.E., Reynolds, S. and Startup, M. (1994) 'Effects of treatment duration and severity of depression on the effectiveness of cognitive-behavioral and psychodynamic-interpersonal psychotherapy', *Journal of Consulting and Clinical Psychology*, 62: 522–34

Shapiro, D.A., Barkham, M., Reynolds, S., Hardy, G. and Stiles, W.B. (1992) 'Prescriptive and exploratory psychotherapies: Toward an integration based on the assimilation model', *Journal of Psychotherapy Integration*, 2: 253–72.

Siegel, P.F., Sammons, M. and Dahl, H. (2002) 'FRAMES: The method in action and the assessment of its reliability', *Psychotherapy Research*, 12(1): 59–77.

Siegelman, E.Y. (1990) *Metaphor and Meaning in Psychotherapy*. London: Guilford.

Siegfield, J. (ed.) (1995) *Therapeutic and Everyday Discourse as Behaviour Change: Towards micro-analysis in psychotherapy process research*. Norwood, NJ: Ablex.

Silverman, D. (1997) *Discourses of Counseling: HIV counseling as social interaction*. London: Sage.

Sloane, R.B., Staples, F.R., Cristol, A.H., Yorkston, N.J. and Whipple, K. (1975) *Short-term Analytically Orientated Psychotherapy vs. Behaviour Therapy*. Cambridge, MA: Harvard University Press.

Smith, M.L. and Glass, G.V. (1977) 'Meta-analysis of psychotherapy outcome studies', *American Psychologist*, 32: 752–60.

Snyder, W.U. (1963) *Dependency in Psychotherapy: A casebook*. New York: Macmillan.

Spence, D.P. (1982) *Narrative Truth and Historical Truth: Meaning and interpretation in psychoanalysis*. New York: Norton.

Spence, D.P. (1993) 'Traditional case studies and prescriptions for improving them', in N.E. Miller, L. Luborsky, J.P. Barber and J.P. Docherty (eds), *Psychodynamic Treatment Research*. New York: Basic Books.

Stern, P.N. (1994) 'Eroding grounded theory', in J. Morse, (ed.), *Critical Issues in Qualitative Research Methods*. Thousand Oaks, CA: Sage.

Stiles, W.B. (1999) 'Signs and voices in psychotherapy', *Psychotherapy Research*, 9: 1–21.

Stiles, W.B. (2001) 'Assimilation of problematic experiences', *Psychotherapy*, 38: 462–5.

Stiles, W.B. (2002) 'Assimilation of problematic experiences', in J.C. Norcross (ed.) *Psychotherapy Relationships that Work. Therapist contributions and responsiveness to patients*. New York: Oxford University Press.

Stiles, W.B. and Angus, L. (2001) 'Qualitative research on clients' assimilation of problematic experiences in psychotherapy', in J. Frommer and D.L. Rennie (eds), *Qualitative Psychotherapy Research – Methods and methodology*. Lengerich, Germany: Pabst Science Publishers.

Stiles, W.B., Barkham, M., Shapiro, D.A. and Firth-Cozens, J. (1992a) 'Treatment order and thematic continuity between contrasting psychotherapies: Exploring an implication of the assimilation model' *Psychotherapy Research*, 2: 112–24.

Stiles, W.B., Elliot, R., Lewelyn, S., Firth-Cozens, J., Margison, F., Shapiro, D.A. and Hardy, G. (1990) 'Assimilation of problematic experiences by clients in psychotherapy', *Psychotherapy*, 27: 411–20.

Stiles, W.B., Honos-Webb, L. and Surko, M. (1998) 'Responsiveness in Psychotherapy', *Clinical Psychology Research and Practice*, 5: 439–58.

Stiles, W.B., Meshot, C.M., Anderson, T.M. and Sloan, W.W. (1992b) 'Assimilation of problematic experiences: The case of John Jones', *Psychotherapy Research*, 2(2): 81–101.

Stiles, W.B., Shankland, M.C., Wright, J. and Field, S.D. (1997) 'Aptitude-treatment interactions based on clients' assimilation of their presenting problems', *Journal of Consulting and Clinical Psychology*, 65: 889–93.

Stiles, W.B., Shapiro, D.A., Harper, H. and Morrison, L.A. (1995) 'Therapist contributions to psychotherapeutic assimilation: An alternative to the drug metaphor' *British Journal of Medical Psychology*, 68: 1–13.

Strauss, A. and Corbin, J. (1990) *Basics of Qualitative Research: Grounded theory procedures and techniques*. Newbury Park: Sage Publications.

Strauss, A. and Corbin, J. (1998) *Basics of Qualitative Research: Techniques and procedures for developing grounded theory*, 2nd edn. Thousand Oaks, CA: Sage.

Streeck, U. (2002) 'On subtle means of diagnostic interaction'. Paper given at Society for Psychotherapy Research International Conference, Santa Barbara, California.

Strong, S.R., Hills, H.I., Kilmartin, C.T., De Vries, H., Lanier, K., Nelson, B.N., Strickland, D. and Meyer C.W. (1988) 'The dynamic relations among interpersonal behaviors: A test of complementarity and anticomplementarity', *Journal of Personality and Social Psychology*, 54: 798–810.

Strupp, H.H. (1990) 'The case of Helen R.', *Psychotherapy*, 27: 644–56.

Sullivan, H.S. (1940) *Conceptions of Modern Psychiatry*. New York: Norton.

Sullivan, H.S. (1953) *The Interpersonal Theory of Psychiatry*. New York: Norton.

Tallman, K. and Bohart, A.C. (1999) 'The client as a common factor: Clients as self-healers', in M.A. Hubble, B.L. Duncan and S.D. Miller (eds), *The Heart and Soul of Change: What works in therapy*. Washington, DC: American Psychological Association.

ten Have, P. (1999) *Doing Conversation Analysis: A practical guide*. London: Sage.

Toukmanian, S.G. and Rennie, D. (1992) *Psychotherapy Process Research: Paradigmatic and narrative approaches*. Newbury Park: Sage.

von Wyl, A. (2000) 'What anorexic and bulimic patient have to tell: The analysis of patterns of unconscious conflict expressed in stories about everyday events', *European Journal of Psychotherapy, Counselling and Health*, 3(3): 375–88.

Vygotsky, L. (1978) *Mind in Society: The development of higher psychological processes*. Cambridge, MA: Harvard University Press.

Wacholz, S. and Stuhr, U. (1999) 'The concept of ideal types in psychoanalytic follow-up research', *Psychotherapy Research*, 9(3): 327–41.

Wallerstein, R.S. (1989) 'The psychotherapy research project of the Menninger Foundation: An overview', *Journal of Consulting and Clinical Psychology*, 57: 196–205.

Watson, D.R. (1993a) *Pragmatics of Human Communication*. London: Faber & Faber.

Watson, D.R. (1993b) 'Some potentialities and pitfalls in the analysis of process and personal change in counselling and psychotherapeutic interaction', in J. Siegfield (ed.), *Therapeutic and Everyday Discourse as Behaviour Change: Towards micro-analysis in psychotherapy process research*. Norwood NJ: Ablex.

Watson. J.C. and Rennie, D.L. (1994) 'A qualitative analysis of the clients' subjective experience of significant moments of therapy during the exploration of problematic reactions', *Journal of Counselling Psychology*, 41: 500–9.

Watzlawick, M.P., Beavin, J.H. and Jackson, D.D. (1968) *Pragmatics of Human Communication: A study of interactional patterns, pathologies and paradoxes*. London: Faber & Faber.

Weiss, J., Sampson, H. and the Mount Zion Psychotherapy Research Group (1986) *The Psychoanalytic Process: Theory, clinical observations, and empirical research*. New York: Guilford.

Welkowitz, J., Cohen, J. and Ortmeyer, D. (1967) 'Value system similarity: Investigation of patient-therapist dyads', *Journal of Consulting Psychology*, 31: 48–55.

Westerman, M. and Foote, J. (1995) 'Patient co-ordination: Contrasts with other conceptualisation of patients' contribution to the alliance and validity in insight-orientated therapy', *Psychotherapy: Theory, research and practice*, 32, 222–32.

Wexler, D. and Butler, J. (1976) 'Therapist modification of client expressiveness in client-centred therapy', *Journal of Consulting and Clinical Psychology*, 44: 261–5.

Wiggins, J.S. (1982) 'Circumplex models of interpersonal behavior in clinical psychology', in P.C. Kendall and J.N. Butcher (eds), *Handbook of Research Methods in Clinical Psychology*. New York: Wiley.

Wiggins, J.S. (1996) 'An informal history of the interpersonal circumplex tradition', *Journal of Personality Assessment*, 66(2): 217–33.

Wilczek, A., Weinryb, R.M., Barber, J.P., Gustavsson, F.P. and Asberg, M. (2000) 'The core conflictual relationship theme (CCRT) and psychopathology in patients selected for dynamic psychotherapy', *Psychotherapy Research*, 10(1): 100–13.

Winnicott, D.W. (1953) 'Transitional objects and transitional phenomena: a study in the first not-me possession', *International Journal of Psychoanalysis*, 24: 89–97.

Winnicott, D.W. (1986) *Holding and Interpretation*. London: Hogarth Press.

Worthington, R.L. and Atkinson, D.R. (1996) 'Effects of perceived etiology attribution similarity on client ratings of counsellor credibility', *Journal of Counselling Psychology*, 43: 423–9.

Index